Chapter 1
Why study Christian worship?

Initial definitions

We are alive at a time when an educated person ought to know a considerable amount about the world's **religions** and how they function for individuals and in society. This textbook is an introduction to the study of a central feature of the **Christian** religion: its patterns of **worship**. The emphasis in this textbook is on the primary Sunday morning worship of Christian communities in the United States. Sunday worship intends to assemble members of the Christian **church** so that they praise God, offer prayers, and strengthen their identity as an inspired community of faith and action.

It may be that for you a course in Christian worship is required by some outside agency, such as your academic major or future employer. Some students have freely chosen to take this course. Yet many historic, cultural, and personal arguments might pull students away from attention to the 100,000 Sundays on which Christians have assembled for **services** of **word** and **sacrament**. Why study the weekly **liturgy** of the church?

religion
a communal worldview about ultimate reality, enacted in rituals and expressed through ethics

Christianity
a worldwide religion based on faith in the resurrection of Jesus Christ

worship
religious exercises honoring the divine and uniting the community

Reasons against the study of Christian worship

A list of reasons against such a study can begin by listening to Ralph Waldo Emerson. Emerson lived in the Boston area in the nineteenth century and is famous in American intellectual history for advocating the worldview called transcendentalism. According to transcendentalism, each individual can receive divine truths by listening to God, who is found within the self and throughout nature. Emerson had trained at Harvard Divinity School to become a minister in one of the most **liberal** groups of Christians in nineteenth-century America. But after a few years he resigned the ministry, having decided that even a church with rational **doctrines**, minimal **symbols**, and few **rituals** stood in the way of receiving divine truth. Emerson judged that although the Christian **Bible** is in some places beautifully written, its morals were flawed and its symbols outdated, and he judged that the church's religious doctrines obscured rather than revealed divine truths.

Emerson expressed his difficulties with Christian public worship in his address to the Harvard Divinity School in 1838. In this speech delivered in the chapel of his alma mater, Emerson developed the position that the moral goal of human life is to live out "the sentiment of virtue." This sentiment, which is "the essence of all religion," is most fully and profoundly found not in books, not even in the Bible, not in churches, but rather in the self, which is good and sweet and houses the "indwelling Supreme Spirit." Jesus is no more divine than is every human person: in his nineteenth-century prose, Emerson said, "Man is the wonderworker." At the beginning and conclusion of the speech, Emerson invoked nature: in order to connect with divine truth, a walk in the woods is better than an hour in church. The implication of his address is that every person with integrity will replace participation in religion with introspection of the self.

> It seemed strange that the people should come to church. It seemed as if their houses were very unentertaining, that they should prefer this thoughtless clamor. . . . We have contrasted the Church with the Soul. In the soul, then, let the redemption be sought. In one soul, in your soul, there are resources for the world.
>
> —*Ralph Waldo Emerson, 1838*[1]

We now listen to Emily Dickinson, one of the greatest poets of nineteenth-century America. Dickinson was raised in Amherst, Massachusetts, in a strict Protestant community that expected her as a young adult to make public confession of her faith in Jesus as the center of her life. Her community also assumed that on the basis of this conviction, she would then publicly join the local church as an adult member. However, Dickinson had no such personal religious conviction, and she chose not to fake it. After age thirty she stopped attending Sunday worship services, and she remained outside the religious obligations of her community. Much of her poetry adopts the pose of the lone individual, somewhat contented in its isolation and facing death without the consolation of religion. Especially in poem #324, she questions the value of Sunday worship, its symbols and rituals.

Bible / the Scriptures
a compilation of some seventy books that constitutes the sacred writings of Christianity

The writings of Emerson and Dickinson present ideas that, although controversial at the time, became increasingly mainstream over the following 150 years. Urban life and the Industrial Revolution led to nostalgia for untouched nature. A pleasant walk in the woods, quite different from the backbreaking labor of the farmer, was idealized. Increasingly, Americans viewed the human being as basically good and wholesome, rather than as essentially sinful. The religious doctrine brought to America by the Pilgrims, that humans are born in sin and "totally depraved," was being abandoned. The idea that God is a stern judge was giving way to belief in God as a loving parent. According to such thinking, since people are good and God is nice, there seemed to be less need for organized Christianity.

Some keep the Sabbath going to Church—
I keep it, staying at Home—
With a Bobolink for a Chorister—
And an Orchard, for a Dome—

Some keep the Sabbath in Surplice—
I just wear my Wings—
And instead of tolling the Bell, for Church,
Our little Sexton—sings.

God preaches, a noted Clergyman—
And the sermon is never long,
So instead of getting to Heaven, at last—
I'm going, all along.

—*Emily Dickinson, 1864*[2]

That the American founding fathers supported the new idea of governmental separation from religion has deeply influenced American life. Thomas Jefferson believed that Jesus was an eminent teacher, but he maintained that what one thought about Jesus was personal opinion. If religion is a set of ideas about one's private connection with God, it is perhaps best kept in one's head. This understanding of religion has led many Americans to assert that they can believe something about God without affiliating with a group that maintains and cultivates this belief.

Adding to these attitudes was the actual living situation of decades of pioneers. Many white settlers occupied geographical areas that did not yet have any resident Christian churches, and so these nonnative immigrants to the prairie and West Coast could not attend meetings for worship even if they had wanted to. Homesteaders were required by law to live in houses that were on their 160-acre allotment, rather than in a town, as had been the European pattern in farming communities. When a church was established in the area, it may not have been the church of the family's heritage, and so persons may have found it difficult or distasteful to participate in its symbols and rituals.

liturgy
the format of text and action used by a Christian community in its worship

liberal
an attitude marked by an open-minded approach to change

doctrine
stated authoritative belief of an association

symbol
a concrete word, image, or object that represents an abstract truth or value; see chapter 2

When churches arrived, there was not one, but several, perhaps many. In previous centuries and locales throughout most of human history, everyone residing in a certain area participated in the same religious symbols and rituals, with more or less personal interest or dedication. Yet for the last two centuries, many places in the United States offer a diversity of Christian **branches** and **denominations**. This array of possibilities encourages a critical view of religious practice, since when choice is offered, persons must use their judgment about their preferences. Such a critical attitude has led many people to reject religious practice entirely.

Many forces within the modern world sought to disregard historic symbols and ancient rituals as being hopelessly retrogressive, and traditional religious practice was blamed for holding back the progress of civilization. Americans wanted to be freed from all the shackles of the past, and for some people that included religion. A scientific worldview that equates truth with fact has led many people to reject religious proposals and traditional scriptures as no more than escapist fantasy. A tour through a major art museum makes clear that the Christian symbols in the medieval art of the European sixth through fifteenth centuries are nearly completely absent from the art of the last two centuries. American society cultivated an increasing focus on the individual. Technology allows a single person to accomplish tasks that used to require cooperation within the group. Great value is placed on individual freedom and preference among options. When a society places considerable emphasis on the individual, any obligation that tradition or the community lays on the individual receives a smaller slice of the pie.

The rise of radically **conservative** religious groups has led to an increase in the number of commentators who describe religion as an entirely negative force in human society. The media publicize scandals in religious communities more often than reasonable and faithful belief and practice. Much in society speaks positively about a life guided by a generalized sense of **spirituality**, rather than by commitment to any organized religion. An increase in marriages in which the two persons come from different religious communities leads to the formation of many families in which the adults do not concur about any Sunday morning obligation. The children of such families may be raised without the habit of attending any one church, or any religious service at all, and may judge that attendance at worship services affords them nothing beyond what they have already received through some other activity.

Over the centuries many Christians attended church services

... wondering, too
When churches fall completely out of use
What we shall turn them into, if we shall keep
A few cathedrals chronically on show ...

—*Philip Larkin*[3]

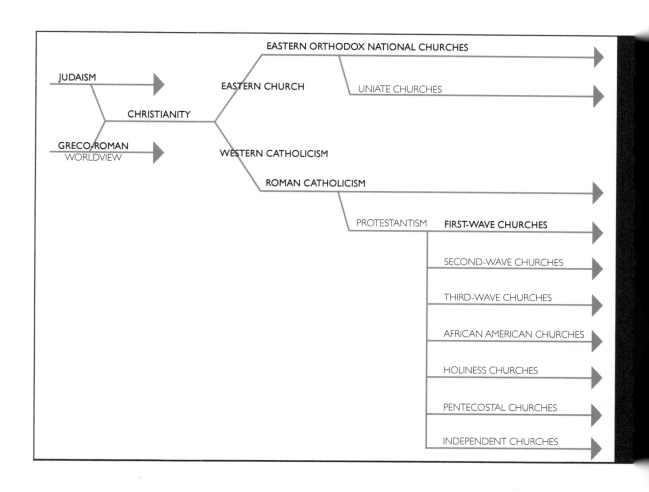

because there was nothing else socially acceptable for them to do on Sunday morning. Church attendance provided a culturally significant occasion for people to connect with others. Although there are still some places in North America where local pressure encourages Christian participation, most locales have greatly diminished or completely removed an American pattern of reserving Sunday morning for church attendance. Sports activities in some public high schools require Sunday morning participation. Stores are open on Sunday morning, and those who staff them then cannot attend worship if they want to.

Technology has played its part. Thanks to the practice of broadcasting services over the air, any individual who cares about hearing a preacher can simply tune in to the sermon while relaxing at home or doing the laundry. People can watch a Roman Catholic service on television. Some Christians now sponsor interactive Web sites with instructions to set "something to drink" and "something to eat, like a cracker . . ." next to the computer screen so as to participate in the ritual privately at home. If religion is largely information, then we can access it without having to assemble with others on Sunday, and much in our society suggests that information is the road we must take to reach what is good.

Some people have been raised within Christian practice, but had a disturbing or stupefying experience with organized religion. They may have been abused by a religious leader, disgusted by a local scandal, or humiliated in a worship setting. They might assume that what is distasteful about one group of Christians will prove distasteful about all Christians, and so, despite their rearing, they have ceased any practice of the faith.

To the degree that organized religion is discredited, the practice in Christian churches of weekly meetings for the worship of God and communal religious inspiration will suffer. If students adopt an attitude of spirituality rather than the practice of a religion, or if they are uninterested in Christianity, or if they are drawn toward other fascinating course options, students may judge that a course

Some churches have been converted into restaurants and other entertainment venues.

dedicated to the study of contemporary Christian symbol and ritual is not a high priority. If students reflect negatively about their own experiences of worship, their attitude for a semester's study may be negative.

> The service ended with the handshake of peace. You had to stand up and shake hands or even hug the people around you. This was a horrifying moment for me, because it meant I had to make eye contact and skin contact with all these strangers. . . . I never tried to go to church at Vassar again.
>
> —Nica Lalli[4]

Reasons for such study

Educated American citizens do well to know something about what Christians do when they assemble on Sunday. Citizens of other countries remark on how central to American life religion is. Yet because of the concern that public schooling might privilege one religion over another, many American students attend sixteen or more years of school and never encounter much information about the religious patterns that influenced world history and are reported in the daily news. The primary source of most people's personal religious experience, whether it is minimal or life-transforming, is the public ritual activities of their religion. The United States embraces a bewildering variety of Christian groups, and students either are themselves Christian or encounter daily believers for whom public worship is a central feature in life. Some of these worshipers can make articulate speeches about why and how they worship, but many cannot.

> Early on the first day of the week, while it was still dark, Mary Magdalene came to the tomb. . . . When it was evening on that day, the first day of the week, Jesus came and stood among them and said, "Peace be with you." . . . A week later his disciples were again in the house. . . . Although the doors were shut, Jesus came and stood among them and said, "Peace be with you."
>
> —John 20:1, 19, 26

Here are some of the many possible questions that a course in Christian worship may help to answer:

Imagine yourself walking down Main Street, USA, and on the boulevard are five different Christian churches. Each one advertises its services on Sunday morning. You wonder, Why are there so many different types of Christians? It seems that two of them have the same group name: Why are there two, if they are the same? You are reading the newspaper: What goes on at worship that influences a section of Americans to vote a certain way at elections? You read in national news magazines about megachurch worship: What is it, and why does it matter? In a movie theater, you see a film in which Christian ritual is featured: Has the depiction been accurate?

You have been raised in a religious tradition other than Christianity: What do Christian people do on Sunday morning? You regularly or occasionally attend one church: How is its Sunday morning experience similar to and different from the worship of other churches? One of your parents left one religious group to join with that of your other parent: What symbols and rituals were left behind? With a friend or colleague, you visit a church that is new to you: What should you wear? How should you act? You have been away from worship for some years, and upon returning, you encounter changes in the ritual: Why have these changes occurred? How might you reflect on these changes? You have been bored to death whenever you went to church: What in the world do others see in this exercise?

You are a faithful worshiper in your church: Where did these symbols and rituals come from? You are committed to your religious tradition and intend to become a leader in your church: What should you be proud of in your tradition? What needs criticism? You are aware of the controversies within your Christian group, some of which are evident on Sunday morning: Who has the authority to make what kind of changes to public worship? How is worship connected with the group's core values?

As a young American, you are expected to make your own way, growing away from your childhood into an adult life of your own choice: Will Sunday morning worship be part of your future life commitments?

This list suggests that your questions at the outset of this course may be wholly intellectual: Why do Christians meet to do whatever it is that they do? On the other hand, your interest may be primarily personal: What is the meaning of my Sunday morning experience? A semester study of Christian worship hopes to assist you as you probe these and other questions about the role of religion in human life.

The intention and method of this textbook

This textbook focuses on why Christians attend weekly communal worship, what happens during such worship, and how worshipers speak of the value of

Why are all these people here?

such worship. It means to serve as the primary text in undergraduate courses in Christian worship, a secondary text in a course on the Christian tradition, or an introductory resource in a **seminary** worship course. Most books about worship are written from within a denomination, for its own members; however, this textbook is **ecumenical**, crafted without preference for any one type of Christian worship. This textbook highlights the symbols and rituals in mainstream Christianity, rather than those of the many faith communities that are in some substantive way idiosyncratic. For example, the practice of **Quaker** silent meeting reflects a belief system so distinctive that some Quakers do not consider themselves Christian. Such exceptional practice contrasts with the general worship consensus of Christians, the topic of this textbook.

It is important here to clarify the terms *symbol* and *ritual*. This survey of Christian worship has adopted these categories from the academic study of phenomenology, that is, the examination of the phenomenon of religion. For phenomenologists, the categories *symbol* and *ritual* are wholly objective descriptors of the central features of religious practice. If people speak in a negative way about "just a symbol," or claim that their communal behaviors are other than "mere ritual," they are not using the terms as would a phenomenologist. Some Christian theologians have refused to use these terms to describe their own practice, explaining that "symbol" is not a profound enough word or "ritual" too secular a category for their sacred worship. However, this textbook

seminary
an academic institution for training leaders in Christian churches

ecumenical
applicable to all Christians worldwide

Quakers, the Society of Friends
a religious community that recognizes God in the self and assembles for silent meditation

will continue to use these academic labels. Members of different Christian denominations may check to what degree their church uses or refuses these objective categories.

As an introductory text, this book does not intend to be a thorough examination of any of its specific topics. The prose of this book recognizes that students may not be knowledgeable about Christianity, ancient geography, or world history, and so definitions are provided in the sidebars. Of the many meanings these words have, the definitions given apply particularly to the use of these words in the study of Christian worship. Quotes that illustrate a point or offer an alternative view are in the inset boxes. Illustrations and cartoons can prompt class discussion. Each chapter's "Suggestions" include discussion topics, essay assignments, and activities to enrich the semester's study for either the collegiate or the seminary student. Appropriate biblical passages, short stories, and films are suggested that can enhance the discussion of each chapter. Endnotes and chapter bibliographies suggest further study.

Students are encouraged to attend worship services at a variety of Christian communities. Many people find that being a visitor at an unfamiliar ceremony is more or less unsettling. Yet visiting churches on Sunday can be a valuable learning experience. Worship is not words on a page, but rather a group of participants who are honoring a set of symbols and enacting specific rituals. Most people cannot experience music by merely looking at the musical score; they must attend a musical performance. Worship is something like a Bach cantata: to begin to know it, you must experience it, and to know it well, you need to experience it repeatedly. Students who cannot visit different churches should view such worship over the Internet, while remembering that watching a screen does not replicate attending a service.

When visiting a service, it is well to show respect for the event by dressing as you would for an important appointment. In some churches, members will be dressed in "Sunday best" as a sign that they are meeting with God, and attire that is too casual may be offensive. Students may choose to go with a member of that church or with a classmate. At some churches, you will be met by a greeter from whom you may ask assistance. You might tell the greeter that you are present because of a classroom assignment. Usually it is acceptable to stand or sit throughout the ritual in respectful silence. Do not feel that you must participate. In some churches visitors will be asked to introduce themselves to the entire assembly. These churches understand that attending worship is more like going to a dinner party than like attending a movie: everyone wants to know who is present. Depending on the church, the Sunday service may last anywhere from a clipped forty minutes to a meandering three hours.

Churches of even a single denomination are not like McDonald's, at which customers everywhere order from an identical menu. Churches are comprised of people who have unique backgrounds, who see things differently from their neighbors, whose history and personalities influence their beliefs and activities. The church you visit might be self-consciously liberal or especially conservative. Thus, visiting one church of a denomination will not necessarily inform you about the worship in all the churches of that denomination. Each Sunday in each church is in some way a unique event. Perhaps on the Sunday you visit, the usual leader or musician is out of town, or the Girl Scouts have an unusual role to play. Leaders of worship may make mistakes, and some may conduct worship poorly. A worship leader may be trying out a new idea that turns out to be ineffective. Even at McDonald's, customers may judge that one manager or employee ought to be replaced.

The goal of this textbook is to equip a contemporary person with knowledge and understanding about the many variations of Sunday worship available in the United States. Chapters 2–3 consider what symbol and ritual are and how they function. The textbook proceeds by investigating how and why the different types of Christian worship developed as they did. Since we inform the present by looking to the past, chapters 4–8 check back through Christian history by asking what symbols and rituals have been around for 100,000 Sundays, that is, since about the year 150. Which ones for 75,000 Sundays, since about 600? What about for 50,000, 25,000 and 10,000 Sundays, about the years 1000, 1550, and 1800? Chapter 9 examines the practice of baptism, and chapter 10 considers worship during the week. Chapter 11 compares and contrasts Christian worship with some of the practices of other religions in North America. The textbook concludes by exploring the claims made for how one's daily life from Monday through Saturday is influenced by participation in Sunday worship.

> Religious experience is absolute. It is indisputable. You can only say that you have never had such an experience, and your opponent will say: "Sorry, I have." And there your discussion will come to an end. No matter what the world thinks about religious experience, the one who has it possesses the great treasure of a thing that has provided him with a source of life, meaning and beauty and that has given a new splendor to the world and to mankind.
>
> —C. G. Jung[7]

You are walking down Main Street, USA, on a Sunday morning in the twenty-first century. Many churches invite your participation. This semester's study hopes to help you decide whether to attend one and what that attendance means, so that whether you worship regularly in your home church or find yourself making a one-time visit, you do so with knowledge, understanding, and perhaps even appreciation.

Suggestions

1. Review the chapter's vocabulary: Bible, branch, Christianity, church, conservative, denomination, doctrine, ecumenical, liberal, liturgy, mystery, ordinance, Quakers, religion, ritual, sacrament, Scriptures, seminary, services, spirituality, symbol, word, and worship.

2. Compare this textbook's definition of the word *Christianity* with other definitions and present arguments for and against each.

3. Summarize and analyze several significant twentieth-century persons, ideas, or events that encourage or discourage participation in Christian worship.

4. Discuss how a contemporary political issue has been influenced in one direction or another by what happens at Sunday worship.

5. Write a personal essay analyzing why you are where you are on Sunday morning.

6. In the Bible, the prophet Amos speaks harshly against the symbols and rituals of worship. Discuss Amos 5:8-24 in light of this chapter.

7. Discuss Anne Lamott's "Why I Make Sam Go to Church,"[8] a chapter in *Traveling Mercies*, in which the author describes the value of church attendance.

8. Discuss the 1989 film *Romero*, the story of the 1980 assassination of Archbishop Oscar Romero. How does worship function for the people? Do you know enough about Christian worship to understand the movie?

9. Attend any Sunday Christian worship service, and write a report of it. Below is an outline for such a report.

An outline for writing a worship service report:

A. Cite the full name of the church and its national or international affiliation, if any. Cite the date, the time, and the type of service attended.

B. Describe the building, its design, its art, its appointments, and any printed matter that is handed to you.

C. Describe the people who are assembled, the size of the group, and its conduct.

D. Describe the leaders, their functions, and their attire.

E. Describe the event itself, its symbol and rituals.

F. Discuss any aspect of the worship service that you found contradictory to the stated intentions of the community, or discuss anything that you found negative about the experience, and give your reasons why.

G. Conclude with a discussion of what you found positive for the community or for yourself, and give your reasons why.

For further study

Berry, Carmen Renee. *The Unauthorized Guide to Choosing a Church*. Grand Rapids: Brazos, 2003.

Matlins, Stuart M. and Arthur J. Magida. *How to Be a Perfect Stranger: The Essential Religious Etiquette Handbook*. 4th ed. Woodstock, Ver.: Skylight Paths Publishing, 2006.

Mead, Frank S., Samuel S. Hill, and Craig D. Atwood. *Handbook of Denominations in the United States*. 12th ed. Nashville: Abingdon, 2006.

Prothero, Stephen. *Religious Literacy: What Every American Needs to Know—and Doesn't*. San Francisco: HarperOne, 2007.

Reitenbach, Gail. *How My Neighbor Worships: A Grand Tour of Faith Communities*. Sante Fe: Right Hand Communications, 2006.

Shea, Suzanne Strempek. *Sundays in America: A Yearlong Road Trip in Search of Christian Faith*. Boston: Beacon, 2008.

Stenger, Victor J. *God: The Failed Hypothesis: How Science Shows That God Does Not Exist*. Amherst, N.Y.: Prometheus, 2007.

Chapter 2
What is a symbol?

Defining and describing symbol

One of the primary reasons that humans can construct myriad and elaborate social structures is that they are capable of complex communication. We humans not only indicate to each other where the food is. We give some foods celebrative value; we craft a beautiful plate on which to serve the food, and we lay a tablecloth; we dress up in special clothes; we hang a painting on the wall of the dining room; we designate one person to sit at the head of the table; we say special words at the beginning and conclusion of the meal. In these and other ways, humans add significant objects, persons, and language onto the necessity of eating. The species is preserved by the eating of food, and the community is nurtured by the sharing of the values that attend the meal. Without the communal bonds that are strengthened by such meanings, human culture as we know it would be threatened.[1]

Scholars customarily distinguish two types of specialized meaning. The more simple type is the **sign**. A red octagon with the letters STOP tells drivers in the United States to apply the brakes on the car, and to make sure that

sign
a communally agreed-upon display with a single referent

See Plate I in the gallery. How many symbols on this church mosaic can you identify?

sacred
embodying and conveying
divine power

drivers would never be confused, laws forbid the use of this design for any other notice that might be posted along the roadway. An icon on a computer screen is a sign: learning the single meaning of the tiny picture eases our word processing. Signs point in one specific direction. A sign is practical. Signs simplify communal life by means of shorthand labeling.

Scholars call the more complex form of human interaction the symbol. The word *symbol* comes from the Greek "to throw together." Meanings are thrown together, layered on top of each other, and as the individuals agree on the layered complex of meanings, the people are thrown together in and through the symbol. Cultures can be described as communities of shared symbols: one becomes at home in what was an alien culture when one can respond to its symbols. A symbol not only is something, it does something. A symbol is consequential. Symbols expand and deepen communal life by their accumulation of value and purpose. Far from being "just a symbol," symbols reflect and intensify human meaning, and they constitute the matrix of human society.

A religion is an immense symbol-system about the meaning of the past, value in the present, and imagination about the future. Religions propose to the community what ought to be considered ultimate and mysterious, what is worthy of our focus and authoritative enough to govern our lives. Since this system of the ultimate and mysterious is, by definition, beyond human knowledge, religion relies on symbols to radiate something of this ultimate mystery. When the religious symbols are displayed and rehearsed, the community is bonded together. Symbols are bridges. By the power of an especially effective symbol, the past is brought into the present, the commonplace is transformed by the exceptional, the individual is united with the community, and sorrow meets up with joy.

What is a sign for one person may be a symbol for someone else. For some Americans, the national flag is merely a sign of the nation. But other Americans have invested the national flag with symbolic importance, and for them the treatment of this concrete object corresponds precisely to the way that the citizen values the nation. For these people, flying the flag both announces one's national loyalty to one's neighbors and builds up patriotism in everyone who sees it. A law to punish the desecration of the flag construes the flag as nearly **sacred**. Marring the symbol would be a disgraceful offense against the ultimate value that is contained in the symbol.

Over time, the meaning of a symbol may change. In the ancient Mediterranean world and still today in some cultures, brides were heavily veiled, since they were shown first to their husband only after the marriage contract was completed. A memory of this is seen when an attendant moves the bride's veil back from her face after the couple speaks the vows. Some brides wear a lace mantilla because in their tradition women always cover their head at worship. However, the white net veil worn by many American brides now signifies the value of traditional garb and its preference for extraordinary attire. When the World Trade Center was under construction, it was a touchstone for angry arguments about the future of New York City's skyline; while it stood, it became a symbol of civic prosperity; when destroyed, it had more symbolic value than before, evoking layers of emotion worldwide about the possibility of destruction and the fear of what is alien. Because the symbol is alive, it changes.

Religions are adept at taking an existing cultural symbol and altering its meaning to serve their own purpose. In the ancient Mediterranean, because a snake sheds its skin, it was used as a symbol of the life-giving goddess. Rejecting this religious system, biblical religion turned the serpent into a symbol of evil. Centuries later Sigmund Freud suggested that the snake is nearly always a phallic symbol. Yet contemporary Aboriginal Australians dismiss Freud's proposal, since in their traditional religion, the rainbow serpent encircles the globe and holds it together. Of course a snake is literally merely a snake. But a symbolic snake is something else again, and one needs to know who is using the snake symbolically in order to approach its meaning.

Because of this layering, the meaning of symbols is usually ambiguous. The red on a stoplight has one clear meaning. But red-colored attire may indicate a medieval king, a Hindu bride, a devil costume, a specific Christian festival, Native America identity, gang affiliation, Chinese nationality. Because symbols are multilayered, it is said that symbols give rise to thought. We see a man wearing a diamond ring, and as humans we think: Is that an engagement ring? A sign of personal wealth? Perhaps instead we are reminded of slave labor and the European oppression of Africans. Many ancient cultures have a legend similar to the biblical tale of Noah's ark, in which a flood destroys nearly all human and animal life on earth. In these stories, is the water a symbol of a cleansing of the earth? Do we think of womb waters, birthing a new world? Or is the water rather the flood of death, drowning those who deserve divine punishment? Perhaps these flood stories are mythologized memories of the

> Symbols, being roomy, allow many different people to put them on, so to speak, in different ways. Signs do not. Signs are unambiguous because they exist to give precise information. Symbols coax one into a swamp of meaning and require one to frolic in it.
>
> —Aidan Kavanagh[3]

Anthropologists can only guess at the meanings of this rock art made a thousand years ago in the American southwest.

flooding that followed the end of the Ice Age. The cosmic flood flows along, acquiring symbolic meanings along the way. Because we cannot say all the truth simultaneously, the symbol presents the community a complex of meanings that are beyond words.

The more significant a symbol is, the more layers it has accumulated, and the more effort must be expended when trying to explicate it. The symbol of the cross is an example. In some symbol systems, the cross calls to mind the earth's four directions: north, south, east, and west. On the robe of the shaman, the tribal visionary healer, the repeated cross pattern may symbolize the far-reaching sight of the flying eagle. In the first centuries of the Christian church, the cross was never depicted, since it was the cultural symbol of the power of the Roman Empire to execute criminals in a particularly cruel way. After all, in our time, probably only seriously disturbed people would wear a pendant of a tiny replica of an electric chair. In the fourth century C.E., however, the Roman emperor came to favor the Christian religion, and as a result he outlawed crucifixion as a method of execution. Only then did Christians begin to use the cross as a symbol.

Over the centuries dozens of different designs of the cross have become beloved by different groups of Christians. Some crosses are gruesome, some beautiful, some shocking, some comforting, each design capturing something of the meaning of the death of Jesus. The more layers to any specific cross—Is there an **INRI** at the top? Is Jesus dressed in brocade? Does the figure appear more female than male? Does the cross have branches like a tree?—the more explication is called for. Yet the most laden symbols always have more in them than any simple explanation can clarify.

Given the complexity of symbolic communication, the symbols in a church may give little or no religious feeling to a first-time visitor. Non-Christians may be shocked to see a centrally hung statue of a tortured man, and Christians accustomed to unadorned walls may find sacred statues and paintings distracting. Yet because symbols have deep roots and many branches,

INRI
acronym for the Latin words "Jesus of Nazareth, king of the Jews"

The Greek Cross
has four equal arms.

The Double Cross
recalls the title placed on Jesus' head on the cross.

The Forked Cross
suggests both the Trinity and arms uplifted in prayer.

The Multiple Cross
suggests the four corners of the earth.

The Latin Cross
has a lower vertical arm.

The Byzantine Cross
is a double cross with a footrest.

The Papal Cross
adds an arm to the Double Cross.

The Jerusalem Cross
suggests the five wounds of the crucified Christ.

The Tau Cross
resembles the Greek letter T.

The St. Andrews Cross
recalls the tradition that Andrew was martyred on such a cross

The Ring Cross
incorporates the Egytian hieroglyphic for life to denote the cross as life.

The Anchor Cross
suggests hope.

Each type of cross layers a specific meaning onto the crucifixion of Christ and is favored by a specific group of Christians

This cross is the tree of my eternal salvation nourishing and delighting me. I take root in its roots, I am extended in its branches. This cross is my nourishment when I am hungry, my fountain when I am thirsty, my covering when I am stripped, for my leaves are no longer fig leaves but the breath of life. This is the ladder of Jacob, the way of angels. This is my tree, wide as the firmament, which extends from earth to the heavens. It is the pillar of the universe, the support of the whole world.

—*Second-century anonymous sermon*[4]

devout believers can climb higher and dig lower into the meanings of their religious symbols each year of their worship life.

An example: the tree of life

Although some symbols are unique to one religion, other symbols are used by many different peoples through the millenniums and around the globe. Yet each religion layers the symbol with its own specific meaning. Although a symbol may welcome us, we approach it with respect, attentive to both its sameness to others and its difference from them. Taking the archetypal tree of life as an example, in some cultures and religions the symbol elaborates a genuine natural tree, while in others the tree is wholly a figment of human imagination.[5]

In traditional Chinese storytelling, the peach tree grants immortality to mortals. According to the Huichol legend of the Gathering of Souls, after death our souls go the tree of life, which exchanges all the sexual organs we have been connected with for pomegranates that benefit the living. The Kuna people of the islands near Panama tell of the paluwala tree of life: a creation tree, it flourished at the beginning of time, and all the animals emerged from its branches. The Mayans depicted a tree of life growing out of the reclining body of the dead king, because the life of the people is rooted in the reign of the monarch. According to the Norse legends, Yggdrasil is the world tree that holds together all the levels of the universe, and the high god Odin hanged himself on it, in the hope that he would gain knowledge through the sacrifice of his own suffering.

The Gyaba people of Cameroon use the soré tree in purification and reconciliation rituals, since it symbolizes the life of a healthy community. The Hopi spirit-dancer called the Morning Singer runs through the village at dawn carrying a branch from the spruce tree, a symbol of the life of the new day and of the community's hope for rain. At festivals, the Kwakiutl people of British Columbia wear blanket capes on which buttons are sewn in elaborate designs, many of which use the cedar tree as the primary symbol, since traditionally the cedar provided the northwest coastal people many of the necessities of life. The Lakota tribe has revived the summer Sun Dance ritual, during which the people celebrate around a cottonwood tree that symbolizes the center of the universe: "All our hopes and griefs are placed on the tree," said one dancer.

Some men hang from the tree by leather thongs, and their suffering cleanses the community. Wiccans participate in a tree of life ritual, in which imagining themselves as trees, they realize their rootedness in the earth. Swedes continue the ancient ritual of dancing around the maypole tree at the summer solstice to celebrate the return of flowers and fruits.

The Hindu story says that when the god Krishna appeared on earth, he was first seen in a kadamba tree, so now the kadamba tree is a symbol of the god himself. The Buddha sat under the bodhi tree and finally achieved enlightenment, and so for Buddhists the bodhi tree symbolizes the possibility of enlightenment for everyone. To aid their meditation, Tibetan Buddhists sit before a painted or embroidered banner called a *thangka*, one of which pictures a tree with the Buddha in the center surrounded by all the beloved bodhisattvas. According to Shinto beliefs, the divine spirits called *kami* arrive on the back of a deer in a sakaki tree, which at Shinto shrines is revered as a symbol of the ancestors' blessings.

At Hanukkah (see chapter 11), Jews light eight candles on a menorah to remember the miraculous flames that lighted the temple, and many of these candelabras are designed to resemble a tree. The Jewish mystics of medieval Europe described the emanations of Almighty God as an upside-down tree, its roots in heaven, and the earth as its branches; and thanks to this tree, humans are connected to the divine, an idea that Orthodox Jews question. In Islam, the prayer rug with its abstract tree symbolizes the paradise that one enters when kneeling on the rug during prayer.

In the Bible, Genesis 3:22 says that the specific reason that the LORD God expelled the man and the woman from the Garden of Eden was to ensure that they could not eat from the tree of life and live forever. Revelation 22:2 describes this tree of life at the end of time, with twelve different fruits, a different kind each month, and leaves that heal the nations. In the Gospel of Mark, when Jesus talks about the mustard plant, he uses a traditional description of the tree of life, in which "the birds of the air can make nests in its shade"; yet the mustard bush is a scrubby annual. A Jesse tree, a common piece of Christian art, is a genealogical tree on which are named the most important ancestors of Jesus, beginning with Jesse, the father of King David. The tree of life is cited in texts at Christian worship, painted on walls of churches, woven into crosses, embroidered onto fabrics, and chiseled into stone, this universal symbol conveying a uniquely Christian meaning to those who gather around it.

Theories about the human tendency to symbolize

Several of the many theories about human symbolizing are particularly relevant for the study of Christian worship. In the thirteenth century,

LORD
the traditional English rendering of *YHWH*, the four consonants of the Hebrew name of God;

vs.

Lord
the traditional English rendering of *Kyrios*, the Greek word for master

See Plate 2 in the gallery. What is your reaction to this church art? Why?

Thomas Aquinas
(c. 1225–1274) friar,
priest, theologian, and
author of the *Summa
Theologiae* whose writings
strongly influenced
Christian theology

to consecrate
to set apart by prayer for
religious use

Protestantism
the branch of Christianity
that began in protest
against the Western
Catholic church, now with
many denominations

ambo / lectern
a reading stand used in
churches

pulpit
a podium, usually with a
waist-high enclosure, at
which the preacher stands

Roman Catholicism
a worldwide branch of
the Christian church
centered in Rome

lectionary
a book containing
the biblical selections
appointed for use at
worship

communion
the assembly's eating the
bread and drinking the
wine

Thomas Aquinas wrote critically about this human tendency. Aquinas reasoned that when Christians refer to God as Father, they are using language that is factually inaccurate. God is not literally a father: God is God, far beyond what our word *father* means. Thus, although believers had to use such imaginative speech, Aquinas judged this practice to be problematic, because the symbol of "father" carries so many varied connotations. It is better, he wrote, to use philosophically accurate labeling, especially when speaking of God. So God is best referred to as "the One who is."[6] But in the twentieth century, theorists working in the fields of psychology, philosophy, religion, and linguistics judge the habit of symbolizing to be perhaps the most uniquely human characteristic. The human imagination inevitably and perpetually creates and projects symbols to communicate its values to others.

The fact that humans dream—and that depriving a person of dream-sleep can soon render that person incoherent—suggested to twentieth-century psychologists that the human mind never stops symbolizing. Sigmund Freud viewed our mental imaginings to be symbolic primarily of our sexual identity, rearing, and desires, and since Freud judged human behavior as being in great part determined by matters of sexuality, these symbols are of extreme importance.[7] For Freud, that Christians often symbolize God as a father indicates that most people both desire and fear their father and his sexual role.

Carl Jung came to disagree with his teacher Freud as to the overwhelmingly sexual interpretation of human symbolizing. Jung proposed that in some way that we cannot fathom, humans have hard-wired into their consciousness what he called archetypes. These archetypal images—such as the old man, the mother, the hero, the monster, the river, the shadow, the number four—exist in our brains and pervade our thought processes throughout life.[8] Humanity's use of the tree of life exemplifies Jung's proposal that "a collective unconscious" of such archetypes directs our species. Jung suggested that more attention to this symbolic world helps persons to experience a psychic wholeness that many modern people lack.

During the twentieth century, scholars of religion called phenomenologists sought to describe religious phenomena with objective precision. Mircea Eliade focused on religious symbolism, exploring especially symbols of the center—so, for example, the cottonwood tree of the Lakota Sun Dance or the Muslim Kaaba in Mecca—around which a community's life revolves and from which the people receive the meaning of their corporate existence.[9] Eliade claimed that such centers function as primary communal symbols, becoming more than they literally are by means of the layers of interpretation and practice they embody.

Other scholars of note offer important insights for the study of worship.[10] The social anthropologist Emile Durkheim analyzed how symbols focus the collective power of the group. Branislaw Malinowski examined the practical results in tribal life of the functioning symbol system. The philosopher Susanne Langer wrote that symbols have the power to transmit through a culture its primary values and that a culture without profound symbols has no access to its deepest values. The cultural anthropologist Clifford

> Symbols are not proxy for their objects, but are vehicles for the conception of objects. In talking about things we have conceptions of them, not the things themselves; and it is the conceptions, not the things, that symbols directly "mean."
>
> —*Susanne Langer*[11]

Geertz claimed that human behavior is culturally constructed: that is, people act, not how they as individuals decide to act, out of personal freedom, but rather as their culture directs them to act, and that these directions are conveyed through symbols.

Symbolic objects in Christian worship

Just as some individuals thrive on symbols and fill their homes with art, some churches enrich their worship with as many symbols as possible. The items used in worship or the clothing worn by the leaders may be **consecrated** to mark them as symbols containing and conveying something of God. For other people, the fewer symbols, the better. Some **Protestants** maintain that instead of connecting God and worshipers, such objects obstruct the believers' access to God. In many European churches, Protestants covered over the medieval wall paintings with whitewash because the images were said to distract from people's attention to worship. Some churches cultivate a middle position, valuing only a few symbols. This disagreement about symbols constitutes one of the primary differences between one church on Main Street and another. Which symbolic objects are most valued ought to reflect the specific theology and tradition of the church.

Most Christian churches agree that one object with considerable symbolic power is a book. In most Protestant churches, that book is a large Bible. It may rest on an **ambo** or formidable **pulpit**. With large print easily seen by the reader, the Bible may have gilded edges and be beautifully bound. Its extraordinary appearance symbolizes that the words it contains are valued as having come from God and as bringing the people to God. In **Roman Catholic** churches, the beautifully bound book will likely be a **lectionary**. Some lectionaries have jeweled covers or impressed gold images. This book will be carried high in procession, perhaps bowed to and kissed.

In most churches, the bread and wine used for **communion** carry extraordinary symbolic significance. The bread symbolizes staple food, what we need for survival, and wine festive drink, what we share in joy. On a deeper level,

tabernacle
a storage box used for consecrated bread

monstrance
a container that displays the consecrated bread for private devotion

vessels
the plates, cups, and pitchers used in serving the bread and wine

chalice
the goblet used for distributing the wine

Eastern Orthodoxy
the branch of Christianity that includes the national church bodies founded in Greece and Eastern Europe

pew
a backed bench used for seating in churches

leaven
yeast or baking powder that by producing gas during baking raises and lightens the bread

host / wafer
a small circle of unleavened bread used in communion

altar
a piece of furniture that has evolved from a table on which the bread and wine are prepared

holy
filled with divine power

churches speak in a variety of ways about the bread and wine carrying God to the participants: the bread and wine symbolize or embody God. Some Protestant churches have replaced the wine with grape juice, which symbolizes that every individual can receive this gift of God, even children, recovering alcoholics, and those who consider alcohol consumption sinful.

For some churches, the symbolic power of communion works in the consciousness of the persons participating. Leftover bread may be eaten after the service or fed to birds, and leftover wine drunk by the leaders or respectfully poured out onto the ground. In other churches, God has transformed the bread and wine into the most powerful vehicles of divine visitation. The mystery has occurred, not in the person, but in the bread and wine. Leftover bread is reverently stored in a **tabernacle**. One piece of consecrated bread may be inserted into the glass center of a **monstrance** and so continue its symbolic power beyond the Sunday service in chapels or festival processions. In some churches, the wine is fully consumed, so that there is none left over.

The containers for the bread and wine are usually called **vessels**. The **chalice** may be gold or silver and may be set with jewels. The chalice is symbolic, not only of the assembly's unity, but of Jesus himself, since it contains and presents the wine to believers. Medieval legends about the Holy Grail, the cup that Jesus used at his last supper before he died, show to what extent the chalice has been revered. In some churches, the chalice might be a large beautifully shaped wine goblet bought at a local store, thus symbolizing that God is available also in our time and place. Some churches use tiny individual glasses, to symbolize contemporary concern for hygiene. In **Eastern Orthodox** churches, the wine is spooned into the worshiper's mouth.

The method used to commune the worshipers is itself symbolic. Some churches pass a tray with pieces of store-bought bread from one hand to another, as people sit in their **pews**. In some churches, participants come up to the altar and are handed small pieces of bread. Some churches use bread specially baked for communion; it is **unleavened** and formed into perfect white circles called **wafers** or **hosts**, symbols of divine perfection. In some churches, worshipers do not touch even their own piece of bread, but are fed directly into the mouth.

The **altar** is a significant symbolic object in Sunday worship. In an Eastern Orthodox church, what is called the **holy** table is considered so filled with divine power and the actions conducted at that table so sacred that there is a room divider to shut it off from the people's area. In some churches, a robed person will process around the altar with incense. Here the altar is honored as symbolic of Christ himself. Some Roman Catholics have the tradition that a **relic** is

There are a variety of ways that the fruit of the vine can be served.

embedded somewhere into the altar itself. These altars are draped with damask hangings and embroidered linen cloths. Many Protestants—for example, some **Presbyterians**—use a wooden table on which they lay a tablecloth. Here the table symbolizes the meal that believers share with the risen Christ and connects communion with daily dining.

Another item with symbolic resonance is the **baptismal font**. The font may be a bowl on a stand. If shaped to resemble a womb, the font symbolizes that the baptized person is being reborn. **Baptist** churches, as well as a growing number of churches in other denominations, have large tubs designed to accommodate the full immersion of adults. Such fonts may be in the shape of a cross, thus symbolizing that when one is baptized, one enters into the cross of Christ. Others are eight-sided, relying on the ancient symbolism that since seven is the number of the secular week, eight is the number of the new life of the resurrection.

Any of these symbolic objects may be adorned with pictorial symbols— so, symbols on a symbol. There are dozens of such symbols, most of them based on imagery found in the Bible. One common symbol is a downward pointing hand, to symbolize God as Creator. The walls or stained glass windows may show a symbolic image of Christ, perhaps as a king, a good shepherd, or a lamb. Many churches will display the first and last letters in the Greek alphabet, *alpha* and *omega*, as symbols that Christ is the beginning and the end. Common also

Presbyterian
a Protestant denomination following some of the teachings of John Calvin

John Calvin
(1509–1564) French Protestant theologian who organized a theocracy in Geneva

baptism
the ritual of washing used when one becomes a Christian; see chapter 9

font
the container filled with water used for baptism

Baptists
a Protestant denomination characterized by the baptism of only professing believers

Trinity
the Christian mystery of one God as three, Father, Son, and Holy Spirit

Gospel
a biblical book that narrates the meaning of the life of Jesus

gospel
the good news of God's love; also, a style of American religious music characterized by simple melody and harmony and rigorous beat

disciples
the inside circle of Jesus' followers, usually numbered twelve; also, all faithful followers of Christ

are the Greek letters *chi* and *rho*, the first two letters of the word *Christ*. Many churches have an image of a dove, to symbolize the Holy Spirit. A geometric design of three interwoven circles is a common Christian symbol for the **Trinity**.

Somewhere may be an arrangement of four figures—an angel, a lion, an ox, and an eagle—that since the second century have symbolized the authors of the four **Gospels**: Matthew, Mark, Luke, and John. Some churches display images of **saints** that include a symbol of the life and work of the saint. The altar may be adorned with images of stalks of grain and bunches of grapes, to symbolize the bread and wine. Many churches depict a seashell as a symbol of baptism. The font may have engraved into it a picture of Noah's ark, to symbolize that those who are baptized are, like Noah and the animals, brought through the water into new life.

Numbers have symbolic meaning in Christian worship. The numbers one or three suggest God, four the Gospels, seven the gifts that the Holy Spirit sends. Twelve is the number of completion: so, the twelve tribes of Jewish tradition, the twelve **disciples,** the twelve gates into the perfect city. A long period of time is almost always forty: forty days for the flood, forty days for Jesus' time in the wilderness, forty years for the Israelites' period of nomadic wanderings. One consequence of regular worship participation is that the assembly learns more and more about its community's symbol system.

Symbolic persons in Christian worship

Christians teach that since the Holy Spirit enters each believer, every **layperson** is in some way a symbol of Jesus Christ and can convey sacredness to others. But nearly all Christians also designate specific leaders who function as symbolic persons. These are the **ordained clergy**. Orthodox, Roman Catholic, and **Episcopal** churches call their clergy *priests* or *presbyters*. Male priests are often addressed as Father, and sometimes female priests are called Mother. Some Protestants, especially **Lutherans**, call their clergy *pastor*, a word that means shepherd. Protestant clergy can be called *preacher*, *minister*, or *reverend*. In some churches, the ordained include *deacons* and *elders*, who depending on the church have varying responsibilities. Each denomination has its own expectations for clergy, its own requirements for training, and its own efforts for maintaining quality control. One exception is the **Amish**, who consider every male able to lead worship, and annually one minister is chosen by lot.

Most churches vest their clergy in symbolic attire. A common vestment is the **alb** that symbolizes one's baptism. Over the alb is probably a **stole** that may be a color designated for the season. The leader may wear a **chasuble** that matches the stole in color. The fabric of the chasuble might be anything from golden brocade to cotton batik. Its fullness symbolizes the embracing love of God. Some clergy, to symbolize that they are educated teachers of the faith, wear a black academic robe called a **Geneva gown**. In some churches, ethnic garb is worn to symbolize the homeland of the assembly. In each case, the vestment announces that the individual has taken on a symbolic role, which is more important for the event than that person's body shape or preferred clothing style. The uniform covers the individual with the role. Some churches want their clergy to symbolize middle-class American professionalism, and their ministers will be dressed in business clothing. At a Sunday service at camp, the minister might be in jeans, thus symbolizing that worship of God can be anywhere, anytime, in any attire.

In those churches that maintain a hierarchy of ministers, a geographical area has an overseer called a **bishop**. Some churches maintain a hierarchy of bishops: so, **archbishops**, **patriarchs**, a **pope**. Such persons usually have regalia symbolic of their position: a **crosier** suggests that the bishop is like a shepherd for the people. The centrally located church that is home for the bishop is called a **cathedral** because it houses the chair of authority. Several large Protestant churches that have no bishops call the largest of their church buildings cathedrals.

Symbolic speech in Christian worship

One type of symbolic speech important to some Christians is called **glossolalia**. Already mentioned in the Bible, this "speaking in tongues" is understood as being beyond human language and thus appropriate in communication with God. It symbolizes the extraordinary nature of conversation with God.

When regular words are used symbolically in worship, they function not as label, but as metaphor. Metaphor is actually counter-label. A metaphor calls something what it is not, in order to suggest a surprising similarity. Although we know that a rock is a rock, we employ metaphor when we call God a rock; and the hearers reflect on how God, who is not a rock, is like a rock, and so they now think of God in a new way. Because the metaphor opens up and layers on human perceptions, the group that shares the metaphor is bonded together by and in their expanded and shared universe. Especially the linguistic

> It is in the actual celebration, the very doing of worship, that the voice and power of a symbol is realized and released.
>
> —*Christopher Irvine*[14]

saint
in some churches, an eminent dead Christian who inspires devotion and who can intercede for the believer before God; in other churches, any dead Christian; in other churches, any baptized Christian

laypersons / laity
the regular members of the Christian church

ordination
the process of designating authoritative leaders in the Christian community through a ceremony of prayer

clergy
designated leaders in the Christian community

Episcopalian / Anglican
a Protestant denomination that arose in sixteenth-century England

Lutheran
a Protestant denomination following some of the teachings of Martin Luther

philosopher Paul Ricoeur taught that, far from being an unnecessary addition to human speech, metaphor is the basic building block of human communication and the primary method that humans use for sharing creative insight. "It always takes two ideas to make a metaphor,"[16] and it is this superimposition of two ideas that is common in the symbolic language of religion.

Poetry is literature that with few words conveys many layers of meaning because it uses so much metaphor, and Christian worship is filled with poetry drawn from the Bible. Most Christians quote some of the biblical book of **Psalms** in their Sunday worship. The most famous psalm is 23, "The Lord is my shepherd." Tradition says that the poem was composed by a shepherd named David. Ancient Near Eastern texts commonly referred to the monarch as a shepherd. Even when many Jews became urban dwellers, no longer nomadic herders, the community carried in its consciousness the memory of shepherding, and they relied on this metaphor to address the deity who cared for and governed them.

Fast-forward two thousand years: when on Sunday morning Christians sing of God being like a shepherd, they imagine God as the hard-working caretaker of the animals that were central to the economy and diet of ancient people. A painting of Jesus as a shepherd intends to assist the verbal metaphor; yet a shepherd pictured with bare feet and a long white robe is so unlike any genuine shepherd that perhaps the painting only shrinks the metaphor. The many metaphors one encounters in the speech of Sunday worship call for considerable knowledge about the language of the Bible, as well as education about how Christians use this language. For example, when Christians praise God for the city of Jerusalem, they may be referring literally to the contemporary city in the Middle East or metaphorically to the church, that is, the place where God dwells. Just as "shepherd" is a symbol for God, "Jerusalem" functions as a symbol for the church or for heaven.

Because God is transcendent, beyond the universe, many words used in worship about God will be metaphoric. To use the image of "king" for God, who is beyond all human categories, or for Jesus, who was a teacher and healer, is to employ a traditional metaphor borrowed from the world of politics. Conservative Christians resist changing their worship language in any way, because they have spiritually benefited from these metaphors and want to repeat them Sunday after Sunday. Liberal churches add new metaphors in their address to God, judging that more metaphors will enlarge their understanding of God.

Some Christians prefer that the language used on Sunday morning be other than their vernacular: an ethnically historic language or, like Latin, a denominational marker. This specialized language symbolizes an ideal otherness that comes alive during worship. Most American Christians pray in English or Spanish, their vernacular, and some continuously update their words with ones more resonant with contemporary culture. Increasingly, churches in the United States are developing bilingual worship, not only to serve a bilingual assembly, but to symbolize that the Christian church is a worldwide community and that God is beyond the boundaries of one language.

How symbolic speech is employed on Sunday morning is one of the markers of Christian churches. Some churches require only approved texts to be used, and others affirm that the Holy Spirit inspires new phrasing each week. Some use countless metaphors, confident that regular worshipers will appreciate them. Other churches judge that the Sunday service should have less, rather than more, language that is metaphoric, so that the meanings of worship will be accessible to the newcomer. Some repeat beloved metaphors, some value new songs with culturally based metaphors, and some try to balance the old with the new. Most churches maintain that learning all the connotations of their metaphors is a long-term project for worshipers. Metaphors are symbols, perhaps opaque to outsiders, but to insiders the metaphors of their faith are brilliantly faceted glass through which worshipers glimpse a vibrant and sacred reality.

Sacraments, like metaphors, are possible because thought and feelings can be led into imaginative leaps through language. The results of these leaps are identities which otherwise would not exist.

—Robert Jones[18]

chasuble
a poncho traditionally worn by presiding clergy

Geneva gown
black academic robe first worn by clergy in the churches of Geneva

bishop
geographical overseer of a group of clergy and local churches

archbishop
in some Protestant churches, the bishop overseeing other bishops; in Roman Catholicism, the bishop of a significant city

My God, thou art a literal God, a God that wouldst be understood literally and according to the plain sense of all that thou sayest; but thou art a figurative, a metaphorical God too; a God in whose words there are such a height of figures, such voyages, such peregrinations to fetch remote and precious metaphors, such extensions, such spreadings, such curtains of allegories, such third heavens of hyperboles, such harmonious elocutions, . . . thou art the Dove that flies.

—John Donne, 1624[19]

Suggestions

patriarch
usually, the bishop of a significant city in the Eastern Orthodox churches

pope
usually, the bishop of Rome and international bishop of the Roman Catholic church

crosier
a shepherd's crook carried by a bishop

cathedral
a church building that houses the bishop's ceremonial *cathedra,* Greek for chair

glossolalia
an ecstatic babble used to praise God

Psalms
a biblical book containing 150 Hebrew poems

1. Review the chapter's vocabulary: alb, altar, ambo, Amish, Anglican, Thomas Aquinas, archbishop, baptism, Baptists, bishop, John Calvin, cathedral, chalice, chasuble, clergy, communion, consecrate, crosier, deacon, disciples, Eastern Orthodoxy, elder, Episcopalian, Father, font, Geneva gown, glossolalia, Gospel / gospel, holy, host, INRI, laity, leaven, lectern, lectionary, LORD, Lord, Lutheran, Martin Luther, minister, monstrance, Mother, ordination, pastor, patriarch, pew, pope, preacher, presbyter, Presbyterian, priest, Protestantism, Psalms, pulpit, relic, reverend, Roman Catholicism, sacred, saint, sign, stole, tabernacle, Trinity, vessels, vestment, and wafer.

2. Present arguments for and against praying to God as a rock or a mother.

3. Report on twelve examples in the world's religions of the sacred mountain.

4. Identify all the symbols in your classroom and on the people who are in it.

5. Write a personal essay about your attitude towards symbolism. Are you a person who prefers more symbols, or fewer symbols? Why? Give examples.

6. In the Bible, Exodus 25–28 describes the construction of the ancient Israelite tent for worship and all its furnishings. Discuss these symbols.

7. Discuss Nathaniel Hawthorne's classic short story, "The Minister's Black Veil."

8. Discuss the 2006 film *The Fountain,* which interweaves three narratives with the symbols of the ring, the fountain of youth, and the tree of life. For the Holy Grail versus the swastika, enjoy the 1989 *Indiana Jones and the Last Crusade.*

9. Visit a shopping mall and write an analysis of American culture based on twelve symbols of our society that you encounter there.

For further study

Chauvet, Louis-Marie. *The Sacraments: The Word of God at the Mercy of the Body*. Collegeville, Minn.: Pueblo, 2001.

Dilasser, Maurice. *The Symbols of the Church*. Collegeville, Minn.: Liturgical, 1999.

Eliade, Mircea. *Images and Symbols: Studies in Religious Symbolism*. Trans. Philip Mairet. Princeton: Princeton University Press, 1991.

Irvine, Christopher, ed. *The Use of Symbols in Worship*. Alcuin Liturgy Guides 4. London: SPCK, 2007.

Jung, C. G. *Psychology and Religion*. New Haven: Yale University Press, 1938.

Taylor, Richard. *How to Read a Church: A Guide to Symbols and Images in Churches and Cathedrals*. Mahwah, N.J.: Hidden Spring, 2003.

Womack, Mari. *Symbols and Meaning: A Concise Introduction*. Walnut Creek, Calif.: Alta Mira, 2005.

Chapter 3
What is a ritual?

Defining and describing ritual

When religious people assemble to honor what they believe to be ultimate and to strengthen their communal bonds, they tend to do similar actions each time they meet together. These activities are called rituals. Colloquially, English speakers sometimes use the word *ritual* to refer to a precise series of actions an individual makes, for example, the routine one follows every morning when rising and readying for work. In the academic study of religion, however, "ritual" has the specific meaning of defined actions that are repeated, communal, and symbolic.

Rituals are repeated activities. Like other animals, humans need to accomplish some tasks regularly in order to survive. Someone must walk to the stream to get the water that the family needs, and carrying the heavy water in the early morning makes more sense than lugging it in the heat of the afternoon. So the women who carry the water establish a pattern of going together at dawn for the water. The same shows are broadcast on television the same time each week; college classes begin on the hour or the half hour. Whether building bridges

or hiring wait staff, communities assume that people will do in a similar way what they have done in the past. Such repetition is psychologically consoling by providing security both to those who act and to those who watch.

Rituals are communal activities. The community is bonded together by its participation in ritual action. A parade held annually on the Fourth of July brings the town's people together. Encouraged away from personal isolation— for humans are not turtles spending most of life alone—everyone connects with one another. It is likely that not the parade itself, but rather everyone meeting during the parade holds most significance for the community. The rituals glue the society together. Replacing celebrative attendance at the baseball stadium with individuals watching the games on personal television sets substantially alters the role that baseball has in the culture.[1]

Rituals assist in the smooth running of communal life by supplying a repertoire of actions and phrases that can be used when the occasion arises. When a friend's family member dies, people are not expected to invent something creative to say or do. Instead, one attends the funeral or memorial service. Even if I know that I will never wear the sweater Aunt Suzie gave me, I am saved from brutal honesty by merely sending a thank-you note.

Although someone may claim that such a thank you is hypocritical and thus unwarranted, the ritual completes the connection that the gift initiated. The connection between persons, rather than one's opinion about the gift, is the operative issue.

Rituals carry symbolic value. That all human communities decide what to do with dead bodies is a natural need. We use the word *ritual* to describe the specific symbolic actions that the community undertakes: adorning the body with flowers, wearing the expected mourning clothing, journeying with the body to the grave, joining in a meal after the burial. When high school students place personal items in the casket of a dead friend, they are not assuming that their friend will use these objects in the afterlife, as apparently some ancient Egyptians did. Rather, the items are symbolic of the life of the deceased. The ritual holds the symbol, and so holds also the community.

> The meaning of ritual is deep indeed. He who tries to enter it with the kind of perception that distinguishes hard and white, same and different, will drown there.
>
> —*Xunzi, third century* B.C.E.[3]

Rituals embody our social values. While getting rid of the dead body, we engage in a ceremony that not only honors the dead with meaning and reconstitutes the community, but also confirms us in our beliefs and announces those beliefs to the world. One can now purchase caskets emblazoned with the logo of the sports team that was valued by the deceased. Participating in the Pledge to the Flag is the most common way for American young people to practice citizenship. For most religious people, their rituals are the central source of personal and communal religious experience through which they gain knowledge of the faith and associate with other members of their religion. Rituals communicate group values, and participation in the rituals reinforces those values.

Some rituals are powerful enough that they actually accomplish social change. Not only the couple being married, but everyone in the community are significantly altered by a wedding. Many rituals seek to perpetuate society in its traditional ways. So contemporary couples who are living together may get married because of the social significance of weddings and the many gifts they will receive. Some rituals are mandated by society: a new president of the United States must speak the precise words of the oath of office, a ritual precisely administered by a judge, even if the oath is being administered in an emergency in an airplane. Yet the words are not magic: outside of the ritual situation, speaking the oath of office today will not make anyone president. It is the communal validation of the ritual that renders the action effective. Some rituals have degenerated into what is called ritualism, a complicated set of actions that seem to have little or no meaning for the participants. A British citizen who hopes to end the monarchy may judge that a coronation is merely expensive ritualism.

Some rituals have as their primary responsibility the separation of the insiders from the outsiders. For example, some churches request that no visitor participate in their meal of bread and wine, since they see the ritual as bonding together the members. Some rituals intend to transform participants from outsiders to insiders. Initiation into groups is oftentimes celebrated in elaborate, even secret, rituals. Many sorority and fraternity members refuse to describe to outsiders their ritual of initiation. One common function of social ritual is to reinforce the community's ideas about gender. Some Hispanic families celebrate lavish coming-out parties for their daughters, while Orthodox Jews ritualize the coming-of-age of their sons. In each case, the ritual announces to everyone the community's attitudes about the role of their mature women and men: the children, who had been outsiders of the adult community, are now insiders, with the rights and responsibilities thereto appertaining.

Usually rituals are primary occasions for storytelling. At the ritual meal after a burial, the mourners tell stories about the deceased. Annually on the Fourth of July, the *New York Times* dedicates a full page to reprinting the handwritten Declaration of Independence, so that avid readers can review the story behind the holiday. Religious festivals include narrations of traditional heroes and heroines. At the Jewish festival of Passover, the ritual begins by the youngest child asking, "Why is this night different from all other nights?" To answer this question, the story of the ancient Hebrew exodus from slavery in Egypt is told. At the ritual gathering, the rehearsal of the story reinvigorates the community of believers.

Although rituals tend to be conservative, that is, valuing the past and honoring tradition, rituals can also be innovative, that is, training their participants into a new way of thinking. When in 1954 the Pledge to the Flag was altered to include the words "under God," the revised ritual intended to make clear that God would protect the United States from communism. During the twentieth century, many Christian churches revised their Sunday rituals, hoping that a newer ritual would be more congruent with the worldview of the participants, making the occasion not nostalgia about the past, but encouragement in the future. Rituals must do something in the lives of the participants, or the rituals are abandoned. That many Americans claim to be Christians yet

Someone can have an insight, and rather than its being lost, it can stay alive through ritual. The sun comes up in the morning, and we can hold up our oryoki bowls with three fingers in the same way that people have been doing for centuries. It's like a thread running through your whole life, holding up your oryoki bowl with three fingers.

—*Pema Chödrön, Buddhist nun*[4]

do not participate in Christian rituals has led some churches to make considerable changes in their ritual practices. Some members are glad of these changes, and others are quite distressed, because they view the traditional rituals in a positive way.

Examples of religious ritual

The primary example of human ritualizing is the feast. In a prehistoric painted cave in northern Spain was found a four-by-one-inch piece of bone onto which was carved, approximately twelve thousand years ago, a picture of a bison feast. The depiction is extremely simple: six human stick figures flank the backbone and skull of the bison. Until frozen meals and microwaves, preparing and eating food were largely communal activities. For the health of the community, for depth of life, the group gathers annually, or weekly, or daily, at table, perhaps for a celebrative feast with a traditional menu, perhaps for regular dinner fare. At ritual meals, the ordinary is turned into the extraordinary: a turkey roasted, wine poured, a lavish dessert enjoyed. To make dinnertime more festive, a family may light candles on the table. We celebrate the birthday even of a one-year-old, who has no clue what is going on. When two contemporary people meet for conversation, they usually talk over food or drink. The community of those who followed Jesus had the practice of the eating meals together.

Religious communities have developed four main types of rituals. The first are rituals that situate the people within the cosmos. Among the most ancient rituals that anthropologists describe are those that celebrated the equinoxes and the solstices, and especially in the Northern Hemisphere the winter solstice. Imagine the dread that infected a prehistoric tribe in northern Europe as the sunlight lessened each day, the weather grew colder, and plants went dormant. We know that elaborate rituals developed in which the community gathered on the date that, with remarkable accuracy, they had determined to be the shortest day of the year, to celebrate the returning sun. Did the shamans think that they were actually bringing about the rebirth of the sun? These rituals place the human community within the natural cycle of the cosmos, since there could be no sustained health for everyone if nature was ignored. One theory is that the immense stone circle of Stonehenge was a calendar for marking the solstice.

Other cosmic rituals developed at the time of hunting, planting, or harvesting. The earth needed to cooperate so that humans would get enough meat and grain for survival. So the community gathered to laud the herd or the sun and rain. Anthropologists suggest that what became the ancient Jewish festival of Passover with its killing of a lamb for a symbolic, communal meal

Note the art on the wall behind these soldiers keeping the American harvest festival.

had been in prior centuries a springtime nomadic ritual in which the herders killed a lamb and offered it to the deities, in hope that the deities will provide the community with a plenteous year of new lambs.

The seven-day week developed as human participation in the structure of the cosmos. Ancient peoples in the Mediterranean could see with their naked eye seven extraordinary lights in the night sky: the sun, the moon, Mars, Jupiter, Mercury, Venus, and Saturn. The idea was that each of these heavenly bodies had jurisdiction over one-seventh of human life, and so the days of the week were named Sun-day, moon-day, and so on until Saturn-day. Our names Tuesday, Wednesday, Thursday, and Friday are substitutions of the Norse deities for the Roman ones—for example, Woden for Jupiter. Thus, an anthropologist can say that when Christians meet once a week, they are maintaining an ancient pagan pattern of ritualizing their connection with the cosmic order. After the French Revolution, the government attempted to change the week from seven to ten days. This change in human ritualizing failed, because the French people were too deeply and fully committed to the cosmic ritual of a seven-day week.

A second type of religious ritual common in the world's religions connects the community with its historic past. Anthropologists have evidence that for fifteen thousand years, humans have participated in ancestor veneration, for example, with rituals at gravesites or annual memorials on the day of a death. Christian churches vary in how much ancestor veneration is part of their tradition. Most churches have a sense that the dead are somehow mystically connected with them through God, and so prayers or songs on Sunday morning may make reference to "the whole company" of the faithful, both living and dead, as united in praising God. One might think of Jesus as the Christian ancestor par excellence. Rituals that address the highlights of his life have become the primary Christian festivals, and Sunday worship includes biblical narratives of his life. There is comfort for the community in a shared history, and it grounds the people so they can proceed together into the future.

A third type of religious ritual common in the world's religions celebrates events in the lives of members. The term **rites of passage** is the usual designation for rituals in which the community observes the change of status of one of its members. Such rites characteristically occur at birth, at puberty, at marriage, and at death. The entire community helps each member make necessary changes of status and acknowledges these transitions in their midst. Religious communities also conduct rituals at the time of serious illness, once again uniting the community around the isolated individual with support and comfort. Most Christian rites of passage do not take place during Sunday worship, but usually any weekday rites of passage will be mentioned at the Sunday gathering.

In the fourth type of religious ritual, the goal is to connect people with God. One way this was done in both ancient and contemporary tribal religions is with animal sacrifice. The Aztecs **sacrificed** humans as gifts to the sun, cutting apart living persons on the top of their ziggurats and holding up the bloody hearts to the sky. Many theories propose reasons why sacrifices were offered: to appease an angry deity, to offer the deity dinner, to share a meal with the community, to negotiate half of a trade of benefits, to channel the human tendency toward violence, to mimic childbirth. For whatever reasons, many peoples killed and ate an animal as part of their process of connecting with gods and goddesses. Even though contemporary Christians do not engage in literal slaughter as part of the weekly event, the language of

> The Sioux Sun Dance is an annual prayer of thanksgiving to the Great Spirit and to all the powers between the breathing ones and Wakan Tanka.... Because four has a special meaning in Sioux spirituality, the fourth and final day of the Sun Dance brings the culmination of the ceremony—the piercing. You know the six powers will flow their medicine strongly through you during the piercing time. You are giving your pain so that the people may live.
>
> —Ed McGaa, Eagle Man[5]

rites of passage
communal observances of an individual's change of status

sacrifice
a ritual understood as creating sacredness; anciently, the killing of an animal for the deity; more recently, the dedication of goods, time, or money for godly purposes

"sacrifice" lives on, and various Christian groups apply this term in a symbolic way to something of their weekly worship pattern.

Connecting people with God is the major intention of most Christian worship. The worldview of all monotheisms is that the world is separated from God, who is the source of life. Religion presents ways to make the connection, so that people can live. Christianity maintains that Christ has effected this connection, which is received by the community through word and sacrament. The desire of worshipers to "get something out of worship" can be met only if what they want is connection with God. This textbook describes the primary ways that different Christians have constituted their weekly ritual so as best to connect the people, who are aware of their need, with God, who can meet that need.

Theories about the human tendency to ritualize

The past century has witnessed the development of an entire field of academic inquiry called ritual studies. Ritual studies was begun largely by field

Cross-dressed men march in the Philadelphia Mummers Parade on New Year's Day.

anthropologists, many of whom examined the practices of cultures distant from their own in geography and worldview. Many anthropologists sought to analyze why alien groups do things that seem weird to us and to suggest principles of human behavior demonstrated by such conduct. Some studies showed that rituals keep the old ways alive, so that the current power brokers remain in place. So, in the wedding rituals of many societies, brides are heavily veiled to emphasize the fact that the fathers negotiated the marriage, and the bride's appearance has nothing to do with it. Some rituals challenge the powerful in the community, allowing a release of anti-establishment feeling to be celebrated openly. An example is Philadelphia's century-old New Year's Day Mummers Parade, at which working-class men, dressed up as women in flouncy dresses and blond wigs, march down the city's main street drinking beer, and so begin their new year with all the social norms reversed.

Victor Turner's analysis of ritual, especially in rites of passage, emphasized the middle ground, the place between, that he called the time of liminality, through which the ritual carries the individuals, in order to form and cement a new community.[6] Turner judged that the transformations that ritual charts are essential for the maintenance of social order. Other scholars employed a psychoanalytic approach. Here rituals are seen as externalizing a conflict that is inside the human psyche.[7] For example, humans are by nature violent animals, and so religious rituals tame that violence. It may be that attention to the blood of a crucified man releases violent tendencies and makes way for peaceful feelings.

Ritual scholars remind us that the meaning of rituals changes. Those who analyze rituals must beware of falling into the genetic fallacy, the mistaken idea that how something began is what it presently means. For example, historians tell us that burial in the ground arose among people who had nature religions and who saw life as emerging from the earth itself. Yet contemporary Christians, who do not worship mother earth, still bury in the ground. The scholar Catherine Bell stressed that a ritual action or object has no meaning inherent in itself; all the meaning comes from the context.[8] Her work has trained scholars to write, not of "ritual," as if it were a static item to examine, but rather of "ritualizing," the complex human process of symbolic activity.

The work of Roy Rappaport is particularly interesting for the study of Christian worship.[9] He suggested that there are three levels of meaning within human communities. Low-order meaning is *labeling*, and its purpose is to convey precise information. Middle-order meaning is *metaphor*. With metaphor, everything means more than it is, and the effect of metaphor is to enrich human experience of the world. Finally, high-order meaning is *participation*. With participation, people enter into the meaning and embody that meaning, so that both individuals and the community itself become more than they were. Rappaport's examples of such high-order participation are art, love

Muslims adopt this arm gesture in mourning, although some Christian worshipers adopt it when approaching the altar for a blessing.

making, and religious ritual. Thus, in studying Christian worship, we can say that the low-order meaning of bread is the loaf purchased at the bakery before church. According to the middle-order meaning, bread is one metaphoric way that church speaks of Jesus Christ, since he is praised as necessary for human life. Using the high-order meaning, the community together ritually eats the bread and understands itself as being a loaf that is served up for the life of the world. The ritualizing community itself is bread.

Ritual theorists present substantial claims for the power of communal ritual to effect much that is necessary for the individual psyche and for communal health. However, many Christian thinkers warn worshipers not to expect too much of Sunday worship. Realists remind the theorists that there is simply no way that the countless groups of Christians who have assembled on 100,000 Sundays around the world regularly achieve the optimal goals of ritual. Meanwhile, some Christian **fundamentalists** reject any application from ritual studies. To the extent that these Christians believe that their worship pattern has been dictated by God and validated through the tradition, they are not interested in contemporary ritual studies, because they judge their worship as having little in common with other religious rituals.

fundamentalist
a conservative religious believer who, in Christianity, holds a literal interpretation of the Bible and an absolute trust of church authority

Christian ritual time

For there to be rituals, people must know when to assemble. So communities establish ritual time. However, ritual time is not merely a regular time at which rituals are scheduled. If rituals are effective, they actually alter one's perception of time, so that the occasions for rituals feel as if they are somehow time outside of time. When a group of friends gathers around a television with their ritual food to watch the Super Bowl, the event lasts as long as it must, and the fans are not looking at their watches during the game. Clock time is replaced with a psychologically different measure of time, with the number of minutes mattering less than the amount of meaning. People who value ritual time claim that such extraordinary time renews their experience of regular time. Like the dreams that take place during REM sleep, the symbols in ritual time enliven the more mundane hours of our days.

Because for much of American society the sixty minutes on the clock so totally control communal life by setting meeting times and determining the length of activities, many churches conduct their Sunday morning event to last precisely one hour. In contrast, especially African American and Latino Christian communities tend to ignore the clock, relishing however many hours it takes to worship together. In either case, the assembled group values ritual time as an event that conveys high symbolic significance. For monks and nuns who have chosen to live in strict traditional Christian **monastic** communities, where the community gathers two, three, or eight times daily for communal prayer, ritual time occupies an extraordinary amount of their life.

The human experience of time is linear: each hour moves inevitably to the next hour, our days moving steadily toward death. Religious rituals alter this linear movement by looping time in circles. The present is underlain with the past and overlaid with the future. When Christians listen to a biblical reading in which Jesus is quoted, the idea is that they hear Jesus in the room in the present, speaking to them now. When Sunday prayers ask God to bring about a perfect future, that future is supposed to be beginning already now. Deceased relatives and friends who are now with God are somehow present in this room. Our time has been transformed by the presence of God who exists outside of time as our universe knows it.

Christians have achieved this time outside of time by layering their annual religious festivals onto cosmic time. Nearly all Christians celebrate **Christmas** as the day of Jesus' birth. Fourth-century Christians set this festival at the time of the winter solstice in the Northern Hemisphere, not only to provide an alternative to the pagan festival of Saturnalia, but also to transform the communal experience of the darkness of winter with the religious faith in Christ as the light of the world. All Christians celebrate **Easter**, and each year's date of Easter, falling on a date between March 21 and April 25, is calibrated

monastic order
sex-segregated living communities with daily worship, men called monks and women called nuns, having taken life vows of poverty, chastity, and obedience

Christmas
December 25; for Christians, the annual celebration of the birth of Jesus; for secular culture, a winter solstice celebration

Easter / Pascha
the annual springtime celebration of the resurrection of Jesus

after determining the movements of both the earth and the moon. The sacred time of Easter means to communicate that the resurrection of Jesus Christ has more significance for the lives of believers than do cosmic rotations and orbits, just as the time made sacred by the community's ritual is more meaningful than the time measured by clocks.

For nearly all Christians, the primary ritual time is on Sunday. When Roman Catholics assemble for worship on Saturday evening, they are following one ancient way of time keeping, according to which each day begins at sundown. So Sunday is said to begin at sundown on our Saturday. Of course, for every general claim in this textbook, there are exceptions. The Christians called the **Seventh-day Adventists** assemble, like the Jews, on the seventh day of the week, our Saturday. Contemporary Christians who claim that they are not required to participate in Sunday's ritual time experience little or no coercion to go to church services. However, most churches maintain that members are supposed to be present for each week's ritual, and some faith communities teach that missing church is a sin.

Seventh-day Adventists
a Protestant denomination formed in 1844 that emphasizes the second coming of Christ

Some Christian churches maintain that holding fewer festivals is better than holding more. An extreme were the Pilgrims in Massachusetts colony, who outlawed Christmas. In our time, **Jehovah's Witnesses** discourage any celebration of Christmas and such religious holidays. Many Protestant churches keep only Christmas, Easter, and Sunday. The logic of such Christian groups is that other ritual time is not indicated in the Bible. Indeed, in the book of Galatians, **Paul** told early Christians not to keep special festivals and religious seasons that are determined by the sun and moon. Furthermore, these Christians say that such ritual time inevitably encourages activities and excesses that are not particularly Christian, and so churches are better off without them.

On the other end of the Christian spectrum are the churches that observe a full year's worth of ritual time. Roman Catholics and many Protestant churches follow a similar pattern in keeping their **liturgical year**. Even consumers become aware of this calendar because of contemporary marketing emphases.

> Holy Week's liturgies, one after another, have begun to accumulate in me.... We need to revisit our experience over and over again; each time, each visit, another layer is peeled away, another piece or aspect is revealed. Our cells carry memories that rise on anniversaries, demand another look.
>
> —Nora Gallagher[10]

Jehovah's Witnesses
a Protestant denomination formed in 1884, known for personal witnessing, that emphasizes the second coming of Christ

Paul
first-century preacher and author of at least eight books of the Bible

liturgical year
the annual cycle of Christian observances

A common liturgical year:

- Advent = four Sundays to prepare for the coming (advance) of Jesus
- Christmas, December 25 = celebration of the birth of Jesus
- (a variable number of Sundays)

- Epiphany, usually January 6 = celebration of the visit of the Magi to Jesus
- (a variable number of Sundays, depending on the date of Easter)
- Ash Wednesday = a Wednesday that focuses on sin and death
- Lent = forty days of preparation for Easter, usually focusing on amendment of life
- Holy Week = the last week of Lent, observing the last week of Jesus' life
- Palm Sunday = the Sunday before Easter, observing Jesus' entry into Jerusalem
- Three Days / Triduum = commemoration of the death and resurrection of Christ:
    - Maundy Thursday / Holy Thursday = the day commemorating Jesus' last supper
    - Good Friday = the day memorializing Jesus' death by crucifixion
    - Easter = the annual celebration of the resurrection of Jesus
- Ascension Thursday = forty days after Easter, commemorating Jesus' ascension
- Pentecost = fifty days after Easter, celebrating the presence of the Holy Spirit
- (the remainder of the standard Sundays of the year)

Keeping this schedule makes approximately half the year especially ritually celebrative, and many aspects of the Sunday services will reflect these observances. Particular rituals mark these observances in many churches, such as signing the cross in ashes on the forehead of worshipers on Ash Wednesday and the giving out of palms on Palm Sunday. For some churches, not only these special ritual occasions, but each Sunday of the year has stipulated Scripture readings and is symbolized with certain colors of fabric, types of music, and appropriate liturgical art. The idea in these churches is that the more ritual time, the better, for it is within ritual time that the community receives what it needs to live fruitfully in regular time.

The Eastern Orthodox churches have a similar liturgical year. Easter is the center of the year, but since these churches compute their date according to an archaic cosmological calendar, Orthodox Easter usually does not coincide with Easter in the Roman Catholic and Protestant churches. The Orthodox liturgical year begins on September 1 and includes both fixed and moveable feasts that run concurrently. Its complexity is seen by the Orthodox as a positive symbol of divine mystery that is meant to be spiritually experienced, rather than easily explained.

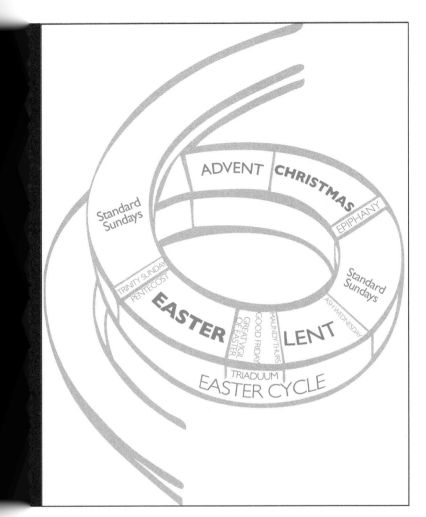

A common liturgical year.

Some churches maintain a daily **sanctoral cycle** that runs concurrently with Sundays and festivals. Usually the commemorations are held on the person's death day, since anciently most people did not know the date of their birth, and since it is said that at their death Christians are born to eternal life. Some churches keep dozens of such saints' days, some few, some none. Especially Orthodox and Roman Catholic churches attend to these annual dates. Many churches are now celebrating St. Francis, a thirteenth-century saint famous for his reverence for the earth, with a ritual of the blessing of animals and pets on October 4. St. Patrick's Day has become a celebration even for people who do not honor the life of that fifth-century missionary who converted many of Ireland's pagans to Christianity. Mexican Christians conduct rituals on November 2, the Day of the Dead, for which images of playful skeletons seek to counter our natural terror of death. Many African American churches keep only two such days: Martin Luther King Jr. Day and a day recalling their **congregation's** founder. Those Christians who observe many saints' days judge that the ritual of remembering the life of a saint supports their present and inspires their future.

Christian ritual space

Some religions, such as Islam, revere a certain place as the most sacred spot on earth, the symbolic center of the universe, to which **pilgrimages** are encouraged or required, but Christianity does not. Although some Protestants choose to visit Jerusalem and the sites associated with Jesus, and Roman Catholics tend to look toward Rome as a symbolic center, in neither case are believers required to travel to these places. The primary Christian idea is that when a group of Christians gather around word and sacrament, ritual space is created. God is in the meeting more than in the physical space.

Yet, when able to do so, people naturally set apart separate spaces for their various activities. So parents urge their young children not to eat in bed. When it comes to religious rituals, this designation of a special place for worship can be an elaborate ritual in itself. Over the centuries, Christians have adapted the buildings common in their culture for worship. Early Christians adapted their homes to better accommodate worship. Fourth-century Christians placed a table, a lectern, and leaders' chairs in large public civic centers, and contemporary **megachurches** construct spaces that resemble movie theaters. Although most Christians have specially consecrated ritual spaces, it is usually understood that worship can be held anywhere—for example, at the beach on a retreat, or a brief service of worship held at a hospital bedside.

In medieval Europe, the ideal in the major cities was to build the tallest, most immense cross-shaped building that was architecturally possible. The size, of course, indicated the power of the city. The cross shape symbolized that when looking down from heaven, God was reminded of the cross of Jesus. Going to church meant ritually being in the cross of Christ. Some churches positioned their buildings to face east, because they thought of the rising sun as symbolizing the resurrection of Christ and of the east as the direction from which Christ would return to earth at the end of time.

Some churches built in the last fifty years have replaced the long rectangular room that raised the clergy at one end with a more circular arrangement, symbolizing that God is in the center, not up and far away. Another alteration has been to give far more space to the font for baptism. Such a redesign of space has considerable effect on the rituals enacted in it. Architects like to say that "the building wins," that is, that the height of the room, its amount and source of light, its arrangement, its art, the color of the walls, all have a powerful and often unconscious psychological effect on people in the room.

People who are accustomed to a certain type of sacred space may not feel ready for religious ritual in a wholly different environment. For example, a Roman Catholic used to a dark room with high ceilings and candles near sacred statues may find it odd to worship in a brightly lit plain Protestant room that resembles a college lecture hall. Each branch of Christianity has developed its own preferred ways to arrange its **sanctuary**. Some churches intentionally separate the clergy from the people, with steps between the **chancel** and the **nave** to symbolize that the altar represents proximity to God. Other churches arrange their space so as to minimize any such distinctions and separations. The theology of a church ought to be apparent by the layout of its ritual space, and altering the interior of a church building may have a considerable effect on the community.

pilgrimage
a religious journey to a sacred site

megachurch
a church, usually independent Protestant, serving thousands of worshipers

sanctuary
the entire worship space, or the area designated as holiest

chancel
the area that houses the altar in the front of the church

nave
the area in which the people stand or sit

Christian ritual gesture

Anyone engaging in international travel knows that symbolic gestures are particular to each community. In Japan, people bow to each other, rather than shake hands. In France, you air-kiss both sides of the face of friends and strangers. The Maori in New Zealand touch foreheads and noses in greeting. When at a Fourth of July concert even the musicians stand as they play "The Star Spangled Banner," a family that remains seated is making a symbolic statement about America. Religious rituals call for specialized body postures, hand movements, and voice projection. As with all other aspects of Christian worship, there is considerable variation in different churches concerning appropriate ritual gesture for Sunday gatherings.

Some people are accustomed to sitting for most of worship; yet until the fourteenth century, most church buildings were open spaces, with only a few benches provided for old people. In eighteenth-century England, **John Wesley** urged worshipers to stand while they sang hymns. Roman Catholics may **genuflect** in the aisle of the church as they enter a pew to show respect for the presence of Christ. At some contemporary churches, it is acceptable to lounge around on the floor. At the time of communion, some assemblies stand, some kneel, some remain sitting, and some file past those who give out the bread and wine. Each church community ought to be able to explain the symbolic meaning of the body postures it prefers.

Hand motions have ritual significance. Since early Christian times, it has been customary for believers to trace on their body a sign of the cross when they begin or conclude a prayer. This cross may be small, on one's forehead, or it may be a full-chest cross: touching the forehead, the center of the chest, and both shoulders in turn, thus symbolically placing one's very body under the cross of Christ. Since medieval times, many Christians fold their hands during prayer, presumably to keep the entire body turned into religious focus. Depictions of Jesus with folded hands are, however, anachronistic. Like all Jews of the first century, Jesus would have prayed in **orans**. This gesture with head facing up and arms and hands upraised is popular particularly in contemporary **Pentecostal** churches as a symbol of reaching toward God and receiving the gifts that come from God.

For thousands of years of religious ritual, the human voice has taken on an extraordinary character. Much speech during worship is carefully crafted to be rhythmic, so that the words capture both the mind and the spirit of the assembly. Churches that print out their texts may edit the words for rhythmic power, and clergy who prefer extemporized prayer rely on traditional rhythmic patterns that they have internalized. Some churches use drums in worship: a beat slightly faster than of the human heart enlivens a group of people, gets them on their feet, and unites them into one vibrant body.

John Wesley
(1703–1791) Anglican clergyman whose "methods" of spirituality led to the formation of churches called Methodist

genuflect
show respect by kneeling with one knee on the floor

orans
prayer posture with arms upraised

Pentecostal churches
a number of Protestant denominations that emphasize the presence and power of the Holy Spirit

See Plate 3 in the gallery. What does her attire suggest to us?

Religions use also melody. Anthropologists report that most ritual speech is sung, rather than spoken. It is as if the words of a religious ritual are so significant that a heightened form of speech is required. Even in Broadway musicals, the actors break into song for the most important speeches. In Christian churches this song was usually **chant**. In some African American churches, the preachers conclude their address by moving from speech to song in a ritual speech called **whooping**. Practically, if in the past the worship space was large, a sung phrase carried farther than did a spoken phrase by raising the pitch level of the male voice. But fundamental to worship are the emotional effects of music, the beauty and power that artful melody and rhythm provide, the role music plays in solidifying memory, and the unity that music creates in a communal gathering.

chant
a method of speaking words to a pattern of musical pitches

Sing lustily and with a good courage. Beware of singing as if you were half dead, or half asleep; but lift up your voice with strength. Be no more afraid of your voice now, nor more ashamed of its being heard, than when you sung the songs of Satan.

—*John Wesley, 1761* [11]

whooping
the exuberant chant used by some preachers

Christians have composed an immense body of religious music for their Sunday rituals. Some churches have kept alive ancient chant, the leaders and the entire assemblies able to sing without rehearsal a notated prose text. Some churches have found the best use of music to be in congregational **hymns** and songs that everyone sings together. In many Protestant churches, a Sunday service includes three or more hymns sung by the entire congregation, some beloved in the tradition, some newly composed. Churches that assume literacy may use hymnbooks that are provided in the pews or may project the songs onto a screen, while other churches prefer **call-and-response** group singing that does not require a printed text. Some churches have relied on choirs to provide the music, especially when the music is complex, with interweaving parts for different singers, and some churches are famous for the exuberant singing of their practiced choirs.

hymn
a Christian ritual song, often characterized by rhymed and rhythmic stanzas

call-and-response
a musical genre in which the leader sings a phrase to which the group sings a simple, repetitive response

At several times in the history of the church, leaders decided that the church music had become so complicated that the worshipers could no longer understand the words being sung, which usually came from the Bible. These leaders then ordered more simple music to be used. Some Protestant churches allow absolutely no musical instruments to accompany the human voice. Yet other Protestants regularly use all the band instruments that might be heard at entertainment venues. One way to study the 100,000 Sundays of Christian worship is to listen to the many different types of music heard around the world in praise and prayer.

Suggestions

1. Review the chapter's vocabulary: Advent, Ascension, Ash Wednesday, call-and-response, chancel, chant, Christmas, congregation, Easter, Epiphany, fundamentalist, genuflect, Good Friday, Holy Thursday, Holy Week, hymn, Jehovah's Witnesses, Lent, Maundy Thursday, liturgical year, megachurch, monastic orders, nave, orans, Palm Sunday, parish, Pascha, Paul, Pentecost, Pentecostal churches, pilgrimage, rites of passage, sacrifice, sanctoral cycle, sanctuary, Seventh-Day Adventists, Triduum, Three Days, John Wesley, and whooping.
2. Present arguments for and against the rituals of your academic institution.
3. Analyze the puberty rituals currently practiced in the United States.
4. Compare and contrast picture books published by churches that teach children the meaning of their Sunday ritual, among which are *A Children's Guide to Worship*, *Shouting!*, and *Sunday Morning*.[12]
5. Write a personal essay about the role of ritual meals in your family.
6. In the Bible, Exodus 12 describes the ritual of Passover. Compare Exodus 12 to the seder text used at a contemporary Jewish Passover meal.
7. Discuss Shirley Jackson's 1948 short story "The Lottery" as a way to think about the negative aspects of ritual.[13]
8. Discuss the 2003 film *Whale Rider*, in which the Maori of New Zealand both retain traditional rituals and alter them.
9. Attend a football or basketball game, and write an analysis of the rituals performed by the fans.

For further study

Bell, Catherine. *Ritual: Perspectives and Dimensions*. New York: Oxford University Press, 1997.

Bowen, John R., ed. *Religions in Practice: An Approach to the Anthropology of Religion*. 3d ed. Boston: Pearson Education, 2005.

Cooke, Bernard, and Gary Macy. *Christian Symbol and Ritual: An Introduction*. New York: Oxford University Press, 2005.

Mitchell, Nathan D. *Liturgy and the Social Sciences*. Collegeville, Minn.: Liturgical, 1999.

Rappaport, Roy A. *Ritual and Religion in the Making of Humanity*. Cambridge: Cambridge University Press, 1999.

Which symbols and rituals have Christians used for 100,000 Sundays?

Although historical records are scarce, scholars have pieced together a proposal about how the earliest Christians worshiped. Some of the symbols and rituals practiced by the followers of Jesus when they assembled during the first century after his lifetime remain in use in the twenty-first century. These symbols and rituals arose from three sources: the culture of the Roman Empire, the religious practices of Judaism, and the memory of the life of Jesus.

Greco-Roman symbols

The term "the Greco-Roman world" refers to the large area of lands and peoples encircling the Mediterranean Sea that was subject to the Roman government for about six centuries. The reason "Greco" is attached to "Roman" is that when Rome conquered the lands that Alexander the Great had subjugated, much of the Greek culture—for example, its religion, mythology, language, architecture, urban life, the Olympic games—was adopted by the Roman Empire. Thus, the culture previously cultivated by the Greeks was now enforced by Roman political power. By the year 70 C.E., the majority of Christians were Gentile, that is, not Jewish, and they adapted some Greco-Roman cultural symbols for use on Sunday.

One Greco-Roman linguistic symbol was referring to God as a father. The polytheistic religion of ancient Greece imagined that the many gods and goddesses were related in a family system, with deities mating with other deities or humans, to bring to birth more deities or demigods. In some polytheisms, the head of the pantheon is the great mother, but in the Greek symbol system, the head was Zeus, called the father of fathers. When this religious system was adopted by Romans, the names of the deities changed, but most of the stories and relationships between the characters remained the same. The head of the Roman pantheon was Jupiter, the name combining two words, Zeus and *pater*, meaning father. Thus, on top of the universe was a divine Father whose authority, like that of the father in the Greco-Roman family, was to be unchallenged and whose word must be obeyed. The streets on which earliest Christians lived were filled with people who spoke about Jupiter as the Father of all.

Pray then in this way: Our Father in heaven, hallowed be your name.

—*Matthew 6:9*

When you pray, say: Father, hallowed be your name.

—*Luke 11:2*

At nearly every worship service for 100,000 Sundays, Christians have addressed God as Father. The Bible records Jesus as calling God *Abba*, an **Aramaic** word perhaps meaning "papa." In the **New Testament**, *Abba* is translated with the Greek word *pater*, father. Two of the four Gospels cite slightly different versions of a prayer that Jesus taught his followers, which begins by addressing God as "Father." Called the Lord's Prayer, the Our Father, or the Prayer of Jesus, this prayer is the most common and beloved in the Christian religion, and some Christians use it as the model for all their prayers. Several English versions are in regular use: one retains sixteenth-century pronoun and verbs forms (e.g., thy, art); one was approved by an international ecumenical committee in 1988; one omits the concluding praise; sins, trespasses, or debts may be confessed. How much to retain the prominence of the title "Father" in worship became a controversial issue in some twentieth-century churches.

A second religious symbol in Greco-Roman religion that became important to Christians was incarnation. Some world religions propose that

Aramaic
a Semitic language related to Hebrew

New Testament
the twenty-seven books about the meaning of Jesus and life in the church compiled into the Christian Bible

although the divine is **transcendent,** the immortal divinity can and does take on flesh, becoming "in-carnate" in a living being. Thanks to such incarnation, the divine is not far distant, but instead is here among us, **immanent.** Greco-Roman religion included stories of divine incarnations, for example, when Zeus-Jupiter took on the form of a male or an animal in order to seduce a human woman. In Greco-Roman religion, the demigods were usually the offspring of a divine father and a human mother. Although such humans were not immortal, they had extraordinary powers. That Christians spoke of Jesus as the incarnation of God and as "the son of God" would be familiar religious speech to many Gentiles.

transcendent
beyond the universe, outside human categories and experience

immanent
present within human experience

At nearly every worship service for 100,000 Sundays, Christians have referred to Jesus as the son of God. In English, "son" is usually capitalized, to demonstrate that although all believers can be described as children of God, Jesus not only had a unique relationship with God, but also shared God's divinity. Over the centuries theologians have labored to explain the symbol of Jesus' sonship. Fifth-century theologians emphasized that although the Greek religious category is used, Christians do not mean that God mated with Mary to produce Jesus in the way that Zeus was said to have mated with Alcmene to produce Hercules. The language is not literal, but uses symbolism to indicate a theological belief about the relationship between God and Jesus.

For its intellectual pursuits, the Roman world used the Greek language. A language organizes reality in the minds of those who speak it by imposing its distinctions on vocabulary and grammar. Since Greek calls a uterus a *hystera*, Greek speakers may expect women to be regularly hysterical. If, following Greek, I live in a *polis*, a metropolis, then it is wise for me to be "polite." During the lifetime of Jesus, educated persons in the Roman Empire were fluent in Greek, and thus Greek categories became foundational in Christian thought. Even Jews in the first century regularly used not the historic Hebrew text of their sacred scriptures, but rather the **Septuagint**.

Septuagint
the primary ancient Greek translation of the Hebrew Bible

At most worship services for 100,000 Sundays, Christian usage reflects especially one Greek word, *kyrios*. In the Roman Empire, this title was used to address Jupiter, the emperor, a male of high status, or a husband. The Septuagint uses the word *kyrios* as the primary title for God, and the New Testament uses *kyrios* to designate both the title for God and the address to Jesus. Since the sixteenth century, the standard English translation of *kyrios* has been "lord." Thus, when the leader of worship says to the assembly,

---

Answering her son's question, the Hasidic Jewish mother says of Jesus, "The goyim believe he was the son of the Ribbono Shel Olom [the Master of the Universe]. They make paintings of him because he is holy to them." "What does that mean, the son of the Ribbono Shel Olom?" "I don't begin to understand it," his mother said.

—Chaim Potok[1]

"The Lord be with you," the term can refer both to the Almighty God and to the revered master Jesus. Some contemporary English-speaking churches continue to sing or speak in Greek the ancient prayer addressed to *Kyrie*.

Greco-Roman rituals

Several types of communal rituals that were significant in the Roman Empire influenced Christian Sunday worship. Roman cities boasted a wide variety of eating clubs, associations that included communal meals and gave their members a strong sense of belonging to a small, defined group in what was a vast, multicultural nation. Some of these clubs, many male only, encouraged philosophical discussions over regularly scheduled meals. Thus, when Christians met for a weekly meal, they were adapting a common cultural practice: what was uncommon, however, was that together at table were slaves and masters, both women and men. Christians in the second century had to defend their weekly meals to governmental authorities, who had come to suspect that all such eating clubs might be subversive to the national interests. Throughout Christian history, this communal meal has sometimes indeed had explicit countercultural intent.

One common Roman practice was to share a meal at the gravesite of the beloved dead. Such a ritual took place at the annual anniversary of the death. Probably these rituals echoed far more ancient beliefs about literally eating with the dead. Thus, when Christians met in the catacombs for a meal, they were not usually hiding from governmental authorities. Rather, they were adapting a common cultural practice of bonding together a group of people near the bones of the beloved. In Christian practice, the bones that became especially beloved were those of the **martyrs**. Still today many Christians have the sense that those who have died in the faith are mystically present with them at worship. **All Saints Day** is kept by some churches as a memorial of those who have died in the Christian faith. Although the bones of the dead may not be present, their memory is.

The mystery religions were a significant feature of life in the Roman Empire. Characteristic of mystery religions were their secrecy and the arduous, lengthy process of their initiation. These religions promised participants salvation from their banal existence and the experience of heightened spirituality. Outsiders were excluded from knowledge of these rites.

It is likely that some aspects of the mystery religions influenced early Christian worship. Some churches have revived the practice of dismissing all the people who are preparing for baptism from worship before the meal is shared. Eastern Orthodox worship, especially when conducted in a foreign language with elaborate symbolism and complex ritual that situates the priest

See Plate 4 in the gallery. How do you react to a depiction of a meal in a cemetery?

martyr
someone killed because of their religious beliefs

All Saints Day
November 1, commemoration of the most eminent or all of the faithful departed

unseen behind a room divider, contains a memory of the otherworldly character of the mystery religions' ritual. The temple worship of the **Church of Jesus Christ of the Latter-day Saints** is closed to outsiders. However, the primary intent of early Christians, to convert all peoples to the faith that was freely given by God, meant that most Sunday worship minimized elements of secrecy.

At the time of the origin of Christianity, Roman cities had numerous temples in which sacrifices were offered to the gods, and authorities scheduled civic rituals during which incense was burned to dead emperors, and eventually also to living emperors, as acknowledgment that the emperors were themselves divine. One reason that some Christians were martyred was that they refused to offer sacrifices to the emperor.

Yet something of the rituals of such sacrifices influenced Christian practice. Although Christians do not burn up dead animals on Sunday morning, they do speak of their worship as "a sacrifice of praise." Some contemporary worshipers speak of the time they devote to worship as "a sacrifice." Some Christians regularly burn incense to enhance their communal prayer, and although the practice probably entered Sunday worship as a way to cover with sweet smells the body odor of an unwashed crowd, the religious idea is that as the smoke of the fire ascends, so prayer goes up to God. Some church services urge believers to give up unnecessary or harmful activities, perhaps as a discipline during Lent, and this abstinence is usually termed "a sacrifice."

Some Christians, especially Roman Catholics, Eastern Orthodox, and Episcopalians, describe the meal of bread and wine as a sacrifice. Bread and wine, rather than a dead animal, are offered to God as a gift, and God responds by blessing the worshipers. Nearly all Christians speak of the death of Jesus as a sacrifice. His execution is understood, similar to sacrifices in Greco-Roman religious practice, as a death that ensured the life of the people. Humans live off the lives of others, and, because of God's self-giving sacrifice, Christians live off the life of Jesus. For some churches, the sacrifice was offered once, when Jesus was executed; for others, every Sunday worship mystically joins into and repeats the "sacrifice" of his death.

Church of Jesus Christ of the Latter-day Saints a variant of Christianity, commonly called Mormons, arising about 1830 under Joseph Smith, who consider The Book of Mormon to be sacred scripture

Jewish symbols

One of the many peoples held subject by the Roman Empire during the first century C.E. was the Jewish population residing in the eastern Mediterranean. The origin of Judaism, as an ethnic identity and

The Christians meet on a fixed day before dawn and sing responsively a hymn to Christ as to a god, and they partake of food—but ordinary and innocent food.

—*Pliny, governor of Pontus, to Trajan, Roman emperor, about 112 C.E.*[2]

a world religion, can be dated variously: from the life of Abraham, about 1800 B.C.E.; or from the tale of the exodus from Egypt under Moses, about 1250 B.C.E.; or from the monotheistic theology of the prophets in about 600 B.C.E.; or from 70 C.E., when the Roman army destroyed the Jewish Temple in Jerusalem, which radically altered Jewish practice from its historic centrality of temple ritual to the contemporary primacy of home ritual.

The books that constitute the Hebrew Bible include many stories about God's dealings with the people. Primarily, according to Jewish belief, God is described as a **covenant** provider. Jews described their relationship with God using language similar to that of ancient Near Eastern overlords: God set up a covenant with the people who gave to God their loyalty, their regular worship, their obedience, even one-tenth of their income, and God gave them what they needed for life. They believed that God would save them from their enemies if they were faithful subjects of divine authority. Often throughout the Hebrew Scriptures, hardships were interpreted as divine punishment that intended to correct human behavior. Even the story of the first murderer, Cain, shows God as a merciful provider. God does not execute Cain, but protects him, exiling him to distant territory, away from the community that he harmed. The foundational Jewish tale is that God helped the people escape from slavery in Egypt, miraculously brought them across a sea, fed them while they lived as nomads, and guided their colonization of Palestine.

At nearly every worship service for 100,000 Sundays, Christians have continued the Jewish practice of praising God as a merciful provider. Each week God is honored for the creation itself, for its continual fruitfulness, for another week of living, for the gifts of the covenant, for health and safety, and for the promise of a supernatural life that conquers death. Some churches stress the obedience required of believers for them to receive blessings. For example, in some church buildings, one version of the **Ten Commandments** is painted on the front wall of the room. Other churches stress the beneficence of God, who is always ready to provide, even to people who are disobedient. How the covenant with a provident God is expressed is one identification mark of different denominations.

Histories of religion usually date the origin of **monotheism** to several Jewish prophets who spoke during the century in which they had been militarily deported away from Jerusalem. The idea that Israel had its own tribal deity gave way to the idea that the one God was above the whole earth. The divine was symbolized, not as in polytheism with a plethora of deities, but with only one. Thus, Jews who were far distant from the Temple were still protected by their covenant God.

Christianity carried on the monotheism of Judaism. "I believe in one God," begins the **creed** that many churches include in worship. The emphasis on only one God has led some Christians to forcibly convert, and even execute, practitioners of other religious traditions, and some contemporary churches affirm that only their kind of Christian is approved by God. However, faith in

covenant
a mutual commitment between God and the people

Ten Commandments
an edited version of Exodus 20:2-17 numbered one to ten

monotheism
the belief that only one God exists and, in consequence, the worship of that one God

creed
a statement of belief

An image of the Trinity by the Christian mystic Hildegard of Binger (1089–1179)

the oneness of God suggests one divine order, one religion, one community, one creedal statement, a mysterious unity that reflects divine being. Focus on the one God also led to the development of **theology** as the correct way to understand the divine.

Over the first four centuries of the Christian church, theologians developed statements that elaborated monotheism with the mystery of the Trinity. Christian doctrine states that God is not only the almighty transcendent creator; God is also incarnate in Jesus; and God is immanent in the church through the Spirit. Although Jews and Muslims see the symbol of the Trinity as tri-theism, Christian theology has always maintained that in a mysterious way this triune being is one God. At nearly every worship service for 100,000

theology
organized study of and teachings about God

years, there will be some reference to the Trinity, some churches focusing
more on the Father, others on the Son, others on the Spirit.[3] In nineteenth-
century Boston, a group of liberal Christians rejected the traditional belief in
the Trinity. They staunchly affirm one God and are called **Unitarians**; some
consider themselves Christian, and some do not.

In Judaism, the written word honored by the tradition is the most valued
symbol of the divine. To approach God and receive divine blessing, Jews are to
read and live out the word of God. The Hebrew Scriptures include the Torah, the
story of the formation of the people of Israel; the Prophets, the narratives about
and the messages of the greatest preachers in the tradition; and the Writings, a collection of poems, short stories, and other works of religious literature. The entire
Hebrew Bible was adopted by Christians as being, or containing, or conveying,
the word of God. One reason why ritual space is less important in Christianity
than in some other religions is that most churches have maintained that wherever
a group of believers gather around the word of God, there is holy ground. When
Christians read in the Hebrew Scriptures terms like the temple of God, the city
of God, the people of God, they include themselves in these phrases.

At nearly every worship service for 100,000 Sundays, Christians have
read from or cited language from the Hebrew Bible, which is included in the
Christian Bible as the **Old Testament**. Some churches read a section from the
Old Testament at each worship service. Christian theology arose as believers discussed what these Jewish words meant for followers of Jesus. By the end of the
first century, there was enough disagreement between Jews and Christians about
the interpretation of these Scriptures that the one religion had become two.

Christian use of Jewish imagery can be seen in the symbol of the lamb.
For hundreds of years, Jews had sacrificed lambs and goats to God as symbols
of their devotion. According to their Scriptures, God had ordered these sacrifices to be conducted in precise ways and overseen by the priests. Because Jews
understood themselves as having been originally herders, a lamb was a symbol
of themselves and of their God-given sustenance, and this they offered to God
with prayer and praise.

The sections in the Hebrew Bible that deal with the sacrifice of lambs
were reinterpreted by Christians as referring to Jesus. Christian theologians
applied the language of sacrifice to explain Jesus' execution: Jesus' crucifixion
was symbolically a sacrifice, and Jesus was symbolically a lamb. Many churches
read each December from New Testament passages in which a preacher called
John the Baptist points to Jesus as the Lamb of God. Many Christian churches
have on a wall somewhere a depiction of a lamb; weekly many Christians sing
or say a prayer asking Jesus, "the Lamb of God," for mercy; and prior to invit-
ing the assembly forward to take communion, Roman Catholic priests hold
up a piece of the bread and say, "This is the Lamb of God, who takes away the
sins of the world."

In Matthias Grunewald's fourteenth-century altar painting, a lamb stands at the foot of the cross, and John the Baptist is pointing to Jesus.

Jewish rituals

Not only Romans conducted religious sacrifices. Biblical Jews also were expected to offer or to pay for animal sacrifices at annual festivals and for various occasions of personal devotion. The Gospel of Luke says that forty days after Mary gave birth to Jesus, she and Joseph went to the Temple in Jerusalem to negotiate a sacrifice of two turtledoves. During the lifetime of Jesus, about two-thirds of the world's Jews lived, not in Palestine near the Temple in Jerusalem, but throughout the Mediterranean world. It is not clear how the Jews who lived distant from the Temple fulfilled these regulations, but all first-century Jews expected that religion included literal sacrifices. Thus, Jews joined polytheists in bringing to early Christian practice at least the language of sacrifice.

Two primary rituals associated with the Jewish **Sabbath** observance became foundational for Christian worship through the centuries. The first was Jewish family meals. Historic Judaism maintained the belief that all food comes from God, who is to be thanked for it. Each Sabbath observance, held

Sabbath
Saturday, the Jewish day of rest

on Friday after sundown, as well as Passover, the primary annual Jewish festival, included a family meal, at which the father of the household offered a prayer of thanksgiving. At the beginning of the meal, God is thanked for bread, which is then distributed to everyone at the table, and at the conclusion of the meal, God is praised for wine, which is then passed around for everyone to drink. For their ritual meal, Christians use bread and wine because Jesus did, and Jesus did because he was observing Jewish religious ritual. The bread and wine symbolize all God's gifts, from the creation of the world down to the present food. Although over the centuries some churches omitted any such thanksgiving prayer, in many churches there is a substantial **prayer of thanksgiving**, descendent from Jewish meal prayer, that the minister speaks or chants over the bread and wine.

Customary parts of a eucharistic prayer:

1. Praise to God for creation
2. Praise to God for salvation through Christ
3. Recital of the New Testament's words of Jesus at the Last Supper
4. Remembrance of the work of Christ
5. Prayer for the Holy Spirit
6. Concluding Trinitarian praise

---

eucharistic prayer / anaphora / canon / great thanksgiving / prayer of thanksgiving

minister's prayer thanking God for the sacramental meal and asking for God's blessing, considered by some Christians as consecrating the bread and wine

synagogue

Jewish institution for weekly assembly around the word of God and communal prayer

An adaptation of the Jewish family meal came about because many early Christian assemblies were not constituted with family units. The New Testament speaks of leaving one's mother and father to follow Christ. So the weekly meal and its thanksgivings were celebrated in what is called a fictive family, rather than a literal family. One joined this family of faith, rather than being born into it. The early Christian practice of a passing around a greeting of peace demonstrated that the worshipers were now brothers and sisters, and thus, quite different from the current practice of a cultural handshake, the symbol was at least in some places a familial full kiss on the lips. This ritual soon devolved into a less startling practice.

The second Sabbath ritual was a **synagogue** meeting. It seems that synagogues arose among Jews who lived far distant from the Jerusalem Temple. During the first century, Jewish males were expected to attend synagogue worship, and funeral citations indicate that women were also important members of the synagogue communities. At these services the people joined in a creedal statement of faith, sang praises to God, listened to the Scriptures, heard a learned teacher preach on the meaning of the text, and prayed for divine blessings. For many Christians, the content of synagogue worship constitutes half or all of their regular Sunday service. Recently a few churches have set up their worship space with two distinct areas: in one the people sit around a reading desk for their version of synagogue worship, and in the other the people stand around the table for their bread and wine. This set-up makes clear that the basic structure of Christian worship combines a synagogue meeting with Jewish table practice.

Over 100,000 Sundays Christians have continued the Jewish use of the psalms for prayer and praise. An essential ritual in synagogues was the use of chant. Psalms were sung to simple repetitive melodies, and biblical selections and prayers were chanted. Early Christian assemblies continued this use of music for their praise and petition, and some contemporary churches are skilled in chanting a psalm each week.

Whoever loves father or mother more than me is not worthy of me.

—*Matthew 10:37*

Whoever comes to me and does not hate father and mother, wife and children, brothers and sisters, yes, and even life itself, cannot be my disciple.

—*Luke 14:26*

Symbols associated with Jesus

Historians agree that during the first century of the common era a man named Jesus from the town of Nazareth in Palestine lived as an itinerant preacher

Pentecostal churches encourage prayer in the style that early Christians adopted from Judaism, their hands upraised.

and healer and died by execution. He was significant enough that still today many societies number the years of the calendar according to the medieval (incorrect) computation of his birth, since although the old abbreviations, B.C. (before Christ) and A.D. (*Anno Domini*, in the year of our Lord), are being replaced with B.C.E. (before the common era) and C.E. (common era), the old numbering that centers human history around the birth of Jesus remains. Christians, however, make ultimate religious claims about this Jesus, and these claims are expressed with symbolic language that reflects what is remembered of his life and mission.

Jesus was a teacher who spoke in parables and offered memorable but controversial interpretations of Jewish religious belief and practice. What we know of his teaching is found in the Gospels that were written thirty to seventy years after his lifetime. His followers, and later the church, believed that he spoke the word of God. Inspired by the Gospel of John, which describes the birth of Jesus as the arrival of the word of God in the world, Christians have called him the Word. In some churches, when the passage from the Gospels is read on Sunday, everyone in the church stands, as if Jesus himself has entered the room and is speaking, and some churches capitalize Word to denote the connection between the Bible and Jesus.

Like several others in the Jewish tradition and the Greco-Roman world, Jesus was a miracle worker and healer. According to ancient understandings of the human person, personal wholeness is not separated from physical health. In Greco-Roman religion, the healer Asclepius was termed "savior," for to be saved is to be made whole. In Plato's *Phaedo,* even Socrates, just before being executed on the charge of atheism, reminds his friends to sacrifice to Asclepius for him. So also Jesus, in bringing divine power to his listeners, healed them of disease and infirmity. That Christian worship refers to Jesus as the Savior symbolizes the faith that Jesus brings to the world the health and wholeness for which it seeks.

Jesus' followers claimed that he was the messiah, sent to deliver the people. Over the centuries during which Jews had been politically subjugated by one empire after another, Jews had nourished the hope that God would raise up from among the people someone who would function like the ancient Israelite kings and lead the people into a time of freedom. These kings had been anointed with sacred oil to symbolize that they embodied the authority of God. The Hebrew word *meshiach*, messiah, means "the anointed one." The Greek word for messiah is *christos*: when English speakers call Jesus "**Christ**," they are speaking Greek. There will be very few Sunday worship services that do not refer to Jesus as Christ, the one elected by God, figuratively anointed, to bring the people to the land of freedom. By calling itself "Christian" the church gives precedence to this symbolic term and places this title onto all his followers.

Christ
messianic title for Jesus, from Greek for "the anointed one"

In ancient Judaism, it was primarily the king, such as King David, who was described as a son of God. This practice paralleled the symbolic language of other ancient cultures, in which the monarch was accepted as the descendent of the deity and consequently ruled by divine right. Early Christian use of the idea of "Son of God" may have arisen out of this royal understanding. But the New Testament includes many passages in which all believers are connected to God, no longer through the Jewish covenant, but rather through baptism, which makes them sons and daughters of God with Christ. Although Greek does not use capital and small letters in the same way we do, English-speaking Christians express the perfect relationship between Jesus and God by capitalizing the word Son when referring to Jesus, and theologians used the imagery of both kingship and sonship when describing the role Christ plays in salvation.

It was not Jesus' crucifixion, but rather faith in his resurrection that brought about the Christian church. After his death, his followers claimed that he was alive again. They experienced his presence in their midst, and his resurrection from the grave proved that, despite his execution, he was the Word of God, the Savior, the Christ, and the Son of God. He was not only their master, their *kyrios*, their lord (small l); he was God among them, their *kyrios*, their Lord (capital L); indeed, Jesus bore the very name of God (LORD), although Greek makes no clear distinction between these meanings.

Sunday worship encapsulates its reverence for Jesus as teacher, healer, messiah, king, the ultimate child of God, and the resurrected Lord in the vocabulary with which it addresses and describes Jesus. Sunday worship will include some or all of this language. Although outsiders may find much of this symbolic speech opaque, Christian communities assume that, as is usual with symbols, instruction is required before participants can enter into all the intended religious meanings.

Rituals associated with Jesus

Jesus is remembered as having prayed to God in both joy and sorrow, and using him as a model, Christian worship includes prayer. But it is especially Jesus' meal practice that became the ritual center of Christian worship. It is not surprising that the fresco painted by Leonardo da Vinci of Jesus eating his last supper with his disciples is one of the most famous depictions in Christianity. Jesus shared a meal with his small circle of followers on the night before he was arrested, tried, and executed. The Gospel narratives that describe this meal quote Jesus calling the bread his body and the wine "my blood of the covenant" (Mark) or "the new covenant in my blood" (Luke). The followers of Jesus saw in this meal a symbol of Jesus himself, and some Christians understand that

See Plate 5 in the gallery for a sixteenth-century altarpiece that contemporized Jesus' Last Supper.

their entire Sunday service is a ritual repetition of this last supper of Jesus. Centuries of Christian theologians have discussed what it means that this meal brings the Lord's death into the present community. At some periods of history, efforts to authorize one meaning of this language led to contentious church councils, persecutions, and even executions. Still today, the way this language is explained is one marker of denominational difference.

Although some churches understand their ritual as reminiscent primarily of the Last Supper, the Gospels narrate many meals that Jesus shared with his followers, and it was because the resurrection of Christ was experienced on Sunday that Christians came to share their bread and wine, not on a Thursday, like the Last Supper, but on Sunday. A commentator in the second century explained that Christians met on Sunday because

---

For I received from the Lord what I also handed on to you, that the Lord Jesus on the night when he was betrayed took a loaf of bread.... For as often as you eat this bread and drink the cup, you proclaim the Lord's death until he comes.

—*Paul, I Corinthians 11:23, 26, about 57 C.E.*

What do you think of this communion table, emphasizing the joyful meal of the resurrection?

on that day God created light, Christ rose from the dead, and the Holy Spirit came upon believers. By the second century, it was evident that Christians were not Jews. Jews observe the seventh day of the week, after a week of work, as Sabbath rest; Christians worship on Sunday, the first day of the week, at the beginning of each cycle. Some churches stress that every Sunday celebrates the resurrection. The meal is the food shared in what is already beginning to be the new life made possible by Christ.

We say, with regard to the Bread, "We thank you, our Father, for the life and knowledge which you made known us to through Jesus your servant. To you be glory for ever. . . . You, almighty Lord, created all things for the sake of your name, and you gave food and drink to human beings for enjoyment, so that they would thank you. But you graced us with spiritual food and drink and eternal light through your servant."

—*The* Didache, *a first-century set of Christian instructions*[4]

Note the differences between I Corinthians and the Didache.

Christian belief that Jesus' body is not in the grave but is raised to life eternal determines the primary vocabulary both for the ritual of the meal and for Christian life. In Christian use, the word *body* has at least four different meanings. First, Christians say that Jesus' body is raised to a new and mysterious life. Second, the bread of the meal is called his body. Thus, the staple of human food is merged with the resurrected life of Christ. Third, the community that shares the food is called "the body of Christ." The idea here is that the transformed life of Christian people embodies the resurrection of Christ in the world. As the theologian **Augustine** preached in the fourth century, "What you receive is the mystery that means you."[5] The body is on the table, and the body gathers around the table. Fourth, the body of the community will demonstrate its faith by honoring the physical bodies of themselves and one another. Some churches stress one usage over the others, but all may be present on any Sunday morning.

Augustine (354–430) bishop of Hippo, Africa, the most influential Christian theologian since Paul

The Sunday synthesis

Although there are exceptions to every generalization, and although some churches developed distinctive practices, most churches maintain much from the symbols and rituals of the first century of Christian practice. Some churches use the full service every Sunday, and others use the full event only on special occasions. The interpretations that communities give to this event have evolved over time. In the earliest Christian assemblies, a strong sense that the world was soon coming to an end meant that the meal was a celebration of the beginning of the new age that had begun in the resurrection of Christ. Such **eschatological** emphasis stressed the presence of the risen Christ in the assembly and the empowerment that the Spirit of Christ gave to the

eschatology belief about the end of the world

Churches name their Sunday ritual meal of communion in diverse ways.

- The Breaking of the Bread recalls first-century references to the meal.
- The Divine Liturgy, a term used by the Eastern Orthodox, stresses the heavenly nature of the event.
- Eucharist comes from the Greek word for "thanksgiving" and emphasizes gratitude for salvation.
- Holy Communion emphasizes the sharing of the community in the meal.
- The Lord's Supper, a term used especially by Protestants, emphasizes the idea of eating with Jesus.
- The Mass, a term used mostly by Roman Catholics, derives from the closing dismissal of the medieval service.

Over all that we take to eat, we bless the Creator of all things through God's Son Jesus Christ and through the Holy Spirit. And on the day named after the sun, all, whether they live in the city or the countryside, are gathered together in unity. Then the records of the apostles or the writings of the prophets are read for as long as there is time. When the reader has concluded, the presider in a discourse admonishes and invites us into the pattern of these good things. Then we all stand together and offer prayer. When we have concluded the prayer, bread is set out to eat, together with wine and water. The presider likewise offers up prayer and thanksgiving, as much as he can, and the people sing out their assent saying the Amen. There is a distribution of the things over which thanks have been said, and each person participates, and these things are sent by the deacons to those who are not present.

—Justin, ca. 150[6]

Justin
lay professor of philosophy whose descriptions of Christian worship are among the earliest extant, martyred in 165

baptized believers. Renewed by the Spirit of Christ, believers were to live in peace with one another and with compassion for all in need. Although subsequent centuries saw this eschatological emphasis diminish, some contemporary churches continue to stress the new age brought about through Christ, and others anticipate that with the end of the world coming soon, worship helps prepare believers for the arrival of the eschaton.

Christian symbols and rituals did not remain static over the centuries. For example, the first Christians shared an entire meal, but by the second century the meal had been condensed into only bread and wine. An evening meeting after the workday became a morning meeting before work. Throughout Christian history, there was often controversy about the contents and meanings of worship that led one group of Christians to split off from another and to form a separate assembly. Some symbols and rituals were dropped over the years; some were so covered over by others that the original intent was obscured; some innovations were short lived; some became standard operating procedure. All communities, however, claimed that they were worshiping the way that best pleased God, the way most appropriate for the situation, the way most true to Christian beliefs. However, there has long been and continues to be considerable disagreement as to what this best way is.

Christian worship 100,000 Sundays ago

1. Worship occurred on Sunday, the first day of the week.
2. It used historic language to make ultimate claims about Jesus.
3. It included praises addressed to God.
4. It included readings from the Bible and commentary on those readings.
5. It included a sharing of bread and wine.
6. It included prayers for God's Spirit in the community and the world.
7. It made some connection with the wider world.

Suggestions

1. Review the chapter's vocabulary: All Saints Day, anaphora, Aramaic, Augustine, Breaking of the Bread, Christ, canon, Church of Jesus Christ of the Latter-day Saints, covenant, creed, Divine Liturgy, eschatology, Eucharist, eucharistic prayer, great thanksgiving, Holy Communion, immanent, Justin, Lord's Supper, martyr, Mass, monotheism, New Testament, Old Testament, prayer of thanksgiving, Sabbath, Septuagint, synagogue, Ten Commandments, theology, transcendent, and Unitarian-Universalist Association.

2. Present arguments for and against the primary Christian worship always being held on Sunday.

3. If Christianity developed out of Judaism, what accounts for the history of Christian discrimination against Jews?

4. Is it a problem that the four Gospels tell the story of Jesus in different ways?

5. Write a personal essay in which you contrast what this chapter says about Jesus with what you previously heard, religiously believe, or encountered in a movie.

6. In the Bible, Luke 24 narrates four events that occurred on the day of Jesus' resurrection. Discuss how Luke 24 has influenced Christian worship patterns.

7. Discuss Ursula LeGuin's short story "The Barrow."[7] What makes something Christian?

8. Discuss the 1973 film *Jesus Christ Superstar*. How is attending Sunday worship different from watching the movie?

9. Attend a Sunday service of the Christian Church—Disciples of Christ, a denomination that claims to model its worship on first-century practices. Compare what you encounter with the contents of this chapter.

For further study

Balentine, Samuel H. *The Torah's Vision of Worship*. Minneapolis: Fortress Press, 1999.

Borg, Marcus. *Jesus: Uncovering the Life, Teaching, and Relevance of a Religious Revolutionary*. San Francisco: HarperOne, 2006.

Bradshaw, Paul F. *The Search for the Origins of Christian Worship: Sources and Methods for the Study of Early Liturgy*. 2nd ed. New York: Oxford University Press, 2002.

Cahill, Thomas. *Sailing the Wine-Dark Sea: Why the Greeks Matter*. New York: Nan A. Talese, 2003.

Crossan, John Dominic. *The Birth of Christianity: Discovering What Happened in the Years Immediately after the Execution of Jesus*. San Francisco: HarperSanFrancisco, 1998.

Heschel, Abraham Joshua. *The Sabbath: Its Meaning for Modern Man*. New York: Farrar, Straus and Giroux, 1951.

For histories of Christian worship, see:

Foley, Edward. *From Age to Age: How Christians Have Celebrated the Eucharist*. Illus. Robin Faulkner. Chicago: Liturgy Training Publications, 1991.

Senn, Frank C. *Christian Liturgy, Catholic and Evangelical*. Minneapolis: Fortress Press, 1997.

———. *The People's Work: A Social History of the Liturgy*. Minneapolis: Fortress Press, 2006.

Wainwright, Geoffrey, and Karen Westerfield Tucker, ed. *The Oxford History of Christian Worship*. New York: Oxford University Press, 2006.

White, James F. *A Brief History of Christian Worship*. Nashville: Abingdon, 1993.

———. *Documents of Christian Worship: Descriptive and Interpretive Sources*. Louisville: Westminster John Knox, 1992.

White, Susan J. *A History of Women in Christian Worship*. Cleveland: Pilgrim, 2003.

Chapter 5
What comes down to us from 75,000 Sundays ago?

Weekly symbols and rituals standardized

Christian worship 100,000 Sundays ago was characterized by diversity in text and style. Christian assemblies in different areas of the greater Mediterranean world proclaimed the word at a meal on Sunday, but since early Christians expected that the world was soon coming to an end, there was no interest in designing worship for the long haul and no reason to aim for widespread uniformity. Justin's description indicates that the presider freely composed the primary prayers on Sunday as well as he was able. Over the next several centuries, some cultural groups came to prefer elaborate rituals with layered metaphor in their prayers, while others modeled their worship on the straight-forward rhetorical style practiced in the civic courts.

From the early centuries of Christian worship, only a few texts of worship have survived, and scholars caution students not to generalize the data discovered. A collection of Sunday prayers from some area in Europe compiled in the fifth century does not indicate how many assemblies used this text. It is likely that accounts of worship from this time period were more prescriptive, a bishop telling clergy what to do, than descriptive, a record of what was actually occurring at worship. Directions for worship in major cathedrals cannot have applied to small village churches. When we read rules that forbid some practice—for example, a regulation requiring that only officially approved texts be sung in worship—we can be sure that what is being forbidden was in fact taking place. These caveats apply also to the contemporary church, in which a specific congregation may not be following the practice that its leaders expect. Aware of how little we actually know of worship in the first six centuries of the church, this chapter presents some of the symbols and rituals that were added by the year 600 and that survive in the twenty-first century on Main Street, USA.

Over the first six centuries of Christianity, Sunday's symbols and rituals came to be somewhat standardized. During this time period, Christian worship moved from small groups meeting in someone's home to a majority of the Mediterranean population meeting in massive church buildings that were adorned with extensive and expensive art. What had been a countercultural, even illegal, Jesus movement became the official religion of the Roman Empire with many government officials attending worship. The freedom that each small assembly had known evolved into formulas that assemblies were expected to use, and many of these formulas are still in use today. Some Christians judge these historic formulas to be ritually helpful and emotionally satisfying, while others, who think that worship should always be newly composed, have little interest in maintaining sixth- and seventh-century practices.

> Women should not approach the altar.
>
> —*Canon 44 of Laodicea, c. 365*[1]

The oldest extant list of the books in the Christian Bible comes from 367. Thus, it took three hundred years before bishops and theologians agreed which of the many Christian writings that were circulating proclaimed most authoritatively the life, death, and resurrection of Jesus. The **canon** was approved to designate which writings should be read at the Sunday service. It seems safe to say that had there been no process of liturgical standardization, there would be no Christian Bible. The Christian Bible includes the Hebrew Scriptures, four Gospels, a book describing the first two decades of the church, letters written by Paul and other first-century church leaders, and one book of **apocalypticism**. Protestant denominations include in their Old Testament only the books that were in the Jewish Bible, while the Eastern Orthodox and Roman Catholics include seven other Jewish texts that were preserved in Greek. Some noncanonical writings from the first and second centuries, especially noncanonical Gospels, have received considerable attention over recent decades. Although on occasion assemblies may read aloud other texts, for example, a letter from the current bishop, normally the solemn reading during Sunday worship is only from the Old and the New Testaments of the Bible.

biblical canon
the authorized list of books that constitute the Bible

apocalypticism
a worldview that employs complex symbolic imagery to describe the cataclysmic end of the world

Contemporary Greek Orthodox churches prefer to read the Old Testament in its classic Greek translation, called the Septuagint, and the New Testament in its original first-century Greek. But given the principle that the word of God speaks to everyone, repeatedly over Christian history church bodies have sponsored new translations into their vernacular language. Many oral languages around the world were first reduced to writing by Christian missionaries, who wanted everyone to be able to read the Bible in their own language. A memory of Hebrew and Greek remains a part of much Christian worship, with the words **Amen**, **Hallelujah** (or *Alleluia*), *Christ*, and **Kyrie eleison** heard on Sundays all around the world.

The most famous Roman Catholic translation of the Bible, called the Vulgate—think "the vulgar" tongue—was completed about the year 400. A translation into Latin was necessary since by that time residents of the Roman Empire spoke Latin rather than Greek. Western Catholics used the Vulgate for over a millennium. In the twentieth century, when only a small number of the educated understood Latin, the Roman Catholic hierarchy authorized language groups to prepare biblical translations in their vernacular.

The most famous English-language biblical translation is called the King James Version (KJV) because it was King James I of England who in 1611 approved that translation for use in the Anglican Church of England. Some churches treasure this translation and use it exclusively in worship, but most Protestant churches use one of the many available contemporary translations. Some denominations require their clergy to have studied Greek, so that in their **sermon** preparation, they can study the original New Testament text.

Early lectionary systems standardized what Scripture selections were to be read on major festivals such as Easter and for important occasions such as baptisms. When in about 380 the Christian pilgrim Egeria traveled from western Europe to Jerusalem for Holy Week, she recorded that sometimes, but not always, these Christians were reading the same Bible selections as her home church did. Today some denominations mandate use of a specific lectionary, and others advise the use of their approved lectionary. Since the Bible is too long to read through even over many years of Sundays, some assistance in selection is helpful, and those who use an approved lectionary are glad to bond with churches around the world reading the same biblical passages. On the other hand, some denominations reject lectionaries as too restrictive

Amen
Hebrew for "Yes, I agree"

Hallelujah, alleluia
Hebrew and Greek for "Praise the Lord"

Kyrie eleison
Greek for Lord, have mercy

sermon / homily
an interpretation of the biblical reading delivered by the ordained leader during worship

The gospels could not possibly be either more or less in number than they are. The Word, the artificer of all things, he who sits upon the cherubim and sustains all things, being manifested to humankind gave us the gospel, fourfold in form but held together by one Spirit. . . . Since this is the case, they are foolish and uninstructed, even audacious, who destroy the pattern of the gospel, and present either more or less than four forms of the gospel.

—*Ireneaus, bishop of Lyons (c. 125–c. 203)*[2]

and instead expect that their preachers will select whichever part of the Bible is most appropriate for that Sunday. However, some local assemblies do not follow the pattern urged by their denomination.

Over the first six centuries Christian hymnody was born. Biblical scholars identify perhaps ten poems in the New Testament as having been the earliest Christian hymns. The most famous **canticle** is the Song of Mary, also called the Magnificat, Luke 1:46-55. Over time more poets and theologians composed Christian poems for Sunday song. Many of these hymns were designed to teach Christians doctrine. The idea is that humans interiorize on a deep level of consciousness that which they know by heart, and that rhythm, rhyme, and tune assist memory. The Latin expression *lex orandi, lex credendi* proposes that Christians should hold together "the rule of praying" with "the rule of believing." That is, what we pray, we believe, and what we believe, we pray. During these early centuries, the *orandi* half was primary; that is, since

canticle

a biblical poem, other than a psalm, sung in Christian worship

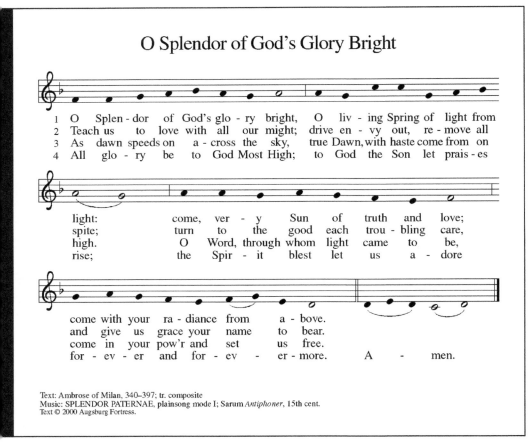

A hymn composed by Ambrose, bishop of Milan (340–397), in a current worship book.

people come to believe what they sing and say in worship, the texts of worship were to teach doctrine. Many contemporary **hymnals** include hymns written from the fourth century on. Some hymns are based on psalm texts. For example, "Joy to the World" is a version of Psalm 98 published in 1719 by **Isaac Watts**. Singing these historic texts is a window into how Christians over the centuries expressed their faith. Some churches are known for their enthusiastic communal song, and some Christian assemblies assign certain historic hymns to be sung on appropriate Sundays. Along with congregational song arose trained choirs and cantors, especially in large churches, and the more complex church music that they could provide. Over the centuries many churches have interspersed simple congregational song with complex choir offerings.

The evidence is that at worship the earliest Christians ate a full meal, either breakfast or supper, on Sunday, which was a workday. Within a century, the ritual had evolved into only the beginning of a meal—breaking apart a loaf of bread and distributing pieces to everyone—and the conclusion of a meal—passing around a cup of wine for all to share. The bread used during these centuries, and by some Christians today, was round loaves of leavened wheat bread. In the fourth century, the Christian emperor proclaimed Sunday a day of rest, at least for some professions, and the ritual had moved out of the home to adapt to the hundreds who gathered in large public assemblies. In so doing, the parts of the meal that were tied to words of Jesus—"This is my body, This is my blood"—received preeminent importance. Whether the Last Supper had been a Jewish Passover meal or not, the Passover lamb was not served at the Christian meal. Rather, Christ was the called "the lamb," and bread and wine were the foods served. A sixth-century set of communion ware now in a Baltimore museum includes a silver bread plate 15 1/2 inches in diameter, suggesting that the size of the loaf served was considerable.

This seventh-century European outline of worship is closely replicated at regular Sunday worship in some American churches:

- opening psalm
- canticle
- *Kyrie*
- canonical prayer of the day
- a reading from the Old Testament
- a reading from the New Testament
- solemn proclamation from one of the gospels
- homily
- **intercessions**
- procession with the bread and wine
- the kiss of peace
- dialogue between the presider and the people

hymnal
a book of hymns

Isaac Watts
(1672–1739) a prolific hymnwriter who versified psalms and composed hymns for the churches in England

intercessions
prayers for the church, the world, and people in need

- song "Holy, holy, holy"
- eucharistic prayer
- communion of the assembly
- **benediction**

benediction / blessing
announcement of God's
favor and protection

Some texts spoken by the priest and the assembly became standard and are still used by many Christians:

Dominus vobiscum. [The Lord be with you.]
The people reply: *Et cum spiritu tuo.* [And with your spirit.]
He says: *Sursum corda.* [Up with your hearts.]
They reply: *Habemus ad Dominum.* [We have them to the Lord.]
He says: *Gratias agamus Domino Deo nostro.* [Let us give thanks to the Lord our God.]
They reply: *Dignum et justum est.* [It is fitting and right.]
—Pseudo-Hippolytus, c. fourth century[3]

The historic dialogue as printed in a contemporary worship book.

elements
the bread and the wine
for communion

Particular attention was given to the prayer of thanksgiving that was said over the **elements**. Standard prayers were developed and an approved text, that is, a canon, was enforced. In some churches, even precise hand motions used by the clergy came to be compulsory. Whether in an elaborate linguistic style or with concise rhetoric, the prayer increasingly became the central act of the Sunday service, since the words of the priest's prayer accompanied or effected the transformation of the bread and wine. Although theologians across the Christian world do not agree at precisely which moment this occurred, increasingly the priest was seen as having the power to bring God's salvation to the people. Repeating the words that Jesus had spoken, remembering the saving actions of Jesus, and calling for the presence of the Holy Spirit were not merely passive mental exercises. Rather, like a birthday party that remembers one's birthday, the prayer and the communion brought into the present assembly the reality of the past event. Some contemporary churches always use an official eucharistic prayer over the bread and wine; some have free choice among many options for this prayer; and some churches do not use any such prayer, judging it to be a clerical addition that detracts from the meaning of the sacrament.

Other texts that arose during these centuries became standardized throughout the Mediterranean world and are still in use today. One example is the **Exultet**, a praise sung at Easter that is included in the contemporary worship books of Roman Catholicism and several Protestant denominations. Although some contemporary Christians think that prayers ought to be drafted newly each year, the annual use that some Christians make of the Exultet exemplifies that historic prayers can be valued as treasures that have served Christians not only in the past, but also into the future. For these churches, what is standard has more communal value than what is locally extemporized for the event.

Exultet
a long poem sung at Easter by a worship assistant that praises God for salvation and attends to a huge candle as a symbol of the resurrected Christ

A significant alteration over the first 25,000 Sundays was the increasing movement of focus from the resurrection of Christ to his death. It became clear that the end of world was not imminent, and the understanding of communion as a meal that marked the beginning of the new age shifted to communion as a participation in the sacrificial death of Christ. Depictions of the crucifixion began to appear in churches. Eucharist was not so much "thanksgiving," as the Greek term implied, but, rather, a salvation meal that replaced the religious sacrifices of pagans or ancient Jews. Jesus' death was the sacrifice that gave believers new life, both now and at the end of time, and communion brought worshipers into the power of his death. The meal replicated not

Mindful of the grace that achieves your salvation which God operated in you, approach communion with fear and trembling. Recognize in the bread what hangs on the cross; recognize in the chalice the water and blood trickling from his side.

—*Attributed to Augustine, bishop of Hippo (364–430)*[4]

so much the Last Supper or Jesus' post-resurrection meals, but rather, the crucifixion.

Annual rituals inaugurated

Early Christians met weekly to celebrate the resurrection of Christ. But over the centuries Christians came to establish an annual festival that especially highlighted the resurrection. In Christian memory was the festival of Passover, at which Jews celebrated their tribal memory that God had saved their ancestors from slavery in Egypt. In several ways, the New Testament connects the death of Christ with the imagery and meaning of the Jewish Passover. By the second century, some Christians had adapted Passover for their own use. After a quarrel between church leaders, the Christian Passover was set on the Sunday following Jewish Passover, thus the first Sunday after the first full moon after the spring equinox. In some years, this ancient calibration is still apparent.

The Passover was altered to fit its new Christian use. What had been a family table ritual was adapted for large groups in a public space. The date was scheduled always on Sunday, since that day is always for Christians the occasion on which to meet the risen Christ. The focus on the liberation of the people from slavery evolved into praise for the salvation of all the baptized from sin and death. The gift of the promised land was reinterpreted as life in the church and the hope for eternal life beyond death. Easter is the primary annual Christian festival. The phrase "an Easter Christian" refers to a person who goes to church only one Sunday a year, which is assumed to be Easter.

Easter concludes a week that is called Holy Week, which begins with Palm Sunday. On Palm Sunday a majority of contemporary churches recall Jesus' entry into Jerusalem on the week of his death and praise Jesus as their king by continuing the historic ritual of processing with palms. By the fourth century, the Easter celebration had come to be spread out over three days. This Three-Day / Triduum celebration included: Maundy or Holy Thursday, the service including both the sacrament of holy communion, as described in Matthew 26, Mark 14, and Luke 22, and the ritual of footwashing, as described in John 13; Good Friday, on which the death of Christ is commemorated by a solemn reading of the Passion story, perhaps from John 18–19, and by some ritual that reverences the cross of Christ; and the **Easter Vigil**, held on Saturday night, understood as the beginning of Easter Sunday. The Easter Vigil begins with a bonfire celebrating Christ as the light of the new year, includes the

Easter Vigil
first Eucharist of Easter, held on Saturday evening

Meanings of the Eucharist:

1. Thanksgiving in the new age inaugurated by Christ's resurrection
2. Participation in the suffering and death of Christ

The Maundy / Holy Thursday footwashing in a contemporary assembly.

ancient poem the Exultet, proceeds with many readings from the Bible that tell stories of God's saving deeds, includes baptisms, and concludes with the first celebrative Eucharist of Easter.

During medieval times the full celebration of the Triduum moved away from local churches into monasteries. However, over recent decades some churches have revived these historic rituals, judging them more profound than other Holy Week rituals, such as **Tenebrae** and **The Seven Last Words**, rites that were constructed several hundred years ago, and the Easter Sunrise Service, which is less than a century old. Churches reviving the ritual pattern from 75,000 Sundays ago see the Easter Vigil as the optimal occasion for baptisms, because especially Paul's letters in Scripture teach that through baptism the believer dies and rises with Christ.

Lent developed during the weeks before Easter as the time for persons to prepare for baptism. When later in history adult baptisms became rare, Lent offered all individual Christians the occasion to amend their sinful lives. Since Christ had to die for their sins, they should try to live more fully in God's Spirit. Lent remains a significant season for spiritual practices, with many even

Tenebrae
a Holy Week service including the reading of biblical passages and successive extinguishing of candles

The Seven Last Words
a Good Friday three-hour service of sermons based on the words of Jesus while on the cross

minimally practicing Christians "giving up" some behaviors so as to amend their life in preparation for Easter.

At the time of the origin of Christianity, the European winter solstice festival was celebrated both as the Roman Saturnalia and as the Birthday of the Unconquered Sun. Historians do not have enough data to reconstruct all the steps along the way, but by the late fourth century, after the church became recognized as the official religion of the Roman Empire, Christians around the Mediterranean world had begun to celebrate the birth of Jesus at the time of the winter solstice. Because the ancient calendar was not accurately synchronized with the solar system, Christmas is celebrated not on about December 21, but on December 25.

In Christianizing the pagan winter solstice observance, Christians borrowed the imagery of the sun to praise Christ as the light of the world, proclaiming that the life we associate with sunlight is symbolic of the life we receive from God in Christ, and the energy expended in wild partying is better spent in prayer and praise to God. Although the traditional Gospel reading for Christmas Eve is the narrative from Luke 2 about the birth of Jesus, the traditional Gospel for Christmas Day is John 1, a poem about the coming of light through Christ. Christmas continues to be the Christian festival most fully shared with the non-Christian society, and many Christians participate in the full panoply of pagan winter symbols and rituals. It is because Christmas always leans toward excessive partying that the settlers of the Massachusetts colony outlawed any celebration of Christmas whatsoever.

By 75,000 Sundays ago, a third type of annual ritual was firmly in place and shared by most Christians. Especially during the first and second century, periodic persecutions were conducted, and eminent Christians were executed by the Roman governmental authorities. These beloved leaders were revered by the people on the annual anniversary of their death. Over the centuries the idea grew that these beloved dead were already in the presence of God and were able to pray for Christians who were still alive. Thus, these annual memorials came to include invocations of the dead, asking them to pray to God for the living. Today, the commemorations in some churches include the ritual of praying to the dead, while other churches use the occasion to thank God for the life of these important Christians. Annual "saints' days" contributed to the popularity of relics, which brought something of the life of the dead person into the worshiping assembly. Some denominations reject any such symbols, and even in his fourteenth-century masterpiece *The Canterbury Tales,* the medieval author Geoffrey Chaucer ridiculed the relic trade. Yet for many Christians today, genuine relics have symbolic power to evoke in the worshiper devotion to God and faithfulness to Christian life.

Buildings for Christian rituals erected

During the first century, Christians met in one another's homes for worship. The evidence is that structural changes were made to the houses so as to better accommodate the rituals of the meeting. The Old Order Amish are among the contemporary Christians who continue the practice of worshiping only in members' homes. Many small groups of urban Protestants have adapted this

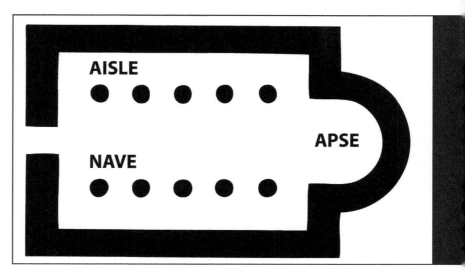

Since the fourth century, Christians have used the floor plan of a Roman basilica for their churches.

This church interior recalls the design of the basilica.

basilica
in the Roman Empire, large rectangular room with one semicircular end, used for civic events; in Christian history, a building of this design used for worship

apse
the semicircular end of a church building

practice by renting a storefront in the neighborhood where the members live and furnishing it to function as their worship space.

However, once the Roman emperor made Christianity not only legal, but popular, private homes were no longer adequate for the large numbers of worshipers, and buildings were adapted or erected to house the weekly worship. In the fourth century, the **basilica** was taken as the structural model for worship space. Visitors in Rome today can worship in some of the church buildings built in the fourth century, and from that time onward, it was usual for Christians to build structures uniquely suited for worship. When the basilica was used as a court room, the government authorities sat in the semicircular end, which functioned as a sound shell, and the people stood here and there in the large open space. Following this pattern, Christian basilicas sat the clergy in the **apse**, while the laity stood around in the nave. Some Eastern

Orthodox churches have maintained the tradition of church buildings that have no seats for worshipers.

The basilica design substantially altered how worship was experienced and how the Christian community was perceived. Within several centuries of basilica use, the clergy sat in elaborate chairs near the altar, which was situated in the apse of an immense room; the hundreds of laypeople stood in their area, men in the center and women around the edges. Not surprisingly, the several men physically elevated at the high end came to be elevated also psychologically. Far from suggesting a community of equals, an intimate fellowship modeled upon Christ's meal practice, the arrangement in the basilica precisely mirrored the hierarchical order of the Greco-Roman world. Furthermore, because the basilica was identified with government functions, Christianity came more and more to parallel the dominant social order. Influenced by the basilica, for more than 75,000 Sundays many Christians have worshiped in a room with an especially holy area for the clergy and have thought about the Christian life as supportive of the status quo.

The earliest Christians had maintained the Jewish practice of obeying what some numbering systems call the Second Commandment: "You shall not make for yourself an idol, whether in the form of anything that is in heaven above, or that is on the earth beneath, or that is in the water under the earth. You shall not bow down to them or worship them." However, other religions in the Greco-Roman world did paint and sculpt holy images, and after considerable discussion, Christians adopted this pagan practice. Such Christian art began in the catacombs, where, following Greco-Roman practice, Christians had met in the early decades to conduct devotions that honored the dead. Many images that Christians painted depicted Old Testament stories now given Christian meaning. Following what Jesus is quoted as saying in Matthew 12:40, the tale of Jonah emerging alive after being in the belly of the fish for three days was interpreted as a picture of Jesus emerging alive after being in the grave for three days. Thus, in the catacombs and in the wall paintings of churches, a depiction of Jonah arising from the fish testifies to faith in the resurrection. Some contemporary Christian churches depict Old Testament stories as one way to teach Christian meaning.

It was not until after crucifixions were outlawed in the Roman Empire that Christians depicted Christ on the cross. The earliest extant depiction of the crucifixion that has been found is carved into the wooden door of Santa Sabina, a basilica in Rome. In this oldest image, Christ is not in agony suffering, but is standing calmly between two thieves with his arms outstretched as if in prayer. When Christians built large interior spaces for worship, and when emperors and wealthy believers contributed large sums of money to make their church building more splendid than one in a neighboring city, Christian art blossomed. Although in the catacombs Jesus is depicted as a young shepherd

See Plate 6 in the gallery. Note the round loaves of bread and large chalice on the altar.

boy, the most common image of Christ in the apse or the dome of a church came to be the *Christos Pantocrator*, Christ depicted as the ultimate divine emperor reigning above the whole world. The mosaics adorning the church buildings in Ravenna, Italy, are among the most prized examples from the sixth and seventh centuries of interior church art. The images include the reigning Christ, symbolic depictions of the four writers of the Gospels, scenes from the life of Christ, and Old Testament narratives that have been given Christian meaning, all bordered with stunning design motifs.

Church buildings like those in Ravenna would have been by far the most majestic interiors ever experienced by nearly all worshipers. The walls' frescos and mosaics were meant both to instruct an illiterate populace about their faith and to deepen the worship experience for all the faithful. Yet some Christian education must have been available, since without explanation, these pictures would have had no Christian meaning for worshipers. For example, a depiction of Abel, said in Genesis to have worshiped God by offering a lamb, functioned as a metaphoric illustration of the church's offering to God the bread of communion and as a reminder that the Bible calls Christ the Lamb of God. The mosaic of Abel over the altar of a church in Ravenna also helped worshipers understand why the priest's prayer likened the Eucharist to the gifts of Abel.

Currently, churches differ in their evaluation of interior art. Some church buildings value the art of their own tradition. Thus, the art in an Italian American church may remind worshipers of churches in Italy. Some churches prize ethnically appropriate art. A church with many African Americans may depict Jesus with dark skin, and Asian Christians show Christ with Asian facial features. Some communities prefer contemporary art, for they want to make clear that the Spirit of Christ inspires us in the present. Thus, sculptures, wall paintings, banners, and windows in some churches would not look out of place in a modern art museum. Because permanent art is so expensive, some assemblies are now projecting onto a white wall or a screen visual images that are especially appropriate for the Bible readings of that Sunday, and several Web sites provide collections of such art to assist local planning committees.

For 75,000 Sundays, not only were the rooms for worship specifically designed and built, but also all the vessels used in the services were crafted for worship. No longer was a wine goblet borrowed from the pantry for Sunday use. Chalices became large enough to hold several cups of wine. Some were crafted out of gold or silver with gems affixed. The clergy wore not merely a warm poncho over a white alb. Instead, chasubles were constructed out of costly brocades and covered with elaborately stitched images, for with the emperor present, only the best was acceptable. Expensive, exquisite adornment has continued in some assemblies up through the present day. Later in history, some denominations rejected such opulence, and of course poor village churches could afford only simple work by a local artist.

Authority structures established

The first century of the church functioned with minimal structures of authority. But as the hierarchy of the church developed, it used its power to shape Sunday worship. By the second century, elections were held to select the bishop of a geographical area. This bishop had oversight of all the local clergy and presided in the downtown church, later called the cathedral. Especially when these cathedrals were in major cities, on central trade routes, or near military garrisons, how the bishops standardized their Sunday worship spread into the surrounding territory. Some bishops came to cooperate with governmental authorities and achieved considerable control over the churches in their jurisdiction. However, just because a bishop wrote an order does not mean that his order was obeyed. Indeed, a ruling usually demonstrates that the opposite behavior is being practiced.

Some bishops took as an essential part of their task to write **catechesis** about the meaning of baptism and the Christian life. Many of these catechetical writings were designed as explanations of worship. The idea was that new members of the community were instructed into ever deeper understanding of what they were doing on Sunday. Such writings show what the most influential clergy thought was going on with Christian symbols and rituals and when those clergy differed from one another about meaning and practice.

catechesis
a study of the meaning of the baptized faith

In the fourth century, the government of the Roman Empire convened councils, conferences of bishops that intended to achieve universal agreement on beliefs and practices. The decisions rendered by such councils influenced and even determined the details of Sunday worship. The **Nicene Creed** was composed at several such councils.

> Each of us gives the Kiss of Peace to the person next to him, and so in effect gives it to the whole assembly, because this act is an acknowledgement that we have all become the single body of Christ our Lord, and so must preserve with one another that harmony that exists among the limbs of a body, loving one another equally, supporting and helping one another, regarding the individual's needs as concerns of the community, sympathizing with one another's sorrows and sharing in one another's joys.
>
> —*Theodore of Mopsuestia, c. 390*[6]

Nicene Creed
ecumenical Trinitarian creed developed by fourth-century councils to affirm correct doctrine about Christ

Apostles' Creed
ecumenical trinitarian creed developed in fourth century from questions asked at baptism

heresy
a teaching about a fundamental item of faith judged contrary to authorized belief

It sets out in three paragraphs the approved faith in the triune God, and it employs language from fourth-century Greek philosophy to explain the relationship between God and Jesus. An earlier fourth-century creed is called the **Apostles' Creed**, and there grew up the legend that the apostles themselves had composed it. The creeds make clear what the issues were at the time of their composition and what **heresies** were being rejected.

Some contemporary churches speak one of these creeds at Sunday worship, and many use the Apostles' Creed as part of their baptismal ritual. Other denominations make the Sunday recitation of these historic creeds optional. Yet most church leaders over the centuries have affirmed that Christian identity not only calls members to honor God with their hearts and to live a Christ-like life, but also to accept with their minds a set of beliefs about the nature of God and the salvation granted through Christ. Since contemporary belief builds upon earlier beliefs, the ancient creeds remain in use. Some assemblies conduct adult classes in which the meaning of these creeds is explored.

Yet because these creeds utilize categories that are not part of current thought, some churches never use them on Sunday. Some Christians have crafted new statements of faith for Sunday use, several of which have circulated widely and become popular with many assemblies. In some contemporary churches a concern about heresy is high, and this attitude may be evident during Sunday worship. In other churches, doctrinal precision is not an issue. Many denominations continue the practice of regular meetings of church leaders to address contemporary issues and doctrinal concerns, and while not composing new creeds, they do make decisions that influence Sunday worship in one way or another.

To epitomize this period of history, Gregory I, pope from 590 to 604, is remembered for his considerable efforts to standardize Christian worship in Europe. History credits his interest in regularizing church music by referring to medieval chant as Gregorian. Many denominations keep alive the traditions from these first six centuries, while continually adapting their heritage for contemporary use.

Suggestions

1. Review the chapter's vocabulary: alleluia, Amen, apocalypticism, Apostles' Creed, apse, basilica, benediction, biblical canon, blessing, canticle, catechesis, Easter Vigil, elements, Exultet, heresy, hallelujah, intercessions, *Kyrie eleison*, homily, hymnal, Nicene Creed, sermon, The Seven Last Words, Tenebrae, Isaac Watts.

2. Present arguments for and against using depictions of Old Testament stories on the walls of Christian churches.

3. Discuss the current controversy about whether Christmas is Christian.

4. When a church building is too large for the number of Christians who gather for worship, what should happen?

5. Write a personal essay about how persons of authority in family, school, church, or society have functioned for well or for ill in your life.

6. In the Bible, 1 Corinthians 10–11, Paul wrote to the Christians in Corinth about their worship patterns. How are Paul's concerns connected with the topics in this chapter?

7. Discuss the essay "Credo,"[8] a chapter in a memoir by Richard Rodriguez.

8. Discuss the 1984 movie *Places in the Heart*. Compare the lifestyle and worship patterns of the Christians depicted in the film with those described in this chapter.

9. Attend a Methodist Sunday service. Many Methodists design their worship to mirror that of the early centuries of the church. Compare and contrast what you encounter with the symbols and rituals discussed in this chapter.

For further study

Bradshaw, Paul F. *Early Christian Worship: A Basic Introduction to Ideas and Practices.* Collegeville, Minn.: Liturgical, 1998.

Danielou, Jean, S.J. *The Bible and the Liturgy*. Notre Dame, Ind.: University of Notre Dame Press, 1956.

Deiss, Lucien, C.S.Sp. *Springtime of the Liturgy: Liturgical Texts of the First Four Centuries.* Collegeville, Minn.: Liturgical, 1979.

Mathews, Thomas F. *The Clash of the Gods: A Reintepretation of Early Christian Art.* Princeton: Princeton University Press, 1999.

Thompson, Bard, ed. *Liturgies of the Western Church*. Minneapolis: Fortress Press, 1980.

Chapter 6
What comes down to us from 50,000 Sundays ago?

East versus West

At the height of its power, the Roman Empire embraced two distinct cultures. What was called "the West" included most of Europe from Italy to the Atlantic Ocean. Rome was its symbolic center, and Latin came to be its vernacular. What was called "the East" included Greece, Eastern Europe, and the Middle East. Byzantium, later named Constantinople and now Istanbul, came to be its central city, and Greek remained its vernacular.

In the centuries that followed the collapse of the Roman Empire, the Christians of the East and those of the West developed their Sunday mornings in ways befitting their distinct cultures. By 800, both Eastern and Western Christians claimed that they alone were the true inheritors of primitive Christianity; both asserted that their worship style, sacramental theology, and church governance were the more apostolic, that is, faithful to the testimony of the first apostles. The bilingual arguments—the East spoke and wrote in Greek and the

West in Latin—became increasingly antagonistic. In 1054, the pope of Rome and the patriarch of Constantinople **excommunicated** each other and brought about what is called the Great Schism. Thus, although Christianity had always experienced local variety in worship, by the year 1100 a world traveler could worship in a Western Catholic church and in one of the Eastern Orthodox churches, and the style of these services had become different enough that the uneducated might not recognize that both events were essentially the same thing: a Sunday meeting of Christians around the word and sacrament.

Today in many American cities both traditions of worship are available: a service in a Roman Catholic or National Polish church, often called "Mass," and an Eastern Orthodox service, called "the Divine Liturgy." Depending on the local immigration pattern from Eastern Europe especially, the Orthodox service might be in an Albanian, Antiochian, Greek, Romanian, Russian, Serbian, Syrian, or Ukrainian Orthodox church. A third tradition called the Uniat churches, for example, the Byzantine Catholics, the Maronite church, and the Ukrainian Catholics, accept the authority of the pope in Rome, yet worship with a style close to that of the Eastern Orthodox. All these churches welcome visitors to attend their Sunday services, but each asks that only members of their church participate in communion.

excommunicate
exclude someone from the sacraments

Symbols important for the Eastern Orthodox

The word *orthodox* means "right worship," and Orthodox Christians maintain that their worship is more authentic than the worship of Western Christians because the Eastern churches have retained more from earlier tradition. Although the worship of the Orthodox churches did develop over the centuries, their preference and pride are for what is most ancient. One example of their preference for tradition is that, following church practice from the first 50,000 Sundays, their clergy are allowed to marry. Another example is that some Orthodox churches maintain the early Christian pattern of providing no seating for the people. For the Orthodox, oldest is best.

We knew not whether we were in heaven or on earth. For on earth there is no such splendor or such beauty, and we are at a loss how to describe it. We know only that God dwells there among men, and their service is fairer than the ceremonies of other nations. For we cannot forget that beauty.

—*Emissaries reporting in 988 to Prince Vladimir of Russia about Orthodox worship in Constantinople*[1]

The symbol system that developed in the Eastern Orthodox churches corresponded to Platonism. According to Plato, everything we see on earth and everything we experience in life are poor copies of what is the deepest, truest, most worthy reality, usually called "the ideals." These ideals, something like eternal patterns that everyday life attempts to reproduce, exist somehow beyond the earth, and they alone constitute unchanging truth. Humans ought to focus not on the things of this earth, but on the ideas that stand behind these things, for example, on the ideals of beauty, goodness, and justice. Most early Christian theologians found neo-Platonism a helpful framework within which to articulate their faith. They reasoned that since the truest, most meaningful reality is the unchanging God, our changeable world is not of highest importance. Life on earth is only a meager version of the heavenly life. During the Divine Liturgy, which celebrates the mystery of the Eucharist, worshipers seek to be carried into the presence of the Almighty. During the otherworldly experience provided on Sunday, believers are transported by the mystery of Christ into the life of his resurrection. The Orthodox use the term **divinization** to describe the transformation of humans back into the image of God. One goal of the mysteries is divinization.

divinization
the process of believers becoming the God-like beings intended at creation

If the deepest reality is unchanging, the church ought not make changes in Sunday worship. The music that undergirds Orthodox liturgy is sung by choirs and derives from ancient chant. The lectionary used in many Orthodox churches is nearly identical to the one developed in the seventh century. The Orthodox churches strenuously object to the Western churches' addition of the phrase "and the Son" to a passage in the Nicene Creed. The type of bread that Orthodox churches use for Sunday communion is like that of the early Christians, round loaves of leavened wheat bread. Of course, there have been changes over the centuries: one is that now Orthodox Christians are fed communion with a spoon. Since the tenth century, the priest places pieces of the bread into the chalice, and then using a spoon he tips the wine-with-bread into the open mouths of the communicants.

Since Orthodox worship seeks a mystical incorporation into the divine reality, the symbols in use on Sunday morning attempt to create an otherworldly experience. One example is the use of incense. The Orthodox churches have made incense into a beloved symbol, and at several places in the Sunday liturgy, profuse incensing of people or objects occurs. The hope is that the sight and smell of the ascending smoke will envelop the room and surround the worshipers, to suggest something of the heavenly atmosphere that surrounds the

The liturgy of the Eucharist is best understood as a journey or procession. It is the journey of the Church into the dimension of the Kingdom. Our entrance into the presence of Christ is an entrance into a fourth dimension which allows us to see the ultimate reality of life. The liturgy begins then as a real separation from the world. The Christ of whom we speak is "not of this world," and that after His resurrection He was not recognized even by His own disciples.

—*Alexander Schmemann, twentieth-century Russian Orthodox priest*[2]

divine presence and to symbolize the Divine Liturgy ascending to the throne of God.

The symbol most identified with the Orthodox churches is the **icon**. When Christians adapted the Greco-Roman practice of drawing and sculpting the divine, the Christians of the East developed their own style of sacred pictures quite different from the statues and realistic paintings common in the West. Icons do not attempt photographic realism, and those who create icons, praying as they apply the brush strokes, are not, as in Western art, to infuse the image with their individual interpretation. Adhering to a tradition that includes an elongation of human facial and body features and an incantatory power in the eyes, the icon means to capture something of the divine image that shines forth in the lives of Christ and the saints.

By venerating an icon of Christ or of one of the saints, the worshiper is drawn into the spiritual reality signified by the image. The icon is a kind of visual incense, like a sacrament pulling the worshiper into what is most important. Orthodox Christians bow to these icons and kiss them, not to worship the image, but to worship the reality that the icon symbolizes. Usually icons are hung on all four walls of the nave and sometimes fully cover the ceiling. Standing or sitting in church, the worshiper is thus surrounded by sacred images. This setting symbolizes what worship is all about. Heaven is what is real, the place where the saints dwell, and in the Divine Liturgy, it is as if we are in heaven. In a beloved icon placed in many Orthodox churches, the Trinity is depicted by means of the Old Testament story in which three angelic figures, who embodied the triune God, came to eat a meal with Abraham and Sarah. For the Orthodox, it is as if worshipers ascend to heaven during the Divine Liturgy to eat with God. Recently, the use of icons has grown in other than Orthodox churches as means to assist in devotional meditation.

To prepare to receive the mystical food of the Eucharist, Orthodox worshipers are expected to have observed a strict vegan **fast** for the preceding three days and to have abstained even from water on the morning before communing. However, because many worshipers have not fasted, many do not regularly commune, and so there has come about an extension of the symbolic bread. Some of the breads are not brought to the altar, but instead are broken into pieces and given out to everyone at the close

icon
stylized depiction of Christ, biblical figures, or saints venerated in Eastern Orthodox worship

fast
abstain from food or other bodily needs as a sign of religious devotion

---

The church was ablaze with candlelight. Every icon, and there seemed to be dozens of them, was surrounded by a glowing aura of slender, amber candles. We were surrounded by vibrant images of Christ's life and death, of vast heavenly hosts, of beloved Bible stories. The music was unearthly and continued to pierce the heart. Somewhere in the midst of such foreign and bewildering ceremony, I somehow managed to stop thinking, to stop analyzing, to stop comparing. I forgot myself completely and was absorbed into a unity of worship unlike anything I had experienced before.

—*Quoted in* **Windows to Heaven**[3]

The icon of the Holy Trinity by Andrei Rublev is used to symbolize the Eucharist. "They are not three angels!" said the Orthodox icon merchant. "That's the Father, the Son, and the Holy Spirit."

of the service. Because this bread has not been sanctified to be the body of Christ, it symbolizes instead all the food that God always provides, and non-Orthodox visitors are welcome to take this bread and eat it.

A primary example of the Orthodox preference for what is old is the symbolic speech of the liturgy. Most Orthodox Christians in the United

States worship in the language of their homeland, with only small parts of the Divine Liturgy in English. Here the use of their historic language symbolizes their national Orthodox identity, and especially when over time fewer of the worshipers are fluent in their ancestral language, the mystique of a foreign language can accentuate the extraordinary nature of worship, thus serving a treasured Orthodox value.

A fundamental characteristic of the worship rooted in Byzantium is its lush style of prayer. In fact, the English adjective "Byzantine" refers to something that is by Western standards overly elaborate, a maze of ornament, so complex as to be indecipherable. So the prayers of the Orthodox Sunday liturgy are filled with adjectives, synonyms, extra phrases, and one descriptor after another. Getting somewhat lost in the syntax is itself symbolic of being taken over by the sumptuous visitation of the divine. A prayer may be repeated, not merely three times, but nine times, or twenty-seven, or even forty times. The Orthodox maintain that such extravagantly layered praises characterize the worship in heaven and so ought to constitute also earthly liturgy. The Orthodox churches like to credit the text of their Sunday liturgy to the most renowned of their historic theologians, **John Chrysostom**. It is a profound respect for the tradition of the Chrysostom legacy, rather than any central governing authority, that makes the worship of the various Orthodox churches similar to each other. So: just as older is better, more is better.

> It is meet and right to sing of Thee, to bless Thee, to praise Thee, to give thanks to Thee, and to worship Thee in every place of Thy dominion: for Thou art God ineffable, inconceivable, invisible, incomprehensible, ever-existing and eternally the same, Thou and Thine only-begotten Son and Thy Holy Spirit. . . . And we thank Thee for this Liturgy which Thou hast found worthy to accept at our hands, though there stand by Thee thousands of archangels and hosts of angels, the Cherubim and the Seraphim, six-winged, many-eyed, who soar aloft, borne on their pinions, singing the triumphant hymn, shouting, proclaiming, and saying . . .
>
> —*The preface to the Orthodox eucharistic prayer*[4]

John Chrysostom (c. 347–407) patriarch of Constantinople, named "golden-mouthed" for his preaching

Rituals important for the Eastern Orthodox

In order that humans can be brought up into the presence of God, the primary goal of the Divine Liturgy is transformation. On their own, Christians are not prepared to be received into God; thus, worship attempts to remake believers so that they embody the divine image that God intends for humankind. The model of such transformation that God gave to the world is Christ's resurrection. Thus, once again, Orthodox Christians retain something of the earliest Christian centuries by claiming that the resurrection is the center of the faith and the ground of worship. Just as the risen Christ embodied the Spirit of God, so through the transformation effected in worship the believer receives the Holy Spirit, is mystically drawn into the life of the Trinity, and participates already now in the resurrection of Christ.

Since transformation by the Holy Spirit is the intention of the baptized life, Easter is by far the most important annual festival, for at his resurrection Christ's divinity was made known and the true image of God revealed on earth. Because of the Orthodox preference for whatever is older, the Eastern churches compute the date of Easter using an archaic cosmological reckoning, which is why the Eastern Easter is usually a different Sunday than is Western Easter. The Divine Liturgy as celebrated at Pascha is extraordinarily elaborate, even by Orthodox standards, and can last from sundown on Saturday through the night until an early breakfast on Sunday. Yet at every Sunday liturgy, there will be multiple occasions in which the priest calls upon the Holy Spirit to bring new life into the assembly and its actions, for during worship the Holy Spirit continues the heavenly transformation experienced in Christ's resurrection. The miracle of resurrection is brought to the worshipers.

The ritual spaces beloved by the Orthodox are ornately decorated. Just as heaven shines with the splendor of God, so church buildings hope to reflect the precious light of the divine. Gold is used wherever possible. The shape of most Orthodox churches follows an ancient pattern for temples, in which the earth is symbolized with a square and heaven with a circle. Thus, the ritual space of most Orthodox churches make clear that we live on the square of the earth, but during worship our souls rise into the dome of heaven. Since for centuries the Eastern emperor and the entire court were regular worshipers in the primary church in Constantinople, the ritual gestures at worship there were formal and elaborate. Clergy vesture was influenced by elegant and expensive court dress, and deep bows to anyone of high rank and anything of symbolic value were required throughout.

The most unique aspect of Orthodox ritual space is the **iconostasis**. In both East and West, the table had moved from the center of the room to the apse and had evolved into an adorned altar, and since no permanent seating

---

After the crucifixion, when the King first arrived below in Hades

His light shone in the darkness and illumined it below,

For the darkness was not able to check Christ; He had ample strength in darkness,

For, just as Jonah was in the belly of his tomb,

So He was carried into the tomb and yet in the grave He was alive,

For His divinity was not separated from the flesh.

Thus, Hades on beholding His awesome miracle,

Cried out, "Come, Death, let us behold

What sort of light He has kindled, He,

The Life and Resurrection."

—*An Easter hymn by Romanos (c. 525)*[5]

---

iconostasis
room divider separating the chancel from the nave on which icons are hung

The church, as the house of God, is an image of the whole world, for God is everywhere and above everything. The sanctuary is a symbol of the higher and supra-heavenly spheres, where the throne of God and his dwelling place are said to be. It is this throne that the altar represents. The upper regions of the church represent the visible heavens, its lower parts what is on earth.

—*Symeon of Thessalonika (d. 1429)*[6]

See Plate 7 in the gallery. Note the two icons that are above the doors.

kept the laypeople in their places, churches erected low fencing to delineate the altar area from the nave. In the East by the fourteenth century, this fencing evolved into a permanent room divider on which to display icons. At the center of the iconostasis are doors, through which the clergy walk when going from the chancel to the nave and back. The doors themselves have symbolic meaning. Usually on one is an icon of Christ as the Savior and on the other an icon of Mary, who is called especially by the Orthodox the *Theotokos*, Greek for "the Bearer of God," and it is through these holy beings that worshipers approach the divine throne. The intercessions are chanted by an assistant standing next to the doors, because in prayer Christians are knocking at the doors of heaven for mercy. Whatever are all the reasons that the low fence became a permanent wall, the iconostasis accentuates the mystery of the Divine Liturgy, since during the most sacred actions of the priests, the laypeople can neither hear nor see what the clergy are doing at the altar. It is as if the place of the altar is too holy for ordinary eyes.

If people are enthralled at a meal with God, they are not watching the time. Like rituals of the ancient world before societies were ruled by clocks, the Divine Liturgy, filled with repetition and continuous elaboration, slowly unfolds and meticulously proceeds, usually over several hours, toward its conclusion. Holiness in heaven is timeless, and so visitors need to be aware that clock time is inconsequential during Orthodox worship.

Symbols important for Roman Catholicism

Roman Catholics also claim that they represent the true church of Christ, but the pattern of thought in the West has been more open to change and development than in the East. Western theologians argue that the Spirit of God continues to inspire the church and that change in symbol and ritual and the development of doctrine are examples of the church's discovering more of what God intends. That the Scriptures begin in a garden and end in a city illustrates the belief that as long as the church is following the way pointed out by God, movement to a new thing is God's will. So Roman Catholics do not apologize for the various ways that their Sunday worship has changed through the centuries.

By the twelfth century, Western scholars had replaced their reliance on Plato with one on Aristotle. Aristotle was a student of Plato, but his style of philosophy differed radically from that of his teacher. Aristotle epitomized an almost scientific search to systematize all knowledge about how the universe functions. His interest in pragmatic learning and rational explanation was explored first by Muslim scholars and then taken over by Christian theologians. Because of the Roman admiration for utility and the Aristotelian devotion to rational thought, the symbols and rituals of the Western church contributed to a religious style different from that in the Eastern churches.

In the East, the clergy who shaped liturgical patterns were mainly monks famed for their profound prayer life, but in the West, it was scholars and educators who influenced liturgical practice. Instructed by learned monks, Roman bishops ordered liturgical changes. When Western theologians decided that "and the Son" stated more precisely how the Holy Spirit comes from the Father, they added this phrase to the Nicene Creed. Annual festivals were added to the Western calendar. One example of the development of worship was that by the late Middle Ages, the festival of Corpus Christi, at which the consecrated host displayed in a monstrance was paraded through the city streets, was more important to many people than communing for their **Easter duty**.

Western theologians taught that the need for salvation arose because humans were sinful. To be saved from the just punishment of hell and to be rewarded with heaven, Christians were to confess their sins during the sacrament of penance, now called **reconciliation**, receive forgiveness, and amend their life. Given this emphasis on sin, the primary symbol in Western churches became the **crucifix**. Some crucifixes were designed as a tree-of-life, with flowers and leaves surrounding the body of Jesus. Some became gruesome depictions of what death by crucifixion was really like. In the present, both Roman Catholics and many Protestants, as inheritors of this Western focus, display a crucifix in a prominent

A crucifix in a Roman Catholic church.

place. The idea is that while gazing on the crucifix, worshipers contemplate the sufferings of Christ on the cross, and this meditation impels them toward confession and amendment of life.

Because the bread used at Eucharist became extraordinarily revered, regular leavened bread was replaced with unleavened bread baked in the monasteries. Western theologians argued for unleavened bread because the ancient Jews had used it in their temple ritual. Furthermore, if the bread was baked into small, single-bite sizes, there would be no crumbs: for since the bread is understood to be the body of Christ, the church does not want any crumbs to be dropped on the floor. Maintaining this medieval development, many Protestant and Roman Catholic churches today use hosts, round white pieces of unleavened wheat, as the bread for communion. The circle, functioning in human symbol systems for millennia as an image of perfection, can be said to symbolize the communicants' whole and perfect union with God. To avoid the wine being spilled, for a short time a straw was utilized, but from the thirteenth to the twentieth century wine was not offered to lay Roman Catholics. A hymn written by Thomas Aquinas in the thirteenth century and sung still today exemplifies the Roman Catholic doctrine of the Eucharist.

> God with hidden majesty lies in presence here,
> I with deep devotion my true God revere;
> Whom this outward shape and form secretly contains,
> Christ in his divinity manhood still retains.
> This I firmly hold as true, this is my belief,
> And I seek salvation, like the dying thief.
> —Thomas Aquinas[7]

After the Great Schism with the East, the Western church continued to schedule councils of bishops who, led by theologians, considered issues related to faith and worship. One development was the decision in 1215 that categories derived from Aristotle be used to explain how the bread and wine become the body and blood of Christ. This complex philosophical teaching can be summarized as follows: We can describe things both by what they are made of and by what they are. For example, a certain thing is made of flour, sugar, shortening, baking powder, frosting, candles; but it is a birthday cake. Using Aristotelian categories, the "accidents" are what something is made of, and the "substance" is what it is. According to medieval Western theologians, although the accidents of bread and wine remain the same, the substance becomes body and blood. Thus arose the technical word **transubstantiation** to render a philosophical definition of what happens when the priest prays the eucharistic prayer. In medieval times, the priest was seen as having somewhat magical power over the elements, and the word *hocus-pocus* derives from a mishearing

transubstantiation
the Roman Catholic doctrine that the substance of the eucharistic elements becomes the body and blood of Christ

of the Latin words spoken by the priest, *Hoc est corpus meum*, "This is my body." Priests were ordered to place the bread in the mouth of the communicant, since it had come about that some worshipers, receiving the bread in their hands, took it home with them as a talisman of holiness, perhaps planting it in their fields to ensure a good crop. Directions to ring a bell at the time of the consecration called worshipers to pay attention during this especially holy action of the priest. Still today for some Roman Catholics, the most sacred moment of the Sunday service occurs when the priest consecrates the bread and wine.

> One morning I had climbed a high hill and was turning around to go back. . . . Thus did Christ once stand on the spiritual mount and offer up to his Father the holocaust of his love and his life's breath. A spiritual mountain still rises, and the hand of God is still stretched out above, and the gifts mount up every time a priest—not in his own person, since he is merely the instrument, of no value in itself—stands at the altar and raises in his outspread hands the paten with the white bread on it.
>
> —*Romano Guardini, twentieth-century Roman Catholic priest*[8]

Another Western development that continues in some Roman Catholic and Protestant churches is the theological formulation of the **theory of atonement**. Theologians taught that God, the almighty Judge of all, demands obedience, and when divine laws are broken, God's honor must be satisfied. Free forgiveness is not rational, and humans cannot possibly pay the debt of all their sins. Because Jesus was holy, he alone could pay the price to satisfy God so that believers can be forgiven. The stronger this idea, the more the Eucharist became a way to enter into a transaction with God the Judge, who at each Mass accepts the sacrifice of his Son and thus forgives the people of their sins.

theory of atonement theological proposal to explain how the death of Christ achieves reconciliation between sinful humans and a righteous God

The **Second Vatican Council** of the Roman Catholic church mandated some changes that meant to return Sunday liturgy to more original practice. As in the early church, worship is to be conducted in the vernacular, and so the Latin of the approved liturgy was translated into local languages. To better ritualize that the Eucharist is a meal, the priest is to face the people, rather than the crucifix on the eastern wall of the room. The lay people are offered the cup. The bread can be a flat, pita-like bread, rather than hosts, and people are to receive the bread in their hands, rather than into their mouth.

Second Vatican Council international meeting of Roman Catholic bishops (1962–1965) that effected many worship reforms

Other changes mandated by the Second Vatican Council introduced innovations into Roman Catholic worship. A new three-year lectionary of biblical readings was developed. At all primary festivals the Gospel is read from John, and in three successive years the Gospel on regular Sundays is taken from Matthew, Mark, and Luke. There is a reading from the Old Testament that complements the Gospel and a reading from one of the New Testament epistles. This Roman Catholic three-year, three-reading lectionary so impressed many Protestants that they developed a variation of it called the Revised Common Lectionary. So it is that on some Sundays, precisely identical biblical readings may be proclaimed in the local Roman Catholic, Episcopalian, Lutheran, Methodist, Presbyterian, Disciples, and United Church of Christ assemblies.

For its ritual speech, the early church in Rome adopted the brusque style required in the Roman governmental transactions. When one addressed the Roman officials, one used concise, somber speech, devoid of any fanciness that would obstruct the main focus. Adopting this succinct style, many medieval Roman Catholic prayers were sleek, with few descriptors of any kind and no extra synonyms, addressing God with the single word *Deus*. This same objective speech characterizes the liturgical language of contemporary Roman Catholic masses. Any extra words usually render a theological explanation of what is going on. Roman Catholic assemblies are expected to use only officially approved texts for most of the Sunday's liturgy.

> Father, it is our duty and salvation, always and everywhere to give you thanks through your beloved Son, Jesus Christ....And so we join the angels and saints in proclaiming your glory: ...
>
> —*a preface to the Roman Catholic eucharistic prayer*[9]

Far from allowing only archaic music during worship, the Western church provided musicians with the primary venue for the performance of their new compositions. Thus, the music heard in church mirrored the music played outside the churches. Instrumental accompaniment was encouraged. A single melodic line gave way to complex musical settings of liturgical texts, with simultaneous interweaving melodic lines of complementary pitches, which were sung by increasingly proficient choirs. Fewer parts of the liturgy were sung by the people. What in Western music is called "a Mass," as in a Palestrina Mass or a Schubert Mass, is a musical setting of usually five parts of the service, and today such pieces are more likely to be heard in a concert hall or on a CD than in a Sunday service. Roman Catholic musicians continue to compose musical settings for the words of the Mass, now usually intended to be sung by the entire assembly, and all manner of instrumental accompaniment can be heard on Sunday morning. Also some Protestant churches continue to sing all or some of these five texts.

Rituals important for Roman Catholicism

Western rituals developed to support the focus on the forgiveness of sins. In the early church, only notorious sinners had to make amends for flagrant public scandal. But later especially Irish monks taught that every Christian was to confess every sin and to say prayers assigned as penance. All worshipers were urged to use the time during Mass to plead for the forgiveness of personal sins.

No one was to take communion if they were not shriven, that is, if they had not confessed to a priest and completed the penitential tasks that the priest had assigned. This contributed to great numbers of the faithful not communing on Sunday, although recently in the Roman Catholic parishes the ritu-

<table>
<tr><td colspan="2">Movements of a musical setting of the Mass:</td></tr>
<tr><td>1. Kyrie—Lord, have mercy</td></tr>
<tr><td>2. Gloria—Glory to God in the highest</td></tr>
<tr><td>3. Credo—I believe in God, the Father almighty . . .</td></tr>
<tr><td>4. Sanctus—Holy, holy, holy</td></tr>
<tr><td>5. Agnus Dei—Lamb of God</td></tr>
</table>

als of private confession are not emphasized. Although there is no evidence that early Christians knelt during public worship, and a fourth-century council forbade kneeling on Sunday since it is always the day of the resurrection, the Western church established the practice of kneeling during many of the prayers, throughout the entire eucharistic prayer, and during communion. Kneeling was judged to be the proper stance expressive of one's unworthiness. Today many Roman Catholics and some Protestants continue the practice of kneeling for prayer and at communion.

Because personal sinfulness was so central, Lent became a sacred time of self-examination and amendment of life. Each Sunday became, not a small Easter, but rather a condensed Lent, a time to confess one's sins and receive forgiveness. This medieval **piety** is evident in many Roman Catholic and Protestant churches to this day. The focus remains, not like in the Eastern churches on the power of the Holy Spirit to transform the believer, but rather on the sacrifice of the Son, whose suffering and death was made necessary by one's sins. However, especially the theologians centered in Latin America have urged that the attention to sin move away from merely personal failings, such as private sexual matters, and attend instead to social sins, such as exploitation of the poor, the perpetuation of racial and gender prejudice, the maintenance of a war machine, and human neglect of the earth's resources. Usually Roman Catholic masses include a short litany asking for forgiveness, and the type of sin confessed varies, depending on the spirituality of that assembly. Many Protestant church services regularly include a ritual of confession and forgiveness.

piety
a style of religious practice

During those centuries that most worshipers could not understand the Latin of the Mass, many Roman Catholics used the time during the service for private devotion. Much of this devotional activity came to be directed toward the Virgin Mary. Roman Catholics view Mary as the saint par excellence, the perfectly obedient believer, who in heaven intercedes for humans in their need. If God was seen as an exacting Judge or a stern Father, Mary became the feminine face of God, the loving and attentive Mother, always ready to embrace sinners with compassion. Popularly it was said that if St. Peter would not let you enter heaven, the Virgin Mary would sneak you in

rosary
a string of beads used in
counting prayers

the back door. The **rosary** developed as an aid for repetitive prayers to guide the worshiper into meditation of the faith. Many Romans Catholics continue to pray with a rosary, although in the United States no longer usually during the Sunday service. Marian devotion became a serious point of contention for Protestants, who discourage any invocation of the saints and reject any such role for Mary.

In the West, the most common design for the building of ritual spaces remained the basilica. By the year 1000, architects were copying especially the arches that they found in the ruins left over from the Roman Empire's expertise in building. Referred to as Romanesque design, these churches were constructed with arches throughout. The naves were long rectangles; the semicircular apse had been enlarged so as to accommodate an immense altar and chairs for the clergy. Cities vied to build higher buildings filled with more exquisitely carved stone images throughout the room, both to praise God in glorious ways and to prove their supremacy over a neighboring city.

But the building design for which the medieval Western church is most famous is the Gothic. In the thirteenth century, architects perfected the pointed arch, which allowed for buildings to be constructed even higher. Outside braces called flying buttresses were added to give support to the walls. Wider and higher windows were filled with stained glass that depicted scenes from the Bible and the lives of the saints. The rectangle became a cross shape, with the side arms and wide aisles used for secondary chapels. The cross shape meant that the altar moved even farther away from the people and became affixed to the eastern wall, eventually becoming massive and elaborately decorated, a kind of throne for the crucifix and the consecrated bread. Throughout his prayers the priest faced this throne of God, rather than facing the people. This accounts for why, on traditional chasubles, the embroidered design is on the back, rather than the front, of the priest's garb. The desire to build the biggest, highest, and most spectacular Gothic cathedral still offers its rewards today, when tourists visit European cities to wonder at the magnificent church edifices.

The Gothic buildings had immense influence on the worship conducted in them. With a building so large, hearing was less important than seeing. The individual worshiper's voice got lost in the empty expanse, and so lay singing was diminished and speaking became whispering. Once permanent seating was introduced, many lay people sat half a football field away from the altar, and even in

> To be in church isn't to be calmed down, as some people say they get when they are at Mass. I'm worked up. I'm excited by being so close to Jesus, but the closer I get, the more I worry about what he wants of us, what he would have us do before we die.
>
> —Dorothy Day[10]

smaller church buildings, worshipers found it normal to sit far away from the activities of the priest. Because in the most spectacular European churches the imagery in the stained glass windows was difficult to decipher, worshipers no longer interpreted the imagery in the church, instead thinking of the colored glass as a kind of gorgeous visual music to rest within. Many European Christians came to equate this design with church, and so even in the twentieth century in the United States, some newly constructed Roman Catholic and

Protestant churches recalled Gothic design. The sanctity of the Gothic ambience continues to influence those Christians who, no matter what the design of their buildings, understand worship as less a communal participation in the body of Christ and more a private contemplation of the holy.

Despite the splendor possible in the most impressive of the Western church buildings, Western liturgies maintained one aspect of their formation in the Roman Empire: time is of the essence. Western services moved along. To save time, the actions of the priest might be conducted simultaneous to the singing of the choir. Usually prayers were said only once, not repeatedly. Periodic reforms had as one of their goals to streamline the liturgy, removing repetition and eliminating accretions. In American Roman Catholic churches, this interest in brevity is apparent. Most parishes conduct a full Sunday Mass in less than an hour, and many worshipers will leave before the service is over if they judge that the service has taken too long.

Creeping individualism

By 50,000 Sundays ago, in especially the West, but also in the East, the sense of Sunday morning as primarily a communal experience was being lost. The churches most famed for their worship practices were immense rooms that dwarfed the individual. One's absence would not be noted. There was no sound amplification. Many Christians were expected to worship using a language they did not understand, and even where the vernacular was used, uneducated peasants had little catechesis as to the meaning of the technical words of their church's theology. Thus, what the original communal event intended—that those who are the body of Christ became strengthened by a meal shared in the Spirit—would not have apparent to many worshipers.

Meanwhile, societies witnessed a rise in societal individualism. The increase of literacy, accelerating urbanization, and the development of capitalism joined other social forces to encourage each individual to recognize and claim at least some authority in the self. This centering in the self has since intensified. The Sunday liturgy often includes the word *you* in the plural: "The Lord be with you" means "you-all," but increasingly this "you" was heard as addressing each individual.

Meanings of the Eucharist, continued:

1. Thanksgiving in the new age inaugurated by Christ's resurrection
2. Participation in the suffering and death of Christ
3. Mystical experience of the triune life in heaven
4. A continuing sacrifice to appease an angry God
5. The occasion for private devotion

The societal sense of the person as primarily a solo performer, rather than as one of the crowd, does not disappear on Sunday morning. An individual could arrive late and leave early without disturbing what the priest was doing. Thus, going to church was more like buying the groceries than like attending a dinner party. Individuals went to church when they chose to, or when their family urged it. There they hoped, in the East, to be brought into the divine presence or, in the West, to receive forgiveness for personal sins; but bonding with others was not their primary goal. To the extent that persons align with a group, they do so out of individual choice, not because of communal pressure or necessity. The sense that worshipers go to church primarily to receive a personal spiritual uplift is rooted not 100,000 Sundays ago, but more like 50,000 Sundays ago, and remains strong in the United States.

However, much that was believed 50,000 Sundays ago is no longer mainstream thought. In the East, the medieval Orthodox worshiper hoped to be drawn into the life of Triune God. But many contemporary Americans judge that, thanks to an interior divinity, they have by nature all that they need of God. In the West, medieval Christians went to Mass to get their sins forgiven. But many contemporary Americans are not convinced that they sin much, deserve divine punishment, or that only through the sacraments can they be forgiven. So theologians grapple with these questions: Ought Christians seek divine transformation? Ought Christians know themselves in dire need of forgiveness? If the answers are yes, how should worship do this in the twenty-first century? If the answers are no, what is goal of Christian worship?

Suggestions

1. Review the chapter's vocabulary: John Chrysostom, crucifix, divinization, Easter duty, excommunicate, icon, iconostasis, piety, reconciliation, rosary, Second Vatican Council, theory of atonement, and transubstantiation.
2. Present arguments for and against the practice of churches requesting that only members participate in communion.
3. Compare the music that accompanies the Orthodox Divine Liturgy with the music used in a Roman Catholic church.
4. Trace the history of the construction of one of the Western Gothic cathedrals.
5. Many contemporary Western churches are now displaying Eastern icons. Write a personal essay in which you describe your reaction to a specific icon.
6. In the Bible, Hebrews 6–7 applies the imagery of the Jewish Temple and its sacrifices to Christian worship. Discuss these chapters.

7. Discuss Andre Dubus's short story "A Father's Story,"[11] which describes a contemporary American who has a strong medieval Catholic piety.
8. Discuss the 1988 film *A Month in the Country*, in which two shell-shocked veterans of World War I are restoring medieval Christian artifacts. What should contemporary Christians do with their old art? Or discuss the 2006 documentary *Monastery: Mr. Vig and the Nun*, about the recent establishment of a Russian Orthodox convent in Denmark.
9. Attend either the Divine Liturgy at any Eastern Orthodox church or the Sunday Mass at a Roman Catholic church, and compare what you encounter with the details of this chapter.

For further study

Baldovin, John, S.J. *Bread of Life, Cup of Salvation: Understanding the Mass.* Lanham, Md.: Sheed & Ward, 2003.

Huck, Gabe, ed. *A Sourcebook about Liturgy.* Chicago: Liturgy Training Publications, 1994.

Macaulay, David. *Cathedral: The Story of Its Construction.* Boston: Houghton Mifflin, 1973.

Taft, Robert, S.J. *Through Their Own Eyes: Liturgy as the Byzantines Saw It.* Berkeley: InterOrthodox Press, 2006.

Ware, Kallistos. *The Orthodox Way.* Crestwood, N.Y.: St. Vladimir's Seminary Press, 1995.

Zelensky, Elizabeth, and Lela Gilbert. *Windows to Heaven: Introducing Icons to Protestants and Catholics.* Grand Rapids: Brazos, 2005.

Chapter 7
What comes down to us from 25,000 Sundays ago?

About Protestantism

Historians call the fourteenth through the seventeenth centuries in Europe the Renaissance, a title that means "rebirth." One cause of this social change was the rediscovery of the arts, literature, and scholarship of ancient Greece and Rome. The wisdom newly acquired from past philosophers, playwrights, and politicians challenged the church's authority and in part displaced the medieval focus on God with a pre-Christian attention to humankind. Scholars scrutinized classical texts, including the original Hebrew and Greek of the Bible, and such intellectual enterprises encouraged the individual mind to reach beyond the dominant structures of religious and social authority. Martin Luther is usually depicted in paintings and statues holding a Bible and wearing a black academic gown: an individual of his age, he is a learned scholar reading a text and taking up the power to teach it.

The rise of nationalism meant that more of a person's circumstances were dictated by one's nation, its governmental policies, economics, social patterns, and language. Part of this political change was a growing importance of cities and the resulting intensification of local identity. Many Western Christians

A stained glass window in a church in Sellersville, Pennsylvania, depicts Martin Luther in his usual pose.

Reformation
sixteenth-century
European Christian
movement that sought
to reform the Western
Catholic church but
instead led to the
formation of several
Protestant denominations

came to care more about the cathedral in their capital city than they did about the basilica in Rome, and consequently their allegiance to Rome and their willingness to send money for its support lessened. The shocking behavior of some of the Roman Catholic hierarchy—for example, three popes reigning simultaneously, or illegitimate sons of popes appointed as bishops—played its part in alienating many Western Christians from a leadership distant in miles and shameful to contemplate. Only given these social conditions can the phenomenon that is called the Protestant **Reformation** make any sense.

The Renaissance led to the intellectual movement called the Enlightenment. This eighteenth-century worldview sought to replace reliance on religious tradition with trust in contemporary reasoning. The past was to give way to the future, and the community to the individual. Only after such thought patterns permeate society can the populace execute its king or a person ignore religious sanctions. In a stark contrast to the spiritual complexity of the New Testament, the edited version of the Gospels that Thomas Jefferson published presented Jesus as a teacher of rational morality. Jefferson removed from his account of Jesus all miracles, all transcendent reality, all communal faith. The spread of this worldview had radical implications for worship patterns that had claimed divine mystery as their authority.

The changes that began about 25,000 Sundays ago in the Protestant churches would not have occurred without the technological advance of the printing press. Prior to the printing press, innovators could be silenced, but now printed copies of their words could be disseminated throughout the Christian world. A reordering of Sunday's worship pattern or the texts of newly composed prayers could now be circulated, and the printed format gave to the texts an aura of authority. Words that might have been seen as magical and known only by the clergy were now read and examined by laypeople. Hymns no longer needed to be laboriously taught over several decades, but could be sung right off the page. Holding a book is an empowering experience for a literate person. The medium of the printed page assumes an individual reader, and so the printed worship order contributed to the growing individualism of the age. Increasingly, to know about anything was to remember what you had read about it, and this new human consciousness had many consequences for historic worship practices that valued traditional symbols and rituals as the sacramental means to connect the human being with God.

A Lutheran says to his neighbor about a newborn: "He's in pretty poor condition, Sorrina tells me. . . . Now look here, Hans Olsa: it's up to you to come over and christen the boy for me. It's all written down in the hymn book—what to say, and how to go about it."

—*O. E. Rolvaag, Giants in the Earth*[1]

Much substance and piety of medieval worship lived on in Protestantism, especially the focus on personal sinfulness. During the first wave of the Reformation, represented in America today by Lutherans and Episcopalians, churches retained much historic practice, deleting only what they believed to be theologically or liturgically objectionable, and so the worship of some Episcopal and Lutheran churches is remarkably similar to that of some Roman Catholic churches. But other Christian communities from the sixteenth century on made considerable changes in Sunday symbol and ritual in order to embody their Reformation ideals. During the second wave of the Reformation, churches discarded much more of the tradition, because they thought that they were replacing the entire erroneous fabric of medieval liturgy with what had been the practices of New Testament believers. This second wave can be seen in the United States in **Reformed churches**, Presbyterians, and the **United Church of Christ**. The third wave is often called the Radical Reformation. It sought to free individual believers from any external control by

Reformed churches
a group of Protestant denominations that follow some of the teachings of John Calvin

United Church of Christ
liberal Protestant denomination founded in 1957 through a merger of Congregationalists and Reformed churches

the government, church tradition, or regional church authorities. The refusal to baptize infants exemplified the conviction that every adult believer stands alone before God. In our day, this movement is evidenced in quite different contemporary churches: the liberal American Baptists, the conservative Southern Baptists, and the countercultural **Mennonites** and Amish.

Over recent centuries in America, Protestant churches have become far more interwoven with one another than is suggested by historic categories. The contemporary Sunday practices of many churches are formed not only by their ancestry in one of the waves of the European Reformation, but also by the emotional imprint of their homeland, the circumstances of their immigration, a history of disruptive church disputes, mergers with other churches, their involvement with current social movements, the seminary that the clergy attended, the style of their church music, even their use of technology. Perhaps the minister was raised in one denomination and then moved to another: positive or negative memories of the childhood church will not disappear. All these influences are stirred together in the stew served up on Sunday morning. Thus, although many cities have over a dozen different Protestant denominations holding Sunday services, the worship practices of some churches are nearly identical.[2]

Symbols arising in the Protestant churches

The preeminent religious symbol in nearly all Protestant churches is the word. According to the Bible, God speaks, first at the time of creation, then at the giving of the law, then through the mouths of the prophets, preeminently in the ministry of Jesus, and then through the writings of the evangelists and apostles. Jews and Christians have taught that God cannot be seen, but God can be heard, and Protestants stress that the word of God is the primary way that the world can access God's promised mercy. "The word" can mean the entire Bible, a selection of passages from the Bible chosen as theologically central to Christian faith and practice, the proclamation of the biblical reading during worship, or the sermon that interprets the reading and applies it to the current situation. When "word" is capitalized, it may refer to Christ himself. Most churches claim that throughout the centuries of the church, God continues to speak words of judgment and grace. Many Protestants maintain that when the Bible is read aloud on

That Christ's Supper is seriously abused has been brought out quite strongly and clearly from the Word of God for a long time: therefore, it will be necessary to remove from it everything which does not conform to the divine Word.

—*Ulrich Zwingli, 1525*[3]

Mennonite
conservative pacifist Protestant denomination that practices believers' baptism

Sunday morning, it is actually God speaking to the contemporary assembly. Thus the medieval patterns in the churches of both West and East, in which the faithful watched a priest perform holy actions and benefited by gazing at religious imagery, were replaced with Renaissance and Enlightenment preferences for words: hearing words, speaking words, reading words, singing words.

In many Protestant churches, the primary architectural symbol set before the people is the pulpit. Because preaching became the central event in Sunday worship, some churches replaced a central altar with a central pulpit, sometimes a massive podium with its own sound shell constructed high above the people's heads, sometimes a reading desk on a stage. Altars came to resemble wooden tables. In some churches, the table is set out only for those services at which communion is celebrated. Protestant theologians placed great store in the dictum that the building wins: the elevated pulpit made clear that looking up and hearing the preacher's proclamation of the word of God was the worshipers' pathway to salvation.

The local lords: "What do you hold concerning our mass?" Elizabeth: "My lords, of your mass I think nothing at all; but I highly esteem all that accords with the word of God."

—*The trial of Elizabeth of Leeuwarden, executed on March 27, 1549*[4]

With most medieval symbols removed, many Protestant churches resemble lecture halls, with little in the chancel or nave regarded as sacred. The clergy sit on a front stage and the people in long straight rows of the now mandatory permanent seating. With pews in place, the normal ritual posture of the people is to sit quietly in their pews, listening. Replacing stained glass windows with clear glass brought light into these candlelit rooms, thus making it easier for worshipers to read. A view from the ceiling would show the worshipers sitting in straight lines on two sides of a central aisle, as if they were lines of type in an open book. When in colonial America services in an unheated room lasted several hours, worshipers brought along foot-warmers, containers that resembled metal lunch boxes filled with hot coals, to keep their feet from freezing. Some contemporary churches have added padding to the pews, to make the sitting more comfortable. Among Protestant churches, it is usually only churches descendent from the first wave of the Reformation that provide some kind of cushions for kneeling.

In most Protestant churches book racks are attached to the pews or seats. Given the expectation that everyone present will be joining in the songs and prayers and may follow along with the biblical readings, many Protestant churches provide hymnals and Bibles in the pew racks. Other churches hand out a service program that includes all the words of the service, except for the sermon. These practices demonstrate the focus on participation in the word.

A colonial church in Philadelphia is still in use each Sunday.

This intense focus on the word led to a devaluing of other forms of religious symbol. That symbols can have an almost magical power over uneducated people was one reason that many Protestants rejected most of them. Church symbols had gained their considerable respect over centuries of European tradition; however, this spoke not for, but against their continued use in churches that strove to discard unintelligible remnants of the past. In the early sixteenth century, the first Reformers began this process in moderate ways, for example, by discarding relics of saints. The Reformers who were influenced by Calvin whitewashed the medieval frescos on the walls of their churches, since they judged that the images distracted from attention to the word. By the mid-seventeenth century, the Quakers designed a morning meeting nearly completely devoid of any symbol whatsoever—although a bare room with clear glass windows makes its own symbolic statement.

Many objects with sacred value within Roman Catholic communities were thrown out. Some Protestant churches have a statue of Jesus or images of biblical characters displayed, but things related to the veneration of nonbiblical saints were removed. A characteristic Protestant comment about the dead is that they were sinners like us, and prayers must be addressed only to God. A shocking example of what happened when the statue was part of the stone wall of the building is St. Steven's Church in Nijmegen, the Netherlands, still used every Sunday by its current Protestant community. During a seventeenth-century riot the townspeople chiseled off the head of every single one of the saints' statues that surround the sanctuary, and so today Protestant worshipers gaze at headless sculptures. Rejection of historic authority, rather than the sanctity of the dead, became a preferred attitude.

Today some Protestant churches light ceremonial candles, and others do not. Gold was sometimes replaced with pewter. Embedded gems were judged, not as worthy worship of God, but as signs of a decadent medieval church, and thus Bibles, liturgical books, and communion vessels were less opulent, more practical. Today in Protestant churches it is usual for the lectionary or pulpit Bible to be large and bound in leather, perhaps with gold-edged pages, but not encrusted with pearls. Some churches have no ceremonial book, but instead readers use the weekly printed folder when proclaiming the word. A woven breadbasket may be used for the eucharistic bread. Jesus was not only divine, but also human, and some Protestants believe that the stuff of regular homes better symbolizes the immanent presence of God than does the ornamentation of a palace.

When few symbols are present, each single symbol can expand its power to fill the symbolic vacuum. Many Protestant churches chose to display not the crucifixes that were normal in medieval churches, but instead plain crosses with no body of Christ affixed. In many Protestant churches, this cross is now the single, sometimes immense, symbol, affixed to the far wall or hanging over the altar. Such a cross is often explained as being symbolic of the resurrection, as opposed to a crucifix being a symbol of the death of Christ. Yet with a large cross attached to the front wall, the building still reflects medieval patterns of

Note the design of this New England church.

thought, in which God was up, beyond, outside the room, and the worshipers faced the front wall to symbolize their standing below the transcendent God.

One fundamental change in Sunday symbol was how the Protestant churches dealt with the bread and wine of communion. Nearly all Protestants assert that the bread and wine are important manifestations of divine presence and communal bonding. Although many first-wave Protestants taught that the elements are both bread and body, wine and blood, many Protestants understood these elements as only reminding worshipers of divine mercy. The main point of Sunday worship was to receive forgiveness, and partaking of the bread and wine, as a memorial of Jesus' last supper, assisted the worshiper in accepting forgiveness. Thus, many medieval practices that reverenced these elements were eliminated. No more was a consecrated host to be set up in a monstrance or carried in procession through town as an aid to spiritual devotion. Most Protestants radically simplified regulations about what to do if the consecrated bread fell on the floor or how to store any leftovers. Both bread and wine were seen as equally part of the communion rite, to be shared by all communicants. The questions about the holiness of the bread and wine and whether to use the word *symbol* continue to this day to differentiate one Protestant denomination from another.

miter
a pointed hat worn by the bishop in the West

The symbols of the priesthood and the church's hierarchy were criticized within most Protestant communities. Some medieval vestments such as the **miter** are seldom seen. Many Protestants replaced the chasuble with the black Geneva gown, the symbol of a university education. Today in the Protestant churches one might encounter full eucharistic vestments of alb, chasuble, and stole—the design either resembling medieval vesture or recast with a contemporary aesthetic—a plain alb with a stole, the black preaching robe, ethnic garb of personal choice, the same business attire an executive wears to work on Monday, or casual clothing.

However, the rejection of a symbol of authority does not mean that the position of authority has been abandoned. The minister may have no power over God, but may still wield considerable power over the people. An example is the Amish, among whom the local bishop has authority over countless practical decisions affecting community life. Only a few denominations function without an ordained clergy. Usually in Protestant churches the clergy are symbols of the genuine need for leadership in a human community, and they are expected to teach the faith and provide pastoral care for their members. The normal practice is for the Sunday service to be led by ordained clergy. Some churches now encourage laypeople to take some leadership roles, but usually the most important functions—preaching the sermon, administering communion—are conducted by the ordained ministers. Nearly all Protestant churches rejected monastic life as a useful Christian enterprise, and so there are only a few Protestant monasteries and convents that might model carefully designed worship.

One striking change of symbols in the Protestant movement occurred in sacred speech. In medieval Catholicism some vernacular preaching in the language of the people occurred, both within and outside Sunday Mass. But for most medieval worshipers, given that the priest's prayers were spoken in Latin, sometimes in low tones and with his back to the people, the alien language associated with worship must have symbolized the vast distance between God and the people, and the work of the priest was necessary to bridge the gap and bring divine grace to the assembly. In contrast, the Reformation churches popularized the vernacular for all the language on Sunday morning. The goal was that during worship every member of the church use a hymnal, which included communal songs, some psalms, and many prayers of the liturgy. These hymnals themselves became symbols of the worship of all the people of God, and many Protestants own a hymnal for use at home. Ancient texts were translated into the vernacular, and new texts were composed. The approved texts of Protestant churches tend toward language that is plain and simple, valuing clarity over exuberance.

> I wish as many of the songs as possible to be in the vernacular which the people should sing during mass.
>
> —*Martin Luther, 1523*[5]

This tendency toward vernacular texts is strong in much, but not all, American Protestantism. The theological explanation for this preference is that God becomes incarnate in the things of this world; the New Testament is written in a colloquial form of Greek; and the language of worship should emulate this accessibility. In the second half of the twentieth century many denominations issued new texts for Sunday worship. In many American Protestant churches, the entire text of the worship service is available to all the worshipers, either in a hymnal or in a weekly printed service folder. The church musician may take time before the service to teach a new song.

Some churches have worked to replace archaic English with contemporary speech. Few Americans realize that referring to God as "Thou" originally was meant to bring God close to the worshiper: in Elizabethan English, "thou" was used to address only one's beloved family, one's closest friends, and God. Since "thou" has now dropped out of colloquial speech and is found only in worship, many worshipers assume that it signifies the sovereign majesty, rather than the intimate love, of God. Because of this linguistic confusion, some Protestant churches have replaced the pronouns Thou-Thine-Thee with You-your-you. "Our Father, who art in heaven, hallowed be thy name" becomes "Our Father in heaven, hallowed be your name." New prayers and hymns present synonyms for traditional theological concepts, so that worship can be meaningful for people who were never taught what, for example, "salvation" is. Publishing houses of some Protestant church bodies have published prayers and hymns that use a variety of both biblical and contemporary titles and metaphors for God.

Because the words chosen for worship are so central to the piety of the people, the decisions regarding the symbolic speech of worship are sometimes what distinguish one assembly from another. In 1559, Queen Elizabeth I, as head of the Church of England, promulgated the Act of Uniformity, which mandated life imprisonment for any priest arrested three times for not using the single approved Anglican text. But now each local Episcopal congregation has some choice about which type of liturgical language it prefers, and many worshipers vociferously defend their preference in symbolic speech. In the authorized worship books of American Episcopalians, *The Book of Common Prayer* Rite I retains some Elizabethan speech, Rite II was crafted in the 1970s, and *Enriching Our Worship* provides intentionally expansive language for God.

> All glory be to thee, Almighty God, our heavenly Father, for that thou, of thy tender mercy, didst give thine only Son Jesus Christ to suffer death upon the cross for our redemption.
> —The opening of the eucharistic prayer, *Book of Common Prayer*, Rite I[6]

> God of all power, Ruler of the Universe, you are worthy of glory and praise. Glory to you for ever and ever. At your command all things came to be: the vast expanse of interstellar space, galaxies, suns, the planets in their courses, and this fragile earth, our island home.
> —The opening of a eucharistic prayer, *Book of Common Prayer*, Rite II[7]

> We praise you and we bless you, holy and gracious God, source of life abundant. You made us in your image, and taught us to walk in your ways. But we rebelled against you, and wandered far away; and yet, as a mother cares for her children, you would not forget us.
> —The opening of a eucharistic prayer, *Enriching Our Worship*, prayer 2[8]

Rituals arising in Protestant churches

Both Roman Catholic and Eastern Orthodox churches count seven sacraments: baptism, reconciliation, Eucharist, **confirmation**, ordination, marriage, and anointing of the sick and dying. In their reevaluation of worship practices, Protestant churches shortened this list. Nearly all Protestants refer to only baptism and Holy Communion as sacraments, because the New Testament

confirmation
a Christian ritual in which young adults baptized as infants publicly affirm their faith and are blessed

connects only those two rituals with the ministry of Jesus. Some churches have replaced the term *sacrament* with the word *rite* or *ordinance*. Most Protestant churches kept doing confirmations, ordinations, marriages, services of confession and forgiveness, and funerals, but these were seen as less fundamental to the faith than were baptism and communion, less tied to Christ, and thus more open to local adaptations.

Since for most Protestants the primary ritual moment had shifted from the priest consecrating the bread and wine to the preacher proclaiming the word of God, the "word" part of the service became more significant than the "sacrament" part. This occurred not only because the culture was marked by a growing trust in the printed page. Many sixteenth-century Christians had made only an annual communion at Easter. This meant that although the consecration of the bread and wine was understood to be the holiest moment of the Mass, what actually had considerable spiritual resonance for them were the vernacular sermons that were preached especially at services of penance. People brought into the Reformation churches their medieval formation, caring more about the preaching than the communing. For the educated leaders of the Reformation, especially the priest's consecration of the bread and wine was viewed as an erroneous power over salvation held by the clergy, and Reformation leaders taught that the saving grace of Christ was more readily available through the word preached by the minister. Even among those Anglicans who hold a communion service each Sunday, it was **Morning Prayer**, an early Sunday service of song, Scripture, and prayer, that became the most popular order of service for many Episcopalians.

Morning Prayer
a morning devotional service built upon the psalms and prayers

The early Reformers hoped for weekly communion by all the faithful, and they rejected the Roman Catholic practice of a priest "saying Mass" alone and communing by himself. Since sixteenth-century people were not accustomed to weekly communion, however, it came about that most Protestant churches scheduled communion only monthly or quarterly. During the settling of the American continent, groups of Protestants could meet each Sunday to read the Bible and pray together, but only if a clergyman visited could a service of communion be conducted, and many Americans lived for decades on the frontier with no resident clergy available. Monthly communion still marks many American Protestant churches. However, several Protestant national church bodies are actively advocating for a return to weekly communion. Their central offices have published resources that speak of "word and sacrament" as together constituting the service of every Sunday. So it is that in one Lutheran or Presbyterian church, communion is weekly, and in another monthly.

The usual Sunday worship in many Protestant churches is a Sunday service of the word without the sharing of bread and wine. Protestant sermons in the American colonies lasted several hours, and now last anywhere

"Excellent sermon."

from fifteen to forty-five minutes. Some churches call their ordained clergy preachers. Often the sermon is understood as Bible study that applies God's word to daily life. In some traditions, the sermon is expected to be a sophisticated exposition of Christian doctrine, a kind of serious adult Sunday school. Some sermons are characterized as "hellfire and brimstone" preaching and can be seen as Protestant replacements of the medieval Catholic practice of assigning strict penances for sin. Many Protestant services now include a children's sermon, during

Meanings of the Eucharist, continued:

1. Thanksgiving in the new age brought about by Christ's resurrection
2. Participation in the suffering and death of Christ
3. Mystical experience of the triune life in heaven
4. A continuing sacrifice to appease an angry God
5. The occasion for private devotion
6. A rendering of the word of forgiveness
7. A reenactment of Jesus' last supper
8. Eating and drinking effecting communal bonding

which children process up to the minister and sit on the floor for a short address or conversation.

When there is a communion service, the method of distributing the bread and wine varies from church to church. In some places, everyone walks forward to a railing around the altar and kneels to receive unleavened wafers and wine. Some churches use regular leavened bread baked by a congregation member or purchased at a local bakery. Some church cut up loaves of white bread into small squares. In some churches, people line up in a queue and receive standing up. In other churches, trays of the elements are passed from one person to another in the pew, and only when everyone has the bread or small glass in hand does everyone consume the elements simultaneously. Some churches hand out printed folders that explain the method of communion and its symbolism. A few denominations with communion four times a year link it with a footwashing, modeling their ritual on the description in John 13 of Jesus' last supper at which he washed his disciples' feet. Although in the sixteenth century taking communion in the Protestant churches was always tied to a private or public ritual of confession, many contemporary churches have replaced a formal confession ritual with a general thanksgiving for forgiveness.

Although the first-wave Protestants maintained the order of service that was rooted in the second century, the second- and third-wave Protestants rejected that order as being too closely identified with Roman Catholicism and too reliant on traditional symbols and prescribed ritual. However, granting that ritual tends to create its own permanent patterns of communal activity, these newly designed service orders are now quite uniform from one church to another.

A typical order of Sunday worship in a **Free Church** is as follows:

Opening hymn or several hymns
Call to worship: usually verses from the Psalms
Introductions: the focus of the morning's worship
Sharing our joys and concerns: personal announcements
Prayer in unison
Choir music
A time for children
Pastoral prayer and prayers of the people
Hymn
Scripture: biblical passage chosen by the preacher
Sermon
Collection of money
Hymn
Blessing and sending[9]

Protestants changed the calendar of ritual time. Although the first-wave Reformers maintained much of the medieval lectionary cycle of biblical readings and the days and seasons of the liturgical year, they eliminated the nonbiblical saints' days. But many of the second- and third-wave Protestants discarded nearly the entire annual cycle except for Christmas, Holy Week, and Easter. Some radical Protestants viewed even Christmas as a malformation that contributed nothing

Free Churches
the Protestant churches that emphasize local freedom from government, tradition, and church hierarchy

but shenanigans to the Christian life. Rather than mandate or even suggest a cycle of biblical readings, most second- and third-wave churches expect preachers to select the passage for each worship service. A proposal to read through the entire Bible at Sunday worship, one Old Testament chapter and one New Testament chapter each week, did not survive. In the United States today, most Protestant churches have reinstituted some annual cycle of festival days, and many share with other churches at least some biblical readings on some Sundays.

One ritual innovation important for some Protestants was the intensification of Sunday as replicating Sabbath rest. Some Protestants introduced strict rules as to what activities besides worship were and were not allowed on Sunday. The idea was to prevent sin, rather than punish it, and Sunday's restricted activities were held up as the model of godly behavior. Some municipalities in the United States still have "blue laws," which, for example, forbid the sale of liquor on Sunday. To counter the frenetic lives of many contemporary people, some churches are reviving focus on Sunday as a day of rest.

Perhaps the most beloved ritual in most Protestant worship is hymn singing. Protestants did not invent this practice, but enormously increased its use. Words that were sung by a trained choir in a medieval cathedral were turned into hymns that everyone sang together. Large pipe organs provided the volume necessary to support congregational singing, and talented church musicians such as J. S. Bach presented worshipers with a continuous supply of new compositions and impressive accompaniments to communal song. Some Protestant worship intersperses songs with each element of the service. Some churches begin their service with perhaps a half hour of singing as a ritual that unites the assembly. Singing certain hymns marks one's specific identity within the wider Christian church, and many Protestants know the beloved songs in their tradition by heart. The text of many Protestant hymns gives honor to "the word." In the well-known hymn "Amazing Grace" by the ex-slaver John Newton, it is the "sound" of the "taught" "word" that "saved a wretch like me." Some hymns had many stanzas, all of which were sung. Putting the biblical message into rhythm and rhyme made it easier to remember.

> A farmer would not think of sowing his seed without first getting the soil in shape. Singing these old hymns can be likened to the final harrowing before planting the crop. It should help in getting our minds into a prayerful receptive mood. What could be a better way to do this than to actively join in singing these hymns?
>
> —*An Amish worshiper*[10]

The onset of option

Perhaps the most significant innovation in Christian worship 25,000 Sundays ago was the element of choice. If one has no option, choice is not a concern.

Since the Great Schism between West and East, there had been two Sunday options, but almost never in the same geographical area. After the first wave of the Reformation, the same pattern was followed. For example, the residents of each locale in Germany were required to follow their prince in being either Roman Catholic or Protestant, and in the sixteenth-century Church of England, Queen Elizabeth I sought to make every Christian residing in England a member of the approved state church. What was operative here is the ancient understanding that religion encompasses the whole of people's lives, and that to ensure a smooth running of society, it is best if all the people who live near one another honor the same symbols and engage in the same rituals.

But once Protestant churches of many varieties were available in cities, individuals could decide which church to attend. Particularly in the United States, one kind of Protestant married another kind, and so the couple was presented with Sunday choice. The fact of choice evolved into the expectation of choice. The term *Protestant* indicates a religious stance that assumes "protest"; in order to protest, one must first critique Sunday worship; and the result of protest

A Mighty Fortress Is Our God

1 A might - y for - tress is our God,
2 No strength of ours can match his might!
3 Though hordes of dev - ils fill the land
4 God's Word for - ev - er shall a - bide,

a sword and shield vic - to - rious;
We would be lost, re - ject - ed.
all threat - 'ning to de - vour us,
no thanks to foes, who fear it;

he breaks the cruel op - pres - sor's rod
But now a cham - pion comes to fight,
we trem - ble not, un - moved we stand;
for God him - self fights by our side

and wins sal - va - tion glo - rious.
whom God him - self e - lect - ed.
they can - not o - ver - pow'r us.
with weap - ons of the Spir - it.

The old e - vil foe, sworn to work us woe,
Ask who this may be: Lord of hosts is he!
This world's prince may rage, in fierce war en - gage.
If they take our house, goods, fame, child, or spouse,

with dread craft and might he arms him - self to fight.
Christ Je - sus our Lord, God's on - ly Son, a - dored.
He is doomed to fail; God's judg - ment must pre - vail!
wrench our life a - way, they can - not win the day.

On earth he has no e - qual.
He holds the field vic - to - rious.
One lit - tle word sub - dues him.
The king - dom's ours for - ev - er!

Text: Martin Luther, 1483–1546; tr. *Lutheran Book of Worship*
Music: EIN FESTE BURG, Martin Luther
Text © 1978 *Lutheran Book of Worship*, admin. Augsburg Fortress.

Martin Luther's hymn "A Mighty Fortress" is his Christianization of the biblical Psalm 46

The colony of Pennsylvania possesses great liberties above all other English colonies, inasmuch as all religious sects are tolerated there. We find there Lutherans, Reformed, Catholics, Quakers, Mennonites or Anabaptists, Herrnhutters or Moravian Brethren, Pietists, Seventh Day Baptists, Dunkers, Presbyterians, Newborn, Free-masons, Separatists, Freethinkers, Jews, Mohammedans, Pagans, Negroes and Indians. But there are many hundred unbaptized souls there that do not even wish to be baptized. In one house and one family, 4, 5, and even 6 sects may be found.

—Gottlieb Mittelberger, a visitor to colonial Pennsylvania who gladly returned to Europe in 1754[11]

may be a change of affiliation. More Christians in the United States attend weekly worship than do Europeans, and one theory to explain American church attendance proposes that the wide range of choice in the United States gives the worshiper an element of personal sovereignty. If I get to choose where and how to worship, I may be more likely to go to church on Sunday.

Suggestions

1. Review the chapter's vocabulary: confirmation, Free Churches, Mennonite, miter, Morning Prayer, Reformation, Reformed churches, and the United Church of Christ.

2. Present arguments for and against the spirit of Protestantism that allows for the proliferation of denominations.

3. Study the historical development of one of the first-, second-, or third-wave Protestant denominations.

4. Compare and contrast what two Protestant denominations teach about the meaning of the bread and wine.

5. Examine and analyze data that records the attendance patterns in contemporary American churches.

6. The biblical book of Galatians is a letter Paul wrote in about 55 C.E., in which he encourages Christians to exercise freedom from religious regulations. Discuss Galatians 3–4, a formative text for many Protestants.

7. Discuss the chapters entitled "Preaching" and "The Bible" in *Amazing Grace* by Kathleen Norris.[12]

8. Discuss the 1987 film *Babette's Feast*, which contrasts the severe life of a small community of Danish Protestants with the sumptuous dinner party prepared by a Paris chef.

9. Attend a Sunday service in a Lutheran, Episcopalian, Reformed Church in America, Christian Reformed, Presbyterian, United Church of Christ, Baptist, or Mennonite congregation, and compare and contrast what you encounter there with the details of this chapter.

For further study

Bower, Peter, C., ed. *The Companion to the Book of Common Worship*. Louisville: Geneva, 2003.

Gilbert, Marlea, Christopher Grundy, Eric T. Myers, and Stephanie Perdew. *The Work of the People: What We Do in Worship and Why*. Herndon, Va.: Alban Institute, 2007.

Lathrop, Gordon. *Central Things: Worship in Word and Sacrament*. Minneapolis: Augsburg Fortress, 2005.

Snyder, Graydon E., and Doreen M. McFarlane. *The People are Holy: The History and Theology of Free Church Worship*. Macon, Ga.: Mercer University Press, 2005.

Wandel, Lee Palmer. *The Eucharist in the Reformation: Incarnation and Liturgy*. New York: Cambridge University Press, 2006.

Welker, Michael. *What Happens in Holy Communion?* Trans. John F. Hoffmeyer. Grand Rapids: Eerdmans, 2000.

Witvliet, John D. *Worship Seeking Understanding: Windows into Christian Practice*. Grand Rapids: Baker, 2003.

Chapter 8

What comes down to us from the last 10,000 Sundays?

Two centuries of American life, more options

From 1800 to 2000 many new denominational groups arose in the United States. Most groups adapted in some way the symbols and rituals of Sunday worship that they had inherited.

Many Protestant African Americans left the churches that were dominated by white authority and by Euro-American preferences and organized their own denominations, which are sometimes called "black church." The mother of this movement is the **African Methodist Episcopal Church (A.M.E.)**. These churches have relied on their memory of African tribal rituals and on the experience of nineteenth-century **revivals** to cultivate an intensely dynamic Sunday event markedly different from that of most Anglo worshipers. Baptists were among the mainstream denominations that split into black and white units. Some congregations with a majority African American membership adopted more characteristics of black-church worship than of their denominational parent.

The **Holiness movement** of the nineteenth century, reacting against the realities of urban industrialization, stressed that the Holy Spirit could inspire

African Methodist Episcopal Church an American Methodist church body founded in 1814 by Philadelphia free African Americans

revival a meeting, sometimes held outdoors, characterized by inspirational song and enthusiastic preaching, with the goal of returning people to active Christian life

Christians for a holy life. The worship of **Methodists**, originally a break-off from Episcopalians, and of other Holiness churches—for example, the **Church of the Nazarene** and countless independent Holiness assemblies—emphasize the individual's role in accepting faith and committing oneself to the Christian life.

A religious revival in Los Angeles in 1906 is usually cited as the source of the Pentecostal movement. The many Pentecostal churches—for example, the **Assemblies of God** and **Church of God in Christ**—infuse their worship with expressions of ecstasy that are understood as natural, even necessary, signs of the indwelling of the Holy Spirit. The term "**charismatic renewal**" is used to describe those churches in mainstream denominations that encourage some level of ecstatic worship. The nineteenth-century movement called **Pietism**, seen, for example, among the **Moravians**, stressed the deep personal devotion that resulted when Jesus entered the individual. Pietist worship, prevalent during the settling of the frontier, is characterized by biblical study, intense self-examination, fervent hymn singing, and communal prayer. Among the many nineteenth-century extensions and adaptations of Christianity are the Restorationists, such as the **Disciples of Christ**, who view their worship as restoring that of the earliest Christians and who thus discarded much of what had accumulated over the centuries. Several groups, such as the Jehovah's Witnesses, Quakers, and Mormons, have in some essential way moved away from the mainstream traditions of Christian worship.

The groups that call themselves nondenominational, such as **Calvary Chapel** and many independent churches, value worship that is free from both the centuries of theological explication and the worldwide alliances that are important to the historic churches. Each assembly is encouraged to design its

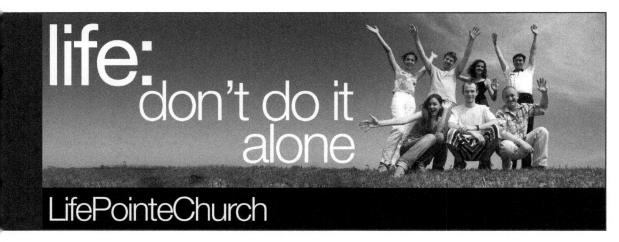

What is and what is not on this church's billboard?

own ritual order for Sunday morning. Such a promise of freedom is attractive to many Americans, and in the twentieth century independent churches proliferated. Most megachurches are nondenominational, independent organizations that advertise a unique style of worship, albeit that the worship of most independent churches closely resembles that of others.

A Protestant grouping increasingly cited in the twenty-first century is the evangelicals. The term *evangelical* is not a denominational label, but instead denotes a style of Protestantism that engages some of the congregations of different denominations. Many evangelicals emphasize a personal experience of conversion called "**being born again**," a literalist interpretation of the Bible, and commitment to a conservative lifestyle. Evangelical churches tend to utilize revival patterns of worship on Sunday.

In America, it is common that worship practices undertaken by one denomination are noted by other Christians, who visit one another's churches or who transfer their membership from one church to another. Thus, churches in perhaps a dozen denominations in one city conduct their Sunday morning with an identical format and in similar ways. Yet when the practices of one group are adopted by others, some alterations in usage and intention occur. For example, originally music in African American churches was provided by the entire assembly singing in harmony. In the 1840s, however, Daniel Payne, who had been reared in the Lutheran church with its long tradition of practiced choristers, became a minister in the A.M.E. Church and introduced choirs into his local black congregation. The African American churches then reshaped the choir tradition to fit their exuberant worship, and now Lutheran choirs are listening to African American church choirs for inspiration.

Another example of this continual borrowing is the assembly's words of greeting. Since at least the third century, the leader of the Sunday worship greeted the people using the biblical quotation "The Lord be with you" to ground the assembly firmly in the word of God, and the people responded with a phrase that meant "the Lord be with you." Over the last century, some churches altered this greeting. Their leader calls the assembly to order with the secular American ritual phrase "Good morning," and the people respond,

> The Pietists modeled a warm-hearted, impassioned, and demonstrative faith that became a hallmark of the emerging pattern of American evangelicalism. They insisted on a religion that could be felt and experienced, on an individual and personal decision to accept baptism, on a dynamic divine presence that could point beyond the hardships of daily life, and on the promise of endless bliss in the life to come. In this new world, where the hardships of frontier and vigorous individualism went hand in hand, what could be more appealing than a Christian vision that cultivated concern for the individual religious experience of every common person?
>
> —*John Witvliet*[1]

Assemblies of God
union in 1914 of largely white independent fundamentalist assemblies that emphasize the transformation of life following baptism by the Holy Spirit

Church of God in Christ
largely African American Pentecostal fundamentalist church founded in 1897

charismatic renewal
an ecumenical movement reviving the biblical rituals of ecstatic speech and prayer for healing

Pietism
a Christian emphasis on the religion of the heart

"Good morning." This practice has spread to churches that had never used such colloquial expressions in their worship. Now in the formal Roman Catholic worship in traditional cathedrals, at the outset of the Mass or in concluding remarks after Mass, the priest may speak "Good morning" into the microphone, and the people respond, "Good morning."

Over the last 10,000 Sundays, American Christians have debated how much of the tradition of Christian symbol and ritual should be retained. How important is it for hundreds, or thousands, or millions of Christians to worship in the same way? How much of the symbol and ritual should assume that the participants are regularly practicing Christians, or to what degree ought worship be transparent and accessible to newcomers? If a certain ritual becomes popular, should other Christian groups adopt its use? As one group of Christians answers one such question in a new way, its proposal becomes a challenge to the many neighboring Christians, for many Christian denominations continually analyze their worship practices in hopes of deepening them and offering greater appeal to potential members.

Symbols developed among American worshipers

Over the last 10,000 Sundays, more everyday objects have been brought into Sunday worship. An expensive pulpit Bible may be replaced with a desk-sized Bible. For distribution of the wine of communion, small manufactured glasses may replace a crafted silver or gold chalice. Secular clothing may replace historic clerical vestments. A rented storefront is seen as appropriately situating the church in the neighborhood, rather than outside of town surrounded by a large lawn. The musical instruments that one hears at a concert or at a nightclub may be the preferred instruments for worship, since they can serve to connect worship with daily life. Guitars, which many people own, can replace organs, which are not personal possessions and are expensive to purchase.

The twentieth century awakened some churches in America to worldwide Christianity. Churches became aware that most of their symbols reflected European practice, and worshipers are widening the sources of their symbols. Thus, the plate holding the communion bread may come from a Third World artist, rather than from an ecclesiastical goods supply company. The cup may have been crafted by a Native American potter. The hope is to insert the local assembly into the worldwide church, so that the community not only recalls its own tradition, but welcomes the traditions of Christians of other cultures.

In an opposite move, many churches placed an American flag in the worship space. This practice began among immigrant Protestant groups, who especially during wartime wanted to symbolize that they were loyal American citizens. Now even some Roman Catholic churches, where the primary identity is meant to be grounded in a worldwide denominational unity, display an American flag. Other churches maintain that national identity ought not be a defining issue at worship, and so no national flags are ever displayed.

In 1869, in the basement of his house in Vineland, New Jersey, Thomas B. Welch invented grape juice. The sugar that is in grapes naturally ferments and produces alcohol, and throughout most of Christian history, granting the difficulty of securing pure drinking water, wine was the normal beverage for anyone who could afford it. Welch developed a method of preventing the natural chemical fermentation of grapes so that nonalcoholic juice was a possibility. On the American prairie, especially Methodist women had led protests against the excessive and socially destructive consumption of alcohol, and encouraged by Welch, some Protestants began to use grape juice for communion as an alternate or replacement for wine. A century later, this practice has widely expanded, with many churches offering grape juice as at least an option for children and for recovering alcoholics. Usually some printed matter that is available for worshipers makes clear what will be served, and if there is an option, how to distinguish the wine from the juice.

The practice of ordaining women to the ministry began about 7,500 Sundays ago. Over the course of the twentieth century, one Protestant denomination after another struggled over this issue. Many Protestant churches now have a large number of ordained women, and some churches have female bishops. In deciding for women's ordination, some have argued that the baptism of all believers suggests that in the church, as in the sight of God, there ought to be no religious preference for males. Others cite evidence in the Bible that women held leadership roles in the early church. Still others claim that the tasks of the ordained ministry draw on abilities cultivated more by women than by men, and so women are more appropriate for the role than men. However, some Protestant churches agree with Roman Catholics and Eastern Orthodox that, in accord with either the Bible or their church tradition, women ought not be ordained. Some of these churches will not allow their building to be used by other Christians for worship if the presider is an ordained woman.

African American assemblies cultivated a participatory style of preaching. In these churches, a sermon, lasting up to an hour, relies on call-and-

> The simple food around which the congregation will gather should be lovingly prepared, despite the pressure of efficiency and convenience. Bread that is delicious and wholesome, firm enough to handle, but easy for all to eat, will be most likely to engage us and encourage our full participation. Wafers, hard unleavened squares, or soft, tiny cubes present a "thin" symbolism, disconnected from real life. A full loaf of good bread has a "thick" symbolism, an expression of real life and a connection with all the meals that sustain us.
>
> —The Work of the People[2]

Barbara Harris was the first female bishop in the Episcopal Church.

response, a ritual dialogue between the preacher and the assembly. The preacher intersperses the text of the sermon with rhetorical devices that serve as clues for the worshipers, who respond with "Amen," "Praise the Lord!" and other phrases. In some churches, the preacher begins the sermon in a soft, low-pitched voice, gradually accelerates the pace and raises the pitch, and concludes by whooping: the speech has evolved into chant; the musicians begin playing on drums and musical instruments; the people join in cheering, clapping, and even dancing in the aisles. Some churches that are not largely African American admire this style and now make some attempt at response from the people during the preaching. The preacher may ask the congregation questions. For about 2,500 Sundays, some sermons have included jokes meant to evoke laughter.

One gift to the worldwide church from African American churches is the symbolic speech of the **spirituals**. These songs and chants, rooted in African tribal song, provided comfort to slaves working in the field. Because of their repetitions, the songs are easily sung without printed texts. The singular pronoun "I" symbolizes the entire community that has become one in its worship. These spirituals, originally sung by the entire assembly, are rooted in biblical narratives, formed through a history of oppression, and supportive of one another through the hardships of life and in a racist world. The story of the suffering and death of Christ unites the worshipers, who like Mary and John were suffering near the cross of Jesus, and the singing moves the worshipers from crucifixion to resurrection. The biblical message of divine justice offers hope in a racist world. These spirituals may be presented by practiced choirs wearing colorful robes. The spirituals are now included in the printed worship resources of largely white denominations.

Some Holiness churches use a style of intercessory prayer called **concert prayer**, during which everyone in the assembly prays aloud simultaneously. The result is a cacophony of sound, seen as symbolic of the prayers of all Christians continuously offered to God. In some churches, a moment of concert prayer occurs during the intercessions, during which worshipers are

spiritual
an emotional biblical song rooted in the experience of African slaves

concert prayer
communal prayer during which participants pray personal petitions aloud simultaneously

encouraged to call out the names of those for whom they wish to pray, and the cacophony symbolizes the people's many petitions to God.

Pentecostal churches, by focusing on the power of the Holy Spirit, encourage and even expect worshipers to have the experience of glossolalia. In extreme emotion, humans tend not to speak words of their learned language, but instead laugh, cry, moan, scream, or make various noises. One such symbolic noise, "speaking in tongues," is an ecstatic babble that can be either a gentle murmur or an uproarious shout. The idea is that the divine has so infused the individual that a primal sound of praise comes forth. The experience of glossalalia gives the individual a profound sense of being visited by God. Being "seized by the Spirit," "getting the blessing," can be so overwhelming that the worshiper jumps around and may even pass out. Churches that expect this conduct have women dressed in white and black to monitor those who succumb to the Spirit, ensuring that they do not harm themselves while in the height of ecstasy. The assembly is bonded together by witnessing the transcendent emotional high. Some non-Pentecostal churches respect glossalalia, and people may be seized by the Spirit during communion.

In some churches worshipers wear their best clothes on Sunday, the men in suits, the women in elegant dresses and elaborate hats, and children dressed as small adults. Here clothing symbolizes the importance of the occasion, with worship far more significant than work or school. In some conservative Protestant churches, women are not allowed to attend worship wearing slacks. Visitors do well to acquaint themselves with the expected dress code, to avoid both offending the members and feeling unduly self-conscious.

Were you there when they crucified my Lord?
Were you there when they crucified my Lord?
O! Sometimes it causes me to tremble, tremble, tremble,
Were you there when they crucified my Lord?

—*Anonymous*

Rituals developed among American worshipers

Over the last 10,000 Sundays, several new interpretations of communion have been added to previous meanings. Churches that were influenced by the intellectual movement of the Enlightenment increasingly saw the Bible as cultivating moral conduct. It has been said that the meaning of much Christian worship is, "Jesus died: be good."[3] These churches were among those that radically diminished the part that sacraments play in Christian life. The Sunday service is a teaching event, and when the bread and wine are served, the ritual is viewed as something like an object lesson used by the instructor to illumine the lesson. Communion is like sending your friends flowers on their birthday: the ritual is a sign of your friendship, but it is essentially unnecessary.

Other churches maintained a strong sense of piety towards the sacrament, and they emphasized that communion reminded believers of the suffering that Christ endured because of sin. These churches usually explained that because the sacramental ritual meant so very much, it ought not be held often, since the intense personal examination of conscience required of the participants would diminish if repeated weekly. Thus, there developed two opposite reasons to have Eucharist only occasionally: it did not mean much, it meant too much. On the frontier, a practicality contributed to scheduling Eucharist seldom: neighbors could meet in someone's home with a Bible for prayer, but they needed an ordained minister for a service of communion. What had been a necessity—only occasional communion—then became the expected practice, after which the practice was defended with one explanation or another.

Over the centuries, theologians have proposed theories of atonement that connect the death and resurrection of Christ with the contemporary believer. Some churches have lessened the medieval stress on God's anger and on the necessity that someone be punished to satisfy divine justice, but most worshipers are still taught that Jesus died for their sins, and this idea continues to undergird the rituals of much Sunday worship. One newer proposal replaces God the angry judge with God the fellow sufferer. The crucifixion of Jesus is seen as the epitome of the endless sufferings of the innocent and of the perpetual reality of injustice, and Christian faith finds God there, suffering and even dying along with all humanity. The death of Christ then comforts believers by placing God with them, and the ritual of the meal nourishes them to model their life on Christ's by standing alongside all who are suffering and by embodying the resurrection to transform the world.

Meanings of the Eucharist, continued:

1. Thanksgiving in the new age brought about by Christ's resurrection
2. Participation in the suffering and death of Christ
3. Mystical experience of the triune life in heaven
4. A continuing sacrifice to appease an angry God
5. The occasion for private devotion
6. A rendering of the word of forgiveness
7. A reenactment of Jesus' last supper
8. Eating and drinking effecting communal bonding
9. An occasional ceremony to interiorize the teachings of Christ
10. An identification with suffering humanity

Because some churches celebrated communion only occasionally, several substitute meal rituals developed. Moravians and Methodists called these rituals **love feasts**; something like the meals of early Christians, these meals emphasize the bonding within the community that proceeds out of commitment to Christ. In African American churches it is common for everyone to eat a full Sunday chicken dinner together after church. Although not a sacrament, this Sunday dinner resonates with ideals of early Christian communities that shared a full meal.

Because during the settling of the American continent many people raised as Christians moved to a location that did not yet have resident churches, itinerant preachers and Methodist circuit riders conducted revivals, which were designed to call Christians back to faithful practice of religion. Some of the ritual design of **frontier worship** continues, even though the conditions of the frontier are long gone. On the prairie, revivals were social occasions that brought everyone together, and one famous comment about the Cane Ridge revival of 1801 was that at it more souls were begot than saved. At these events, the entertainment aspect of preaching and singing grew enormously. How much worship should be entertaining is a question raised in many contemporary churches.

The practice of revivals led to a new ritual order for Sunday worship. According to these ABCs of worship, the goal of Sunday is to Admit your sins, Believe in Jesus, and Commit yourself to Christ. The minister preaches on biblical passages that remind everyone of their sins, and the sermon attempts to inspire everyone to believe in Christ for forgiveness of sin. The more inspiring the sermon, the more likely that people will respond. Thus, these churches prize preachers who excel in inspiring the crowd. The service concludes with an **altar call**, in which sinners are encouraged to walk forward to confess Christ as their savior and begin their renewed life. In many established Protestant churches, the close of the service each week includes some call to recommit one's life to Jesus Christ.

Modeling their ritual speech on the autobiographical writings of Paul and the confessions of adult converts, individuals at such worship services are encouraged to testify to their faith. Many churches include substantial time on Sunday morning for personal **testimonies** in what is called the **devotional service**. Some churches attempt the same personal sharing by including a time called "Joys and Concerns." These rituals encourage participants to tell others their personal stories as a way to value the individual and to tie the community together.

In many of these churches, the ritual of the sermon tries to

One of the advantages of the Love Feast is that any Christian may conduct it. Congregational participation and leadership are usually extensive and important, especially involving children. Testimonies and praise are the focal point in most Love Feasts.

—The United Methodist Book of Worship[4]

love feast
nonsacramental Christian fellowship meal

frontier worship
a Protestant service of song, sermon, and call to commitment that arose on the nineteenth-century American frontier

altar call
the preacher's invitation after the sermon for persons to come forward and commit or recommit to Christ

I next attended and preached several times at a camp meeting, which continued five days. We had pentecostal showers—sinners were pricked to the heart, and cried mightily to God for succor from impending judgment, and I verily believe the Lord was well pleased at our weak endeavors to serve him in the tended grove.

—Jarena Lee, 1823[5]

involve the listeners. As the preacher cites various biblical passages, the people will studiously mark up the Bibles that they brought from home. When crafting their sermons, these preachers assume that believers know the Bible well because they read it daily at home. When delivering their sermons, the preachers may hold their Bible high in the air in a ritual that suggests that this book is the way to heaven.

A significant development of worship among some Christians was the rejection of any printed prayers as being canned and thus not from the heart. Preachers were expected to compose long prayers without using books. These prayers usually followed memorized outlines and included traditional phrasing, and they modeled how believers were to pray daily at home. Much of this prayer focuses on one's personal relationship to Jesus Christ and asks God to strengthen one's faith, and many contemporary Christians prefer extemporized prayer and understand it as conversation with God about their activities and emotions.

Seeker services are a recent ritual adaptation. Such worship includes as few as possible symbols and rituals and only perhaps a single sentence from the Bible, the idea being that to convert an outsider, simple explanations will be more effective than the layered meanings always inherent in symbols and rituals. Some churches that schedule seeker services on Sunday morning conduct more intensely Christian services on Wednesday evenings, which may include communion. Some churches employ a method called **entertainment evangelism**. Since Americans feel comfortable in are-

> The main purpose of the devotional service is to heat things up for worship. There was a deacon in the congregation of which I am pastor who would stand before the people and say, "Come on you all, join in and let us get things hot for the pastor, so he will not have to work so hard." The main desire was to get the people "fired up" for worship and prepared to receive the Word of God.
>
> —Joseph Jones[6]

nas of entertainment, these church buildings are designed to resemble movie theaters, with individual padded seats. The service presents Christian beliefs by means of entertaining songs, skits, and short speeches with a format resembling a variety show.

An increasing number of churches present a menu of services, in which one service, usually termed "contemporary," may resemble seeker services. Sometimes "contemporary" means only that the songs have been composed recently and the accompaniment is provided by a praise band rather than a professional organist. In other churches much of the worship ritual is aligned as closely as possible with the dominant contemporary culture, so as to maximize comfort. Historic denominational markers are laid aside. Even though most participants at this worship are members rather than seekers, the communal event includes little or nothing that is extraordinary, since the idea is that informality and simplicity are preferred by many Americans. However, in some churches, because of relatively recent immigration, the style of worship closely resembles that of the homeland and is resistant to American cultural influence.

Meanwhile, other churches intend to make their worship as out of the ordinary as possible. In Pentecostal churches, rituals that embody the power of divine healing are common, with the ministers placing their hands on the body of the individual who prays for wholeness. In a society in which one's hands are to be kept to oneself, this ritual replaces cultural expectations with sacred actions. This ritual has spread into many non-Pentecostal churches. In some churches, at the time of communion, people can have hands laid on them for a moment of private prayer for healing. Some Christians have found this ritual significant in making communal worship also personal.

Ritual time in current Protestant churches varies greatly. In many churches, worship takes less than an hour. However, among African American, Pentecostal, and Holiness churches, Sunday worship lasts several hours, beginning with a devotion and hymn sing that may itself last over half an hour. Although the service will not include communion, everyone is invited to remain for a substantial Sunday dinner. Those most committed to the faith then attend an afternoon service. Thus, most of the day of Sunday is dedicated to communal worship. It is helpful for visitors to be aware of the expected length of the Sunday event.

The design of some contemporary churches emphasizes the communal aspect of worship. Seat-

> For many of us, "traditional" versus "contemporary" no longer serves very well as a way of setting up the debate. We do not want to be "traditional" if that means nothing new, and we do not want to be "contemporary" if that means poor imitations of American Top 40 tunes with vacuous, repetitive lyrics.
>
> —*Michael Horton*[7]

ing is arranged so that the people see one another and realize themselves as one body of worshipers. Some worship spaces are designed as semicircles, even as full circles, so that worshipers are gathered into one group, with the altar and pulpit in a center position, rather than on a far end. This emphasizes that God is in the midst of the people and deemphasizes a separation between clergy and the laity. Some contemporary churches are famous for innovative exterior design. Rather than resembling a concert hall, striking architecture or artistic elements demonstrate that this is an extraordinary space in which extraordinary activities occur.

In the churches that expect worshipers to come forward at the close of the service to make public confession of their sins and to accept Christ into their life, there may be an open area between the seating and the pulpit called

One Christian lays hands on another during a prayer for healing.

the **threshing floor**. In biblical times, threshing took place at a communal wooden platform called a threshing floor. This metaphoric label compares the sinner to wheat at the harvest. The chaff must be beaten away so that the pure grain remains.

The last few centuries saw innovations in hymn singing. In the Protestant churches after the Reformation, many hymns had numerous stanzas and thus were sung by seated worshipers. But urged on by John Wesley, many Christians now stand while they sing. More churches are including a drum set and other rhythm instruments for accompaniment in the service, and the experience of an ecstatic assembly responding to a rhythm band can come to resemble that of a rock concert.

Common in evangelical churches is a style of song called praise and worship. In some churches, in a pattern reminiscent of Pietist values, praise and worship music constitutes half of the worship event, with an educational sermon the second half. The songs, carefully chosen so as to lead the worshipers through a series of emotions and convictions, seek to create intimacy with God in a way that can be seen as similar to the goal of the Eucharist.

At Holy Rosary Roman Catholic Church near Albuquerque, the people sit on three sides of a central altar.

The encounter with God achieved in song is meant to move the individual toward a life of service in the world.

The world phenomenon of globalization has led to a worldwide sharing of Christian music. Even American churches that do not have a bilingual membership may sing at least a refrain in a language other than English. What is termed "global music" is becoming more common. Hymns and songs sung by the choir and the assembly come from all around the world, with the melody line, the harmonies, the instrumentation, and the imagery of the words from a distant place on the globe. The idea is that these musical practices will bond the local community with all Christians and fill the people with enthusiasm for the worldwide faith, thus in a small way countering Americans' cultural focus on the individual.

In the black esthetic, time is suspended. Black music goes on and on; ritual in the black tradition goes on and on.

—*Irene Jackson Brown*[8]

A ritual introduced about 10,000 Sundays ago is the collection. From the earliest centuries, Christians collected money and food for the poor. For much of Christian history, the cost of maintaining the churches was borne by a combination of state funds and donations from the wealthy. However, with separation of church and state and with the emergence of denominations that had few rich members, the collection of money for both charity and local expenses became a normal part of Sunday worship. A Protestant church that owns property and employs a full-time staff must raise the funds for its considerable budget, usually with no financial assistance from the national or regional church body. Many churches provide envelopes for cash or checks, and some are now instituting systems of direct withdrawal from banks. Usually the collection is termed "an offering" because it is viewed as a gift of thanksgiving to God, a contemporary version of ancient sacrifices in which an animal was offered to God.

One final example of ritual change over the last two centuries: previously men and women stood or sat separately in church. The nineteenth century popularized mixed seating, so that families could sit together. Today only the most conservative Christian groups, such as the Amish, maintain separated seating for men and women. One recent innovation is the practice in some churches to designate a service as for only adults, during which time children attend a Sunday school that includes worship designed for the children. Some churches designate one of the Sunday services especially for families with young children.

Dormant symbols and rituals recovered

Although for 100,000 Sundays there has always been local variation in Sunday worship, the American assumption that the past need not determine the present has encouraged many Christians in the United States to change their worship patterns. These changes are brought about in various ways. The authorities of the church body may mandate or suggest a change, and local congregations may honor or may ignore this authority. A local congregation may vote for a change. Many churches have worship committees that are empowered to lead change. Some clergy are vested with the authority to make changes. Change may evolve over decades merely because of a lapse in worshiping with an earlier pattern, until finally nobody remembers the previous ways of worship. With either symbol or ritual, the culture may urge a change, because in the wider society an image or a gesture comes to have a new meaning, for example, with the meaning of the word *thou*.

One significant phenomenon of the last 10,000 Sundays has been the work of various recovery movements. As churches reflect on how to improve their worship, some have argued that the past had more evocative symbols and more expressive rituals than does the present. For example, a room in the round with a central altar, recalling first-century house churches, may make the communal meaning of Eucharist more evident than can a basilica style. When in the 1960s Roman Catholics moved from Latin to the vernacular, they were replicating the ancient church in its use of common speech. That some Roman Catholics now desire to regularize once again the Latin Mass demonstrates that Christians disagree about precisely which was the better past.

One influential attempt at recovery has been called the ecumenical liturgical movement. Some historians date this ecumenical movement from 1903, when Pope Pius X called for the church to restore the active participation of the faithful to Sunday worship. Especially Roman Catholics and the first- and second-wave Protestants have together discussed how to achieve more profound worship, and liturgical innovations have been shared across denominations. Some churches want their worship to be more ecumenically accessible than denominationally specific. That Roman Catholics have paid increasing attention to the word and some Protestants have reinstituted weekly communion are examples of the effect of the movement's seven principles.

An example of the ecumenical liturgical movement at work can be seen in the greeting of peace. The call to "Greet one another with a holy kiss" is included five times in the New Testament. In the early church, the kiss of peace was a customary ritual at all Christian assemblies. It ritualized the notion that because all were baptized into a single community of brothers and sisters, no antagonisms existed, God's peace reigned, and all were to greet one another with a sign of intimate affection. By the fifth century, at least one theologian judged that, even though men and women were standing in different areas of the nave, the kiss of peace was getting out of hand and taking too long, and he tried to regulate the ritual more tightly. By the medieval centuries, only the presiding clergy greeted one another, by passing between each other a small board on which was written the Latin word for "peace." At the time of the Reformation, Protestant churches introduced the Peace as a verbal greeting, the minister saying, "The peace of the Lord be with you," and the people responding, "Amen." The twentieth-century recovery movement reintroduced the Peace as a communal ritual in

---

The seven principles for liturgical renewal:

1. Christian worship is always centered in the death and resurrection of Christ.
2. Worship is the action of the entire assembly.
3. More of the Scriptures are proclaimed.
4. Holy Communion is celebrated weekly.
5. Baptism is communal.
6. The images of God used in prayer and praise are expanded.
7. When making changes, assemblies at least consider what other denominations do and what from the past has been lost.

---

which everyone greets one another, not, however, with a kiss, but with the cultural sign of formal greeting, which in the United States is a handshake. This greeting of peace is now part of the Sunday service in the churches of many denominations. As with other retrievals, the current ritual both revives and alters the original practice.

The use of the past has become important for a movement called **ancient-future worship**. Reviving ancient symbols and rituals, these assemblies have reintroduced some Latin chants, repetitive litanies, incense, icons, candles around the room. They may add symbols and rituals from other religious traditions: for example, the striking of a Tibetan prayer bowl to mark periods of silence or the use of Hindu chants as background music. Yet looking toward the future, screens are used for the projection of images for meditation. Alternative rock music is common. Usually the event is planned by teams that select not only the biblical readings and theme of the Sunday, but also the Sunday's prayers, music, digital arts, video projections, drama, and teaching components. Many worshipers participate in some leadership role. Worshipers, wearing jeans, may sit on sofas and sip fair-trade coffee during this intentionally eclectic style of worship.

A liberal reform rooted in the earliest century of the Christian church is the feminist liturgical movement. Some biblical scholars and historians agree that the earliest Christians were marked by a countercultural attempt at sexual equality. Only in the second century, to more closely reflect the culture, did male authority become the norm. Feminist Christian worship values women occupying all leadership roles, biblical and noncanonical readings that are in some way emancipatory for women, female-identified symbols, positive use of body imagery, conversational dialogue, participatory ritual, and significant focus on the continuing oppression of women around the world. Considerable attention is given to replacing the male language of Father and Son with either female or non-gender-specific divine imagery. Some of the women who prepare and participate in such worship prefer traditional symbols and rituals that have been purged of sexist bias, while others strive for radically different ways to envision God and to worship together.

Some conservative communities look back to a favored period of history as they confront contemporary ethical questions, and the Sunday worship in those churches may make clear that certain behavior epitomized in that preferred past is required of members. Most often, this has to do with sexual

ancient-future worship
a worship style intentionally blending symbols and rituals from the early centuries of Christian worship with those of contemporary world cultures

---

O tranquil, radiant Sunlight, bring our lives to flower in their
  season,
through the life-giving Spirit breathed on us by Christ,
whom we meet in broken bread and fragmented life. Amen.

—*Ruth Duck*[9]

---

practices. Thus, one church body looks back to the affirmative style of Jesus and welcomes clergy and laity of all sexual orientations. These assemblies may print out such a welcome in their worship folder. Meanwhile, other churches, perhaps of the same denomination in the same geographical area, look back to certain parts of the Bible and to the last century and militate against any acceptance of homosexuality. Both groups mean to recover the true spirit of the faith, but each has chosen a different century to emulate. In these churches, the reigning ethic may be expressed in the prayers or the sermon.

This textbook deals with the worship of churches in the United States. Christians who travel to other countries experience sometimes surprising examples of **inculturation** and a far wider range of symbols and rituals on Sunday than have been discussed here. To broaden the picture of Christian worship, here are several examples. Some Christians in Australia have borrowed from the religion of their Aboriginal tribes the divine image of God as a great snake who holds the earth together by encircling it, and so at Sunday worship God might be called the Rainbow Serpent. Many Asian Christians use their own cultural greeting of the bow, rather than a handshake, at the Peace of the Lord, and some Japanese Christians are using rice cakes and sake, rather than wheat bread and grape wine, for communion. Some Christians in the Southern Hemisphere are discussing whether to reverse their calendar, so that also for them the celebration of Easter will be near the spring equinox and Christmas near the winter solstice. It would require a much longer textbook than this one to cover the many symbols and rituals that Christians around the world are using in worship.

inculturation
adaptation of an inherited pattern to correspond with another culture

See Plate 8 in the gallery for a crucifix presented by a Christian Anishinabe artist. The three birds on top represent the Trinity, and the other birds the living and the dead.

Suggestions

1. Review the chapter's vocabulary: African Methodist Episcopal, altar call, ancient-future worship, Assemblies of God, born again, Calvary Chapel, charismatic renewal, Christian Church/Disciples of Christ, Church of God in Christ, Church of the Nazarene, concert prayer, devotional service, entertainment evangelism, evangelicals, frontier worship, Holiness movement, inculturation, love feast, Methodist, Moravian, Pietism, revival, seeker, spirituals, testimony, and threshing floor.
2. Present arguments for and against the practice of racially or sexually identified worship.
3. Study the role that frontier camp meetings, especially the 1801 Cane Ridge revival, played in American worship.
4. Compare and contrast the positions of those churches that ordain women with those that do not.

5. Write a personal essay about the style of music that puts you into the mood to worship.

6. Discuss how the symbols and rituals described in this chapter correspond to the ideals laid out in the biblical chapters 1 Peter 1–2.

7. Discuss "The Threshing-Floor," the final twenty-five pages of James Baldwin's novel *Go Tell It on the Mountain,* which describes the experience of speaking in tongues.

8. Discuss the 1997 film *The Apostle*, which accurately depicts worship in a Holiness church. The 2004 documentary *Let the Church Say Amen* is also recommended.

9. Attend the Sunday service in an African American, Holiness, Pentecostal, independent, or self-described evangelical church, and compare and contrast what you encounter with the details of this chapter.

For further study

Balmer, Randall. *Mine Eyes Have Seen the Glory: A Journey into the Evangelical Subculture in America.* New York: Oxford University Press, 1993.

Basden, Paul A., ed. *Exploring the Worship Spectrum: 6 Views.* Grand Rapids: Zondervan, 2004.

Best, Thomas F., and Dagmar Heller, ed. *Eucharistic Worship in Ecumenical Contexts: The Lima Liturgy and Beyond.* Geneva: WCC, 1998.

Chupungco, Ansgar, O.S.B. *Cultural Adaptation of the Liturgy.* New York: Paulist, 1982.

Costen, Melva. *African American Christian Worship.* 2nd ed. Nashville: Abingdon, 2007.

Duck, Ruth C., and Patricia Wilson-Kastner. *Praising God: The Trinity in Christian Worship.* Louisville: Westminster John Knox, 1999.

Hawn, C. Michael. *One Bread, One Body: Exploring Cultural Diversity in Worship.* Herndon, Va.: Alban Institute, 2003.

Hollenweger, Walter J. *The Pentecostals: The Charismatic Movement in the Churches.* Minneapolis: Augsburg, 1972.

Jones, Joseph, Dr. *Why We Do What We Do: Christian Worship in the African-American Tradition.* Nashville: R. H. Boyd, 2006.

Kimball, Dan. *Emerging Worship: Creating Worship Gatherings for New Generations.* Grand Rapids: Zondervan, 2004.

Maynard-Reid, Pedrito. *Diverse Worship: African-American, Caribbean & Hispanic Perspectives.* Downers Grove, Ill.: InterVarsity Press, 2000.

Roof, Wade Clark. *A Generation of Seekers: The Spiritual Journeys of the Baby Boom Generation.* San Francisco: HarperSanFrancisco, 1993.

Ruether, Rosemary Radford. *Women-Church: Theology and Practice of Feminist Liturgical Communities*. San Francisco: Harper & Row, 1986.

Webber, Robert E. *Worship Old and New*. Rev. ed. Grand Rapids: Zondervan, 1994.

Westerfield Tucker, Karen W. *American Methodist Worship*. New York: Oxford University Press, 2001.

Wright, Timothy. *A Community of Joy: How to Create Contemporary Worship*. Nashville: Abingdon, 1994.

Chapter 9
What is baptism?

Baptism on Sunday

In many world religions, ceremonial washings express the archetypal meanings of water: water nourishes and cleanses the body, yet water also drowns and destroys. The Christian water ritual, symbolizing death and rebirth, is called baptism, from the Greek word *baptizein*, meaning to dip, to immerse, to plunge into water. For two thousand years most churches have regarded baptism as expected, if not necessary, for every Christian.

The principal Sunday service of a Christian community may include the baptism of one or several infants, children, or adults. This ritual of baptism may take only several minutes, or because of additional symbols and rituals it may take half an hour or more, following upon months or years of preparation. The assembled community may have no role except to witness the baptism, or the assembly may take an active part in the ritual, perhaps by gathering around the font, joining together in the creed, speaking together a speech of welcome, or applauding the candidate at the conclusion of the rite. Before or after the baptism, the congregation may sing a hymn that illumines the meaning of the symbolic washing.

Even without an actual administration of baptism, there are various ways that the importance of Christian baptism may be apparent on Sunday

baptistery
area of the church building or separate structure in which baptisms take place

morning. Some churches have built a small, silo-like addition to their church building that is the **baptistery**. In most churches, the nave houses a small or large baptismal font. The font may be in the narthex foyer, near the main doorway, to symbolize that it is through baptism that one enters the church. The font may be anything from a shallow basin on a stand to an in-ground pool, designed so that adults can step down into the water. If not by the main doorway, the font or pool may be behind the pulpit or in a baptismal niche or chapel.

The font, small or large, may be enhanced with art that depicts stories or images from the Bible to illumine the meaning of baptism. A large mural painting of a river, to recall the Jordan River in which Jesus was baptized, may serve as the backdrop to the pool. At the conclusion of the story of Noah's flood, the peace that God sends to earth is signified by the flight of a dove, and the narratives of Jesus' baptism say that a dove descended from heaven. Thus, many Christians use the dove as a symbol of the Holy Spirit, bringing divine peace into the world, and in many churches the image of a dove is on or near the baptismal font as a sign that in baptism, the Holy Spirit alights on the candidate.

When worshipers enter the church, they may pass by the font, dip their finger into the water, and sign their forehead or chest with the sign of the cross. By this ritual they reinsert themselves into the meaning of their own baptism, since at baptism they were placed under the sign of the cross of Christ. The leader of worship may sprinkle the people with water from the font while announcing the forgiveness of their sins. Such an **asperges** ritual goes back at least to the ninth century, and some churches use a small branch from an evergreen tree to disperse the water, to remind worshipers of the life-renewing aspect of their baptism. Some

Compare this font with the quote on the next page and the font pictured on page 157.

asperges
a rite of sprinkling worshipers with water from the baptismal font

churches have a small receptacle for water located at the entrance, originally the font itself, and worshipers may sign themselves with what has been called "holy water." A prayer had been said over the water, thanking God for the water and asking God's Spirit to enter into it. Such water can then be called holy, because it is connected with the power of God.

There are several ways that baptism might be referred to during the service. A rite of confession and forgiveness may include prayers that speak of baptism. The sermon may include some teaching about baptism. The intercessions may pray for people who are awaiting baptism or ask for God's blessings on anyone who was baptized during the last week. At the beginning of the communion rite,

Small fonts covered, invisible, inaccessible, or with minimal amounts of water, or worse, dry, contradict the theology of baptism. Make it as large as possible, with as much water —moving water—as possible. Think not just of a baptismal font or pool, but of a baptismal space around which the assembly may physically gather, even if it has to process to it for baptism. "Shall We Gather at the River?" What a wondrous image! Let it be the place that says, "from here we come, from here we go."

—*Glaucia Vasconcelos-Wilkie*[1]

Some churches provide a Noah's ark toy for children to play with during church.

an announcement may be made or printed in the service folder that anyone who is baptized is welcome to join in the communion. The biblical texts that serve as the focus of the day's worship may include a description of a New Testament baptism or a selection from one of the epistles that discusses the meaning of this Christian water ritual. After the sermon there may be an altar call that invites people to come forward and accept Jesus as their savior, and this altar call may invite unbaptized persons who seek Christ to become candidates for baptism.

Several documents that have survived from the early centuries of the church indicate that in some places the process of baptism could take as long as three years. Called **catechumens**, the candidates for baptism underwent an intensive study of the faith and proved their dedication to live a new life. If their career was inappropriate for a Christian—for example, if they were actors who played roles in pagan Greek dramas—they were expected to get a different job. Some contemporary churches have revived something of this extensive catechumenal process, and Sunday worship may include a ritual that prays for the catechumens. One such ritual in a church that generally baptizes infants is the Roman Catholic Rite of Christian Initiation for Adults. To symbolize that they are not yet full members of the community, the catechumens may together process out of the service after the sermon and before communion, in order to study with one another the meaning of the Sunday's Scriptures. Attention to the adult catechumens is usually part of the services during Lent, since the baptisms will take place at the Easter Vigil.

Outside of the church services, there may be a baptism party. In some traditions, the baptism of an infant is a significant family event that relatives, friends, and colleagues attend. In some families, the baptism party functions like a classic rite of passage, a ritual that introduces the infant to the wider community. Some Christians maintained the practice that the infant's baptism was the first time that the newborn was brought out of the house, and so the day of the baptism was the occasion for the entire community to meet the new member of the community.

Practicing Christians may serve as **sponsors** or **godparents** of the one being baptized. In some churches, godparents can be any relative or friend chosen by the parents. In other churches, the godparents are members of that

catechumen
a person learning about the Christian faith as preparation for baptism

"Well, then, shall we move on to the subject of sacraments?" says Ming Tao. "I should like to begin with baptism." "Baptism," the younger priest begins, "is a drowning, a death, a surrendering, a going under, as well as a washing, a cleansing, a sign of renewal. When the catechumen is immersed in the baptismal flood, as the earth was immersed in the flood in the day of our ancestor, Noah, the sins of one's earlier life are eradicated." "But I have been told that in baptism there is no real 'going under,' only a sprinkling," says Ming Tao.

—Ingrid Hill[2]

godparent / sponsor
a Christian who assumes some responsibility for a person being baptized

particular parish. The sponsors may be asked to accompany the parents or the adult candidate through the entire baptismal process. About 50,000 Sundays ago, it was usual that the godparents were chosen as the ones to rear the child should the parents die before the child was grown. Currently, churches have various traditions about the responsibilities of the godparents. For the baptism of an infant, a godparent usually holds the baby at the font and answers whatever questions are addressed to the candidate, thus symbolizing the community of faith that will support each Christian throughout life. Usually, sponsors make promises concerning their continuing role in the life of the new Christian, and they are encouraged to take these promises seriously.

The essential symbol and ritual

To learn what Christians mean by baptism, it is necessary to begin with the earliest descriptions of baptism. For the Christians who assembled weekly 100,000 Sundays ago, the Gospels and epistles that became the New Testament contained numerous references to baptism that would have enhanced whatever a particular community heard from its evangelists and leaders. Several dozen New Testament citations have become significant over the centuries as teachings about baptism. Although some of these passages do not explicitly mention baptism, their reference to water has been used by Christian teachers to illumine the meaning of baptism.

See Plate 9 in the gallery. A Greco-Roman-dressed Moses leads the people through the sea: a Christian metaphor for baptism.

    The Gospel of John has a narrative in which Jesus and the woman of Samaria sit by a well and discuss whether there is some water that will forever quench one's thirst. Early Christians used this story when describing baptism as the water that humans need for survival (John 4:14). In another chapter of John, Jesus discusses with Nicodemus how the water of God's Spirit is like the womb waters from which humans are born (John 3:6). To some Christians, the statement that one must be baptized in order to enter the kingdom of God (John 3:5) means that without baptism, people will suffer eternal punishment in hell. In the Acts of the Apostles, a book Luke wrote about the early churches, baptism is a ritual that washes away one's sins (Acts 22:16). Luke wrote that when the Ethiopian eunuch was baptized, he did so in response to his belief that Jesus was the good news that saved him (Acts 8:35-36). Yet Luke records that entire households were baptized, and many Christians have assumed that this included infants who were too young to be able to testify to their faith in Christ (Acts 16:15).

    All four Gospels tell of Jesus' baptism, and theologians have had to explain, granting what baptism does for a sinner, why Jesus needed to be baptized. These baptism narratives say that a voice was heard calling down from heaven that Jesus is God's beloved Son (Mark 1:9-11; Matthew 3:13-17;

Luke 3:21-22; John 1:29-34). Christians have used these passages to claim that in baptism, believers become children of God. Paul's long discussion about baptism emphasizes that in baptism believers enter into the death and resurrection of Christ (Romans 6:3-5), and Luke wrote that the apostles laid their hands on those who were baptized, who then received the power of the Holy Spirit in their lives (Acts 8:17).

The New Testament epistles, some of which were written before the Gospels, discuss baptism, so it is clear that from the earliest gatherings of Christians, this rite was significant. Paul wrote that baptism establishes a covenant with God, something like the covenant that Abraham had with God, an agreement in which both parties joined together with responsibilities and benefits (Galatians 3:29). In another place, Paul describes baptism as something like the covenant Moses had with God, the water of baptism being like the Red Sea through which God brought Moses and the people of Israel (1 Corinthians 10:1-4). A later author likened baptism to the covenant that God established with Noah, after the world had been washed clean by the flood (1 Peter 3:20-21). This section of 1 Peter has made the archetypal story of Noah's flood an image of Christian baptism and God's covenant with creation (Genesis 9:14-15) a parallel with God's grace at baptism.

A mother comes upon her preschool daughters baptizing the two family cats. "But baptism makes you a child of God," says the mother. "So," said the four-year-old, "they are now cats of God."

For Paul, humans are continuously attracted to, even filled with, the power of evil. He speaks of humans as slaves to sin, and baptism makes believers slaves to God instead (Romans 6:22). In another place Paul describes baptism as the entrance rite into the community (1 Corinthians 12:13). Paul envisioned that the Christian community would be marked by a radical equality, in which Jews and Greeks, slaves and free people, males and females, are made one in Christ (Galatians 3:27-28). It was this biblical teaching that led some nineteenth-century slaveholders of the American South to refuse their slaves baptism, since the baptismal equality promised in the Scriptures conflicted with the inequality of persons under the system of slavery. Another biblical passage speaks of baptism as making persons holy, which in the first century meant not sinless, but sacred, set apart for the things of God (Ephesians 5:26). Another passage speaks of baptism as enlightenment, and over the centuries some churches have spoken of baptism as bringing believers from darkness into light (Hebrews 6:4). Finally, in the eschatological imagery of the book of Revelation, baptism is metaphorically referred to as the river of life, flowing from the throne of God, and as the water in which believers wash their robes white (Revelation 22:1, 14).

This list of biblical citations shows that baptism was recognized as a significant, even essential, ritual for believers to undergo. Yet churches evidence a variety of understandings about when, how, and why baptism is performed, and each church can support its practice by quoting the Bible. Originally, most baptisms took place at a river, the flowing water an apt symbol of the living water of life from God. Over the centuries there came to be only two essentials: water, symbolizing the life of God, is poured over the head of the candidates; and the baptizer says one of two phrases, either "I baptize you in the name of the Father, and of the Son, and of the Holy Spirit," citing Matthew 28:19, or "I baptize you in the name of Jesus," citing Acts 2:38. Here, "in the name of" means "through the power of, because of the authority of," as when English says, "Stop in the name of the law." The newly baptized person has now been placed within the mercy of God. However, Christian ritual can be creative if need be. There are instances in deserts of persons being baptized with sand, since no water was available.

About 90,000 Sundays ago, a community of Christians in present-day Syria made some structural changes in a house so that the rooms could better function as a place for Sunday worship. One small room became their baptistery, and recent excavations have uncovered the wall paintings near the bathtub-like font. Although there are no written records or sermons extant from this community, because of these paintings contemporary scholars see what these Christians of Dura-Europas in about the year 230 understood baptism

See Plate 10 in the gallery. Note the art and the size of the font.

to be. The paintings depict: (1) David conquering Goliath, thus suggesting that in baptism individuals can conquer the immense power of evil; (2) the Samaritan woman with Jesus at the well; (3) the paralyzed man healed by Jesus, thus suggesting that in baptism believers receive forgiveness, healing, and wholeness; (4) a young shepherd carrying a sheep, thus suggesting that Jesus cares for the baptized like a good shepherd; and

Meanings of baptism:

1. Initiation into the Christian community of faith
2. Adoption as a child of God
3. Mystical incorporation into the death and resurrection of Christ
4. Infusion with the Holy Spirit
5. Washing away of sin and guilt
6. A new birth into the new covenant

(5), perhaps most interesting, the three women on Easter day who brought spices to anoint the body of Jesus but instead encountered the resurrection. This last image was located near the tub-font, thus suggesting that in baptism the believer joins into the death and resurrection of Christ and so receives the benefits of the mystery of Christ. What was once a dead body is now the life of the resurrection.

Because the New Testament connects baptism with the death and resurrection of Christ, churches about 75,000 Sundays ago designated Easter as the most appropriate time for baptism. Lent then developed as a time to prepare the catechumens for baptism at the Easter Vigil. Some records indicate that the preparation process included serious fasting, as a symbol of the death of one's old self. Many Christians have inherited this connection between Lent and fasting, and some are newly attempting to give genuine meaning to what for some had become a minimal or mechanical practice. Scheduling catechumenal preparation in Lent emphasizes that one's old life is over, one's old commitments replaced by the new life of the resurrection. Some baptisteries were built to resemble mausoleums and fonts to resemble tombs to symbolize that one's old life was dead. Some fonts were shaped like a great cross, into which one stepped down and then out again; some were eight-sided, to suggest that in baptism the believers entered into a new day, a time beyond regular time. In most of the fonts that survive from these early centuries, water would have been about a foot deep, and the catechumens knelt or stood while water was poured three times over their body. Some fourth-century preachers taught that the three dousings signify the three days that Jesus lay dead in the tomb, and others tied the triple ritual to the three names of the triune God.

By 50,000 Sundays ago, the cultural situation in Europe had totally changed, and especially two developments led to a narrower understanding of baptism. Becoming a Christian was no longer a brave act of countercultural import. Instead, every single citizen was baptized shortly after birth. Indeed, because Jews were not baptized, in many localities they were not considered citizens with civil rights. Second, the doctrine of original sin, which teaches that each human is born with the guilt of sin, required that even newborns needed to be baptized in order to avoid hell as punishment of their sinful condition. Especially during medieval times, this interpretation became nearly the sole explanation of the meaning of baptism in the Western church. Thus, it developed that anyone, not only clergy, can baptize, and many medieval infants were baptized by the midwife, who feared that the newborn might not survive. If the child lived, the child was not rebaptized by a priest: the symbol and ritual in the hands of the midwife were valid. The idea that an unbaptized

A report about some Anabaptists in eighteenth-century Philadelphia: "It is their method of baptizing that sets the Brethren apart from other Protestant sects. Baptism usually takes place in the spring of the year; but sometimes, as in that 1723 Christmas Day ceremony in the Wissahickon Creek, the ice must be broken, not once but two or three times, before the ceremony can be performed. The immersion is complete. The bishop places his hand on the aspirant's head and three times dips him face forward under the water. Once baptized, the newly-made Dunkard hurries to a farmhouse, sometimes a full mile away, to change into dry clothes. Tradition among the Brethren has it that no one ever catches cold, let alone pneumonia, from this experience."[3]

Some Christians continue to baptize in rivers.

child went not to hell but to limbo, a neutral eternal condition that was nei-ther heaven nor hell, did not much alter the concern of parents to have their infants baptized soon after birth. Because most persons were baptized as three-day-old newborns, and because these baptisms were conducted at stone fonts with freezing cold water, it came about that less and less water was used and that fonts became smaller and shallower. Finally the medieval church authori-ties decreed that three drops of water on the infant's head were sufficient for baptism to save the person from the damning power of sin.

About 25,000 Sundays ago, Protestants reexamined the rite and inter-pretations of baptism. The churches of the first and second wave maintained the medieval practice that infants should be baptized. However, third-wave Protestants instituted what is called believer's baptism. The biblical narratives in which an adult accepts the good news of faith in Christ and requests bap-tism became the authoritative support for baptizing only professing adults. In the late medieval world, adulthood was considered to begin at puberty. Thus, during the time of the Reformation, some churches administered a second baptism to persons who had been baptized as infants, and so they were called Re-Baptizers, or **Anabaptists**. Churches in the United States today that practice believer's baptism include Baptists, Mennonites, Amish, Pentecostals, and many independent evangelical churches. Because some of these churches are becoming numerous in the United States and around the world, the percentage of Christians baptized as believers, rather than as infants, is growing. Some congregations assemble at a nearby river or pond, rather than around an inside font, for their baptisms. Most of these churches baptize with one immersion of water, rather than three. The candidate is lowered backwards into the water, as if like Jesus being laid in the tomb, only to rise again to new life.

Anabaptist
Protestant churches that baptize only professing believers

In these churches baptism is understood as an act that a person undertakes to signify personal faith. The accent is on the action of the believer: the believer chooses to be baptized in order to obey the command of God found in the Bible. For other churches, baptism is seen as an act of God, a mystical gift of salvation. People are baptized into the mercy of God with no consideration of their age or mental capacity. The ritual is seen as a necessary sacrament that brings God into the person. Whether baptism is viewed primarily as an action of the believer or an action of God is one way that churches differ. Usually now, were a person baptized under one understanding to join a church with the other understanding, the person is not rebaptized, since most Christians stress that baptism is a once-in-a-lifetime event. It does not matter who officiated at the baptism, nor whether the individual remembers the event. However, some churches practice rebaptism for the believing adult, as a sign of having been "born again."

More meanings of baptism:

7. Deliverance from hell
8. The registry of one's birth with the social authorities
9. An act of obedience to Christ's command

Additional baptismal symbols and rituals

In religious practice, symbols and rituals expand and deepen. Over the centuries some churches have added symbols and rituals to the essential water ritual, so that its many meanings were illustrated and enacted for the community. Thus, what might be a ten-second action for a midwife is substantially embellished in some churches. Some enhancements to the essential baptismal rite have become common throughout the Christian churches.

The rite might begin with an **exorcism**. For some Christians, the power of evil is understood as literally emanating from a supernatural being called the devil. The devil embodies and generates evil, working incessantly to oppose God, who is the embodiment and source of all that is good. Ancient baptism rites included physical rituals, such as spitting, that enacted the catechumen's desire to reject the devil's temptations. For some contemporary Christians, the language about the devil is a metaphor for the immense power of evil in the human person and throughout human society. These Christians may not believe in a literal devil, but they still maintain that evil has terrifying power over human life. In either case, it is common for the baptismal ritual

exorcism
a ritual that frees a person from the power of evil

Do you renounce the devil and all the forces that defy God?
Do you renounce the powers of this world that rebel against God?
Do you renounce the ways of sin that draw you from God?[4]

to begin with the catechumen, or the godparents of the infant, answering usually three questions. Each question aims at calling the person to renounce the power of evil: "Yes, I renounce the power of evil."

Many baptisms include another three questions that ask the catechumen or godparents whether they believe in the triune God. Usually this inquiry takes the shape of the minister asking, "Do you believe in God the Father? Do you believe in Jesus Christ? Do you believe in the Holy Spirit?" Over the centuries, these three questions came to be answered in the words of the Apostles' Creed. Although the apostles did not craft this creed, this fourth-century statement of faith is understood as expressing the faith of the apostles and was developed for use in the rite of baptism. In some churches, the entire assembly joins together to recite the creed. Some churches substitute some other statement of faith in the triune God or of commitment to Jesus Christ as part of the rite.

The Apostles' Creed presents a condensed description of the saving actions of the triune God. The first **person** of the triune God is called Father, Almighty, and Creator of all that is. The second person of the triune God is Jesus, named Christ, the Son of God, and Lord, and his incarnation as a human is narrated. The third person of the triune God is the Holy Spirit, whose activity is witnessed in the present and future church. While theologians continue to clarify what the mystery of the triune God means, this simple form of belief continues in use to signify the beginning of one's intellectual assent to faith. As a formula that connects the contemporary believer to the church of the past, reciting the creed is something like hanging on the wall the photos of one's ancestors. Some Protestant churches use this creed regularly on Sunday, even when there is no baptism.

person
theological category derived from the Latin *persona*, designating relationships within God and between God and humankind

Directly before the person is baptized, it is usual to ask for the person's first name, which our society used to call one's "given name," meaning the name given at baptism. In some churches, only approved names can be used as the given name at baptism. Some ethnic groups maintain expectations about a person's given name. Some churches urge use of a saint's name. In some communities it is becoming common to make up a unique name. But clergy would probably not baptize a child who was to be named "God." The practice of formally naming the child at baptism resembles the understanding in some ancient cultures that a newborn was not considered a full human being until it underwent the communal rite of passage. At the naming that is part of baptism, however, the social name of the individual is placed under the sacred name of Christ. Calling baptism "christening" indicates that the person has now adopted the name of Christ.

In some churches, the ritual of baptism includes a short or lengthy prayer over the water. Deriving from the Jewish practice of thanking God for the things of creation, this prayer of thanksgiving characteristically praises God for the waters of the earth, for the water rescues narrated in the Bible, and for the life-giving waters in the font itself. This prayer may call down the Holy Spirit to use the water for salvation. Perhaps the minister's hands are extended over the water, to symbolize the power of God entering the water. The blessed water remains regular water, however, and there would be no concern about the water from the font dripping onto the floor. Some churches add to the local water some drops of water from the Jordan River, since it was in the Jordan that Jesus was baptized, but no churches say that Jordan water is essential.

One ritual that is optional in some churches but essential in the Eastern Orthodox churches is the **anointing**. Descriptions of baptism from the fourth century indicate that a person's whole body was anointed with oil. Perhaps this evolved from the social practice of anointing a body after a bath or oiling a competitor's body before competitive games. In Christian meaning, the ritual recalled the ancient practice of pouring sacred oil over the head of priests or monarchs to signify their special status. Moses' brother Aaron was anointed to be the first priest of the Jewish tradition. Still today in Great Britain, at the coronation ceremony of the monarch, the person is first anointed by the archbishop of Canterbury, and only then crowned. The name Christ means "the anointed one," and so those who are "christened" are also "anointed" with the Holy Spirit, having become royal brothers and sisters of the King Jesus Christ.

Usually for this anointing, the minister traces a cross on the person's forehead with a dab of oil. In some churches, this anointing is postponed until puberty and becomes part of the ritual called confirmation. In other churches, the term *anointing* is only metaphoric: no oil is used, although the language of being anointed is present. However, in the Holiness churches, the term

anointing
pouring over a person's head oil that has been scented and blessed to designate a sacred status

"the anointing" refers to a surge of power from the Holy Spirit that inspires the preacher to deliver the word of God.

A candle is a common symbolic addition. Many early Christian homilies refer to baptism as enlightenment. Before baptism persons lived in darkness, and after baptism they live in the light of God. With this light, one joins with other Christians to shine light in the world. In some churches, a lighted candle is presented to the candidate or the godparents. The family may be invited to light the candle each year on the anniversary of the baptism. During the ritual, the candle may be lighted from the large Easter candle that was ceremoniously lit at the last Easter Vigil and now stands burning near the font.

Many people are familiar with the practice of clothing an infant in a white baptismal gown. This evolved from the earlier practice that when coming up from the water of the font, the naked candidates were clothed with a white robe. The robe symbolized the newly cleansed person and reminded worshipers of the biblical images of the white robes that the saints wear in heaven. Because some gowns became so elaborate that the family did not want them to get wet, little water was used in the ritual. Some churches now provide simple white smocks for either infants or adults that are placed over the body or other clothing after the administration of the water. In those churches where the leaders of worship wear an alb, the white robe means to recall the baptismal garment.

At baptism the candidate receives the gift of the Holy Spirit. Traditionally, this reception was signified by the presider laying hands on the head of the individual and praying that God send the Holy Spirit into the new Christian. It is common to describe this gift of the Holy Spirit as seven qualities of the baptized life: wisdom, understanding, counsel, might, knowledge, the fear of the Lord, and joy. In some churches, this laying on of hands occurs not at baptism, but at confirmation. Such laying on of hands is used in several other church contexts. When a person is ordained to the clergy, or when a clergyperson becomes bishop, or when a person requests the power of the Holy Spirit in a healing rite, the traditional ritual of the laying on of hands may be used. In some communities, the clergy are understood as having a power that is transferred to the recipient. In other communities, the ritual symbolizes a power from God that all Christians share.

Throughout human history, rites of passage in most communities conclude with a feast. There's a new baby in the community? Hold a feast. A

> Hasten to the bath that will purify you thoroughly. Now your mother adopts you to make you her child. Be bathed in the waves of the river flowing over you. You will plunge naked into the font, but you will soon emerge clothed with a heavenly garment, dressed in white. And the one who does not soil the baptismal robe will possess the kingdom of heaven.
>
> —*Zeno, bishop of Verona, c. 350*[5]

person moves from childhood to adult status? Hold a feast. Two persons are marrying? Hold a feast. Even after the burial of the dead, the living hold a feast, to acknowledge that life goes on. Originally, the feast that followed baptism was the Eucharist, at which the newly baptized communed for the first time. In Eastern Orthodox churches, newly baptized infants are given a spoonful of wine with bread crumbs. But in the Western churches, first communion became separated from baptism. Thus, the feast may be the regular communion service, or a festive coffee hour where everyone enjoys the cake that has the names of the newly baptized inscribed in icing, or a family party at home.

Contemporary considerations

Theologians continue to discuss the meaning and process of baptism. Some such conversations are conducted in ecumenical contexts, so that each denominational tradition contrasts its practices and convictions with those of other Christians. One growing consensus is that baptism ought not be thought of as magic, hocus-pocus to transfer people miraculously from hell to heaven. Clergy do not go to a seaside resort and with a megaphone baptize everyone who is swimming. Many churches agree that baptism is not a momentary rite, but is more like a lifelong process that takes place within the community of the church. With the baptism of infants, nurturing in the faith and education about belief follow the sacrament; with adults, the nurture and education both precede and follow baptism.

Because fewer contemporary Christians fear that God will damn an unbaptized infant, there is less pressure to baptize immediately after birth. Some churches that baptize infants interpret their practice not by stressing the sinfulness of the newborn, but by connecting even the infant to the general human condition, as being open to evil, yet ready to receive the mystery of the life of God. Because baptism brings candidates into the community of the church, more churches are urging that baptisms take place in the Sunday service or at baptismal festivals such as the Easter Vigil. This practice heightens the realization that the church is a communal enterprise. As a ceremony celebrating God's gift of water that continuously cleanses and renews all that lives, baptism also awakens believers to the ecological concern for the preservation of clean waters around the globe. Many new hymns celebrate the archetypal force of water in human life, the biblical imagery supporting baptism, and the denominational teaching about baptism. These hymns help the worshipers to sing out a wider understanding of baptism than was common fifty years ago.

The medieval pattern of theologians stipulating the minimal symbol and ritual needed for a sacrament to be valid is no longer recognized as the

Note the method of baptism of this infant.

best way to proceed. Not what is minimal, but what best expresses the full meaning of the sacrament or ordinance is sought. Thus, some churches are replacing small fonts with ones that allow for immersion of at least an infant. While Baptist churches usually contain a tub-sized pool, some churches with different theological understandings of baptism have now installed immersion pools, so that the ritual of baptism more clearly symbolizes the new birth and cleansing desired by God.

A controversial issue involves the triune name of God that is cited during baptism. Some Christians around the world are inquiring whether there might be a theologically appropriate way to name the triune God without using the male terminology of Father and Son, and at baptism some congregations invoke God as Creator, Redeemer, and Sustainer. For other Christians, a baptism is valid only when the biblical language of Father, Son, and Holy Spirit is used, and they may rebaptize a person whose baptism used a nontraditional name of the triune God. Some churches have compromised by retaining the traditional words while adding a congregational response or hymns that use innovative metaphors.

Several other related questions are being addressed. Is communion served only to the baptized, or can persons be welcomed to the meal of bread and wine before they make the commitment of baptism? It is now understood that the prayer for the Holy Spirit at confirmation was originally part of the baptism rite, and only over the centuries came to be separated into a separate puberty rite. For the churches that baptize infants, is confirmation a useful ceremony? If so, should the age of confirmation be maintained, lowered, or raised to twenty-one? Should confirmation have any relationship to first communion? If Christians want to be rebaptized so they can actively participate in the ritual as adults, should this be allowed? Ought a minister baptize anyone who asks, or ought only active members of the church be granted the sacrament? Ecumenical conversation on these and other questions continue to occupy the minds of the leaders of many Christian churches.

Suggestions

1. Review the chapter's vocabulary: Anabaptist, anointing, asperges, baptistery, catechumen, exorcism, fast, godparent, person, and sponsor.
2. Present arguments for and against the baptism of infants.
3. Discuss the baptismal words popularized by the Riverside Church in New York City: "I baptize you in the name of the Father, and of the Son, and of the Holy Spirit, one God, Mother of us all."[6]
4. Interview several godparents / sponsors to discover what, if anything, they promised and whether they have any continuing responsibility to the baptized person.
5. Write a personal essay about an event through which you realized both the creative and the destructive powers of water.
6. Compare and contrast two New Testament passages used by many churches to teach the meaning of baptism: Acts 8:26-39, a narrative describing a first-century baptism, and John 3:1-21, an extended metaphor about baptism as being born from above.
7. Discuss Flannery O'Connor's short story "The River."[7] List all the literal references and metaphoric allusions to baptism in her story.
8. Discuss the 1982 movie *Tender Mercies*. List all the literal references and metaphoric allusions to baptism in this film about Mac Sledge's fresh start in life. Access all three stanzas to the song "Wings of a Dove."
9. Visit at least three church buildings, one of which practices believer's baptism, and compare and contrast their fonts and any attendant imagery that illumines the meaning of baptism. If you can attend a baptism this week, compare and contrast what you encounter with what you have learned in this chapter.

For further study

Benedict, Daniel. *Come to the Waters*. Nashville: Discipleship Resources, 1996.

Meyers, Ruth A. *Continuing the Reformation: Re-Visioning Baptism in the Episcopal Church*. New York: Church Publishing, 1997.

Schreiner, Thomas R., and Shawn D. Wright, ed. *Believer's Baptism: Sign of the New Covenant*. Nashville: B & H, 2007.

Spinks, Brian D. *Early and Medieval Rituals and Theologies of Baptism: From the New Testament to the Council of Trent*. Burlington, Vt.: Ashgate, 2006.

———. *Reformation and Modern Rituals and Theologies of Baptism: From Luther to Contemporary Practices*. Burlington, Vt.: Ashgate, 2006.

Stauffer, S. Anita. *On Baptismal Fonts: Ancient and Modern*. Notthingham, England: Grove, 1994.

Stookey, Laurence Hull. *Baptism: Christ's Act in the Church*. Nashville: Abingdon, 1982.

Yarnold, Edward, S.J. *The Awe-Inspiring Rites of Initiation: The Origins of the R.C.I.A.* Collegeville, Minn.: Liturgical, 1994.

Chapter 10
What Christian worship takes place between Sundays?

Sunday is the primary day on which Christians through the centuries have assembled for worship. But since the beginning of Christianity, church leaders have urged that personal prayer be conducted daily, and over the centuries an increasing number of events have been seen as appropriate times for communal worship. Christian occasions for worship are characterized by enormous variation in symbol and ritual across the Christian world and even among the Christians of a single American city. However, one can expect some Christian underpinning to all these occasions of worship; that is, a wedding that is Christian will be in some way different than a wedding that is not. Yet how much any communal event to which non-Christians are welcome ought to be distinctively Christian is an increasingly controversial question. A traditional position maintains that all non-Sunday worship is a theological and pastoral extension of what Sunday worship is. This means that whenever Christians pray, each believer unites with other believers in Christ to hear the word of God, offer praise for the blessings God sends, and pray for divine assistance.

Worshiping through each day

In the centuries before Christ, Judaism had maintained that males should pray three times each day. Already in the first century, Christian believers, male and female, were encouraged to pray, now in the name of Jesus. The *Didache*, written in the first century, urged believers to pray the Lord's Prayer "as our Lord directed in his gospel"[1] three times each day. This early Christian expectation of daily prayer at morning, noon, and night developed in several different ways over the centuries.

In medieval times, some monastic communities developed daily prayer into a discipline of eight separate services of prayer sometimes called the **daily office**. The historic pattern was comprised of the communal chanting of psalms, a reading from Scripture, and petitions appropriate to the time of day. Both the cosmic pattern of day and night and the events of the life of Christ influenced the content of the prayers. So the office prayed at

---

Pray before your body rests on the bed. Rise about midnight, wash your hands with water, and pray. If your wife is present also, pray both together; if she is not yet among the faithful, go apart into another room and pray, and go back to bed again. Do not be lazy about praying.

—The Apostolic Tradition, *ca. fourth century*[2]

Contemporary monks in traditional garb pray the daily office together.

sunrise likened Christ to light of day, and the office prayed at three in the afternoon recalled the death of Christ on the cross at that hour of the day. The office prayed at bedtime likened sleep to one's own eventual death. Because the book of Psalms was viewed as the primary prayer book of the church, some monks and nuns followed a rigorous pattern in which all 150 psalms were chanted each week.

A few traditional monastic communities maintain this medieval pattern of interspersing all their daily activities with times of prayer, even getting out of bed in the middle of the night to pray one of the offices. Some monastic communities have become places for laypeople to make a **retreat**, affording them occasion for more daily prayer than they would normally experience. During the twentieth century, the Roman Catholic church revised its daily office into a more accessible pattern of three prayer times each day, and Roman Catholic clergy, whether or not they are members of a monastic community, are expected to pray the office each day.

After World War II, a Swiss man named Roger Schutz organized an ecumenical Protestant monastic community in Taizé, France, that has become internationally famous as a Christian place of retreat. Realizing that peoples of many languages would pray at Taizé, the brothers of the community developed a unique style of sung prayer, held daily at morning, midday, and evening, that reintroduced Latin as a universally available language and relied on repetitive refrains for congregational singing. Characteristically the room for prayer is lit with dozens of votive candles, and Eastern icons are displayed as aids to meditation. The Taizé chants have spread around the world, and in most large American cities a church of some denomination will sponsor regular "Taizé worship," particularly during Lent.

Many Protestants also pray two or three times daily, and many worship books provide a service order for Morning Prayer and Evening Prayer for use by the assembly. Some Protestants, especially Episcopalians, schedule regular Morning and Evening Prayer in their churches. Some Protestant churches schedule the classic form of Evening Prayer on Wednesdays during the weeks of Advent and Lent.

At any of these occasions of daily prayer, it is usual for the people to sing a hymn, pray one or several psalms, read a short section of Scripture, and offer prayers for themselves and everyone in need. Often these formats include biblical canticles from the Gospel of Luke: in the morning, the Song attributed to Zechariah at the birth of John the Baptist, called the Benedictus in

daily office / canonical hours / liturgy of the hours
a pattern of psalms and prayers stipulated for communal or personal prayer at times throughout each day

retreat
a period of time designated for intensive religious devotion, lasting usually several days or weeks and conducted at a religious center

Components of any Christian worship event:

1. Praise to God appropriate to the situation
2. A reading from the Bible
3. A statement of faith in Christ's death and resurrection
4. Petitions appropriate to the situation

Latin (Luke 1:68-79), and in the evening, the Song of Mary, commonly called the Magnificat, the poem ascribed to the mother of Jesus when meeting her cousin Elizabeth, in which she praised God especially for saving the poor and oppressed (Luke 1:46b-55). Such services of prayer can be simple for home use or fully embellished, with choir music and a homily, for parish participation. Some churches publish worship materials that overlay the Sunday liturgical season onto the cycle of light and dark that comes with the rotation of the earth. This way one's daily prayer is connected with both cosmic movement and Sunday worship.

Some Roman Catholics attend daily Mass, an abbreviated form of the Sunday service of Eucharist. Usually this is a spoken service that lasts about half an hour. Some Protestants, especially Holiness and Pentecostal churches, schedule regular evening midweek services of communal prayer. These services bridge the gap between the worship on Sundays and usually include considerable Bible study and preaching, and the communal prayers relate to the Bible passage studied. Some megachurches at which the Sunday service is designed for seekers schedule a midweek service designed for the faithful. This event is sometimes a communion service. The chapels at many colleges and universities sponsor daily devotional services that depending on denominational preferences employ a great variety of formats.

In the United States, the daily prayer of most Christians is conducted, not communally, but individually. Sometimes people follow a formula in these prayers, because they value the idea of many persons sharing the same prayer or because they prefer to have their personal prayer directed by the wider church. The Moravian Church exemplifies this in their annual publications that propose a hymn, a Bible selection, and a printed prayer for each day of the year. Over the last century thousands of Protestants have used the daily lectionaries and prayer guides provided by their churches. A **devotional** guide that has been influential among some Christian groups directs the individual's personal prayer over a cycle of forty days, in hopes of probing God's will for the believer. There are calendars that assign a saint for each day's meditation and prayer. Several Internet sites provide ecumenical prayer cycles that broaden and deepen personal prayer to include all human conditions around the world. The hope is that believers will pray to God not only for themselves, but also will intercede for all the needs of the world. During the four weeks

---

DAY TEN: THINKING ABOUT MY PURPOSE.

Point to Ponder: The heart of worship is surrender.
Verse to Remember: "Surrender your whole being
to him to be used for righteous purposes."
Romans 6:13b (TEV)
Question to Consider: What area of my life am I
holding back from God?

—Rick Warren, The Purpose-Driven Life[3]

---

devotion
a religious exercise for the individual or small group that uses a form other than the primary worship event

of Advent, many Christian homes conduct home devotions at the dinner table at which the candles of an **Advent wreath** are lit.

Historically, Christians have prayed before eating. When in the second century Justin described to the Roman emperor how Christians worshiped, he wrote, "Over all that we take to eat we bless the creator of all things through God's Son Jesus Christ and through the Holy Spirit."[5] Some families join in prayer even when eating in restaurants. The habit of calling this prayer "**grace**" arose from the sound of the word *gratia* in the Latin phrase *gratia agere*, meaning "to give thanks."

Perhaps the most common occasion for formulaic prayer is bedtime. Martin Luther composed a morning prayer and an evening prayer for everyone to say when rising from bed and when going to sleep. Bookstores sell picture books of children's daily prayers, and many young children memorize simple bedtime prayers. Traditionally, even children's prayers connected sleep with death: "If I should die before I wake" is one line in the famous prayer that begins "Now I lay me down to sleep."

Some Roman Catholics maintain the historic pattern of daily asking the saints for their aid. According to church teaching, it is not the saint who solves one's problems; rather, the saint intercedes for the believer, just as Christ intercedes for the whole church and each believer is to intercede for everyone in need. Those Christians canonized as saints in the Roman Catholic Church are believed to have successfully interceded in some distress so that a miracle, usually of healing, has occurred. Thus, invocation of persons not yet canonized has become part of the process leading to canonization. Many saints are seen as caring especially for a particular human need. For example, a common **folk religious** practice among Roman Catholics is to pray to St. Anthony for help in finding a lost object.

Many Roman Catholics are assisted in their daily prayer by using a string of prayer beads called a rosary, and the saint invoked is Mary. The **mantra** usually called the "Hail, Mary" pleads for Mary to intercede for the believer now and at the time of death. Included in the Hail Mary are several phrases from the biblical story of the angel's visit to Mary in Luke 1 announcing her miraculous pregnancy. Repetition of the prayers in the rosary is intended to occupy one's mind so that one's soul can meditate on the **mysteries** of the faith. During the centuries that Sunday services were conducted in Latin, many worshipers prayed the rosary during Mass. Recently, Roman Catholics have been urged to pray the rosary throughout the week. For some, Mary becomes the female face of God,

> Here are the two best prayers I know: "Help me, help me, help me," and "Thank you, thank you, thank you." A woman I know says, for her morning prayer, "Whatever," and then for the evening, "Oh, well," but has conceded that these prayers are more palatable for people without children.
>
> —*Anne Lamott*[4]

Advent wreath
a circle of four candles that are progressively lighted in the four weeks before Christmas

grace
the loving mercy of God; also, the prayer before a meal thanking God for food

folk religion
a religious practice popular among believers that is not authorized by religious authorities

mantra
a short phrase repeated for religious devotion

the mysteries of the rosary
five joyful, five luminous, five sorrowful, and five glorious mysteries of the life of Christ that prompt religious devotion

novena
nine-day period of private or public prayer to obtain some particular favor or to procure a certain frame of mind

the Jesus prayer
a mantra repeating the name Jesus and asking for mercy, designed to be prayed continuously

the loving mother not only of Jesus, but also of all believers, and her presence fills their prayer life. However, historically Protestant churches have dismissed, even condemned, this practice, stating that only God should be addressed in prayer.

The communal or private practice of **novenas** extends this invocation of a saint to a nine-day period of prayer. The discipline of a novena usually addresses an appropriate saint and is scheduled on the days prior to a religious or personal event, because of an individual need, at times of mourning, or for forgiveness of one's sins. Some formats for novenas suggest not only daily prayers, but also meditations inspired by the saint to assist one's spiritual growth.

A formulaic prayer common in Eastern Orthodox churches is called the **Jesus prayer**. Used since at least the fifth century, the Jesus prayer epitomizes the idea that a mantra spoken by the mouth frees up the soul to reach toward God. Also called "the prayer of the heart," the mantra is simply this sentence: "Lord Jesus Christ, Son of God, have mercy on me, a sinner," repeated dozens, even hundreds of time a day. Some users learn to coordinate the prayer with their breathing. In quoting this petition that the Gospel of Luke ascribes to the despised tax collector in Jesus' parable, the Jesus prayer means to transform one's consciousness from normal self-centeredness into perpetual humility before God. Like the use of the icon in Eastern Orthodox worship, the Jesus prayer is understood as channeling the believer toward God, thus offering a vehicle that assists in one's focus on God.

Many Christians do not find formulaic prayer helpful and prefer free prayer instead. When contemporary people speak of "talking with God," they are participating in an increasingly common form of free prayer in which they simply talk, silently or aloud, to God. God is believed to be listening to them as they give thanks for the gifts of life, think through what is on their mind, and ask for help in their needs. God is thus imagined not only as the almighty creator who brings about desired changes, but also as the loving grandmother who gladly listens to one's joys and sorrows. Some Christians understand this prayer as conversation, a two-way communication in which they talk from their heart to God and listen for God's response.

This style of free prayer became beloved during the eighteenth century. During the time of the Enlightenment, philosophical Deists maintained that God had completed the work of creation and did not alter the natural processes of the universe to satisfy individual desires. In reaction to this, Christians in the Pietist movement found in the narratives of the New Testament an affirmation that God loved each person and cared for the well-being of all believers, willingly hearing all human concerns and effecting miracles on their behalf. In some Christian practice of daily devotion, the time of free prayer follows a reading from the Bible, so that one's conversation with God has been directed by the word of God. Some Christians open a Bible to any page and point to a passage that then focuses their conversation with God, claiming that the choice of the Bible passage was not random, but directed by God.

Worshiping at the rites of passage

Anthropologists claim that the earliest evidence of behavior that is now considered religious is found at grave sites. Over fifty thousand years ago, Neanderthals laid flowers on the bodies of people they buried. Throughout the millennia, most universal rites of passage in human communities have occurred at the time of disposal of a beloved body. The methods of disposing of the dead and the rituals assigned to mourners have been culture specific, dependent on many factors, including the geography of the area, beliefs about an afterlife, and the wealth of the deceased. What makes sense for the disposal of the dead in one location and time may seem bizarre, even repulsive, to people of other places and times, and this is true even of Christian funeral practice.

Of the several methods of disposal of the dead available to early Christians, their preference was for burial in the ground, in imitation of Christ. The mourners accompanied the corpse to the place of burial while chanting psalms that praised God for life and prayed for a future hope that they saw promised in baptism. The burial of Christians of high status brought about a more elaborate Christian rite, but it was largely the burial of martyrs and the subsequent gatherings at the martyrs' tombs that secured the immense importance of this rite of passage in Christianity. All believers had died in the faith of Christ, but the martyrs had, like Christ, suffered for all the people, and they were especially honored. Christ's resurrection was seen as a

> Nor do we sing any dirges or doleful songs over our dead and at the grave, but comforting hymns of the forgiveness of sins, of rest, sleep, life, and of the resurrection of departed Christians so that our faith may be strengthened and the people be moved to true devotion.
>
> —Martin Luther, 1542[6]

down payment of the resurrection that awaited all the faithful. Thus, in much Christian practice, although expressions of grief were welcome, the mood of a funeral was to be marked by praise for salvation.

In the narrative in Genesis 2–3, God creates the first human out of soil: in Hebrew, human is *adam*, and soil is *adamah*. When the man and the woman are expelled from Eden, God says, "You are dust, and to dust you shall return." Recalling this ancient tale, Christians have used phrases such as "earth to earth, ashes to ashes, dust to dust" to acknowledge that the dead body returns to the soil from which it came. Usually some words to this effect are added: "in sure and certain hope of the resurrection to eternal life." Although Christian funerals were originally marked by praise and hope, in medieval times, dread at the possibility of hell and sorrow over the probability of decades, even centuries, in purgatory turned the mood at Christian funerals to mourning and lament. Among contemporary Christians, the balance between praise and lament usually reflects the historic practices of the specific denominational and ethnic group represented at the funeral. Yet whether the service is marked by sorrow or thanksgiving, the rite of passage usually concludes with a meal, for Christians join with most humans by concluding a burial with a feast in which the living reconstitute the community.

Current American funeral practice usually includes hiring professional undertakers who prepare the body, embalm it, host a **wake**, and transport

wake
a gathering around the corpse, usually the evening before the burial

A contemporary columbarium set up next to a church substitutes for medieval churchyard burials.

the casket to the church and later to the cemetery. Some American churches still bury their dead in their **churchyard**. Although in medieval times the Western churches forbade cremation since it was thought that burning the body would prevent God from raising it up for judgment on the last day, many American Christians are now choosing cremation for their

Components of a Christian funeral:

1. Praise to God for the life of the deceased
2. A reading from the Bible pertaining to death and the afterlife or the resurrection
3. A statement of faith in Christ's death and resurrection as hope for the dead
4. Petitions for God's care of the deceased and for the mourners

departed, and an increasing number of churches are providing one of several types of **columbariums** for their deceased members. Eastern Orthodox Christians expect that the mourners will kiss the dead body, while other Christians always close the casket before the funeral, perhaps covering the coffin with a **pall** that recalls the robe of baptism. A recent trend is to hold a memorial service some days after the disposal of the body. This practice makes scheduling the service more convenient for mourners who must travel, but it distances the event from the reality of the dead body and so is discouraged by some clergy.

None of these practices is mandated by the Christian faith. Characteristic of all Christian funerals, however, will be some reading from the Bible about faith in God through life and death. Many Christian funerals include not only an obituary or eulogy, but also preaching that connects the deceased specifically with the story of Christ. Usually the service includes reference to the **communion of saints** as comfort to the mourners. Since Christians have thought about the afterlife in a variety of ways, some funeral rites speak confidently of the deceased being already in heaven, while others pray for the resurrection at the end of time. Both understandings can be supported by citations from Scripture.

One primary difference among contemporary Christians concerns prayers for the dead. Especially Roman Catholics and Eastern Orthodox encourage the ancient practice of praying for the dead in the months and years afterward. Such intercession suggests that even the dead rely on the mercy of God. Nearly all Protestant churches discourage prayer for the dead, teaching that the dead have already been placed before God, and nothing more can be sought on their behalf. The change over the centuries from a view of God as an angry judge to God as a loving parent influences the practice of prayer for the dead.

According to some Christian piety, all deaths, even of children or after seemingly random tragedy, are directed by God, who is the single arbiter of life and death. For these Christians, language in the prayers will stress acceptance of death as the will of God. Other Christians do not speak of death as

churchyard
traditional synonym for cemetery, indicating burial next to the church building

columbarium
a structure providing niches for holding the ashes of a cremated body

pall
large drape to cover the casket

communion of saints
a phrase used by Christians and found in the creed denoting faith in the bonds in Christ between the dead and the living

part of God's plan, and the words at their funerals construe death an enemy of God. For all Christians, the conquest of death began in the resurrection of Christ, but only at the end of time will death be finally overcome. Some contemporary Christians, aware of humans as part of nature, are replacing the traditional idea that death is God's punishment for sin with an ecological understanding of death as the natural end of life. This attitude may influence the prayers or preaching at a funeral. Thus, just as Christians in one city do not agree on whether to pray for the dead, so also Christians think differently about how death functions in the mind of God.

A second classic rite of passage common to religions and cultures is a ritual at marriage. For the first millennium of Christianity, churches did not hold religious rituals at weddings. Instead, traditional ethnic patterns were maintained. Usually in Europe these rituals involved a party at a home, as the community gathered to acknowledge the new couple. The only role for religion occurred if the priest blessed the bed, in which the couple was reclining, although fully dressed. Yet anyone who knows the play *Romeo and Juliet* is aware of the medieval move toward public church-sponsored rites as the only socially approved method of establishing married life. These church rituals solemnized any private promises that the couple may have made with or without the witness of a clergyman or the approval of the couple's parents. By late medieval times, since issues of inheritance were fundamental to marriage agreements, at least the upper classes were married in the church. In the United States, the government has authorized the clergy to perform the legal ceremony of marriage, and so even many minimally active Christians choose a church for their wedding.

One current issue over historic wedding symbols and rituals is that many of them express the male dominance of earlier societies. For example, the ritual of "giving away the bride" arose in centuries past when the father owned his daughter and in the marriage was transferring legal power over her to her husband. Some contemporary brides have reinterpreted this ritual to signify affection between father and daughter. Some Christian clergy are discouraging use of this paternalistic ritual, and some adapt the ritual by having both the groom and the bride escorted to the altar by their own family members. On the other hand, although in some cultures the bride does not publicly give her consent, the medieval church mandated that the Christian bride could not be vowed before God against her will, and so an early feminist move in

Name, will you have this man to your husband, and to be buxom to him, love him, obey to him, and worship him, serve him, and keep him in health and in sickness, and in all other degrees, be to him as a wife should be to her husband, and all other to forsake for him, and hold you only to him till your life's end?

—*Fourteenth-century marriage vows, York, England*[7]

Christian worship was to require that the bride publicly say yes to the marriage.

A ritual about thirty years old is the lighting of a **unity candle**. While some couples find this ritual a meaningful sign of their newly wed existence, others find that extinguishing the two individual candles misrepresents married life, and so discourage its use. The practice of "jumping the broom" as a ritual at African American weddings exemplifies the use of ethnic traditions that continue being important in rites of passage. Some churches publish wedding guides that help the couple and parents not only choose the biblical readings, but also evaluate critically the pressures of the bridal industry and consider to what degree popular symbols and rituals are congruent with Christian values. In some churches, the engaged couple is required to attend classes that reflect on the religious content of marriage and thus plan for a wedding that is informed by Christian faith.

There is considerable variation in how the different church bodies understand marriage, divorce, and remarriage in the church. Roman Catholics and Eastern Orthodox view marriage as a sacrament, and thus these churches place more requirements on the couple and on the service itself than do most Protestants, who instead consider marriage as a civic ritual at which Christians offer prayers of blessing. For Roman Catholics, the rite of marriage is usually celebrated within the rite of Eucharist. Since Roman Catholics maintain the Western medieval position that a Christian can be married to only one living person, legal divorce is not recognized as a religious condition, and the church has established regulations as to whether a second marriage can take place in the church. On the other hand, Eastern Orthodox churches have a rite for second marriage, which acknowledges the failures of the first marriage. The attitudes toward divorce and remarriage in the church vary significantly among Protestant communities. Some Protestants tolerate absolutely no divorce. On the other end of the spectrum, some Protestant groups hold prayer services at the time of divorce, at which the assembled families pray for God's blessings as the two people dissolve their marriage bonds.

Because the symbols and rituals at Christian rites of passage tend to reflect the participants' social class, ethnic heritage, cultural preferences, education level, family patterns, and personal choices, wide variations in practice exist. The symbol of the wedding ring provides one example. The majority of married Christians in the past did not wear wedding rings because they could not afford them. The European practice of women wearing a ring after marriage

---

Components of a Christian wedding:

1. Praise to God for the couple and for the goodness of sexuality within marriage
2. A reading from the Bible pertaining to marriage or to love
3. A statement of faith that Christ's death and resurrection strengthens human vows
4. Petitions asking God's blessing on the couple

---

unity candle
a set of three candles, two of which represent the unmarried persons and one the married couple, ceremonially lighted at some weddings

At an Eastern Orthodox wedding, the groom and bride are crowned, to reign with love and justice in the kingdom of their home.

derived from the slave ring worn in Greco-Roman households, because the wife was legally the property of the husband. Later the woman's ring came to symbolize her husband's love, the symbolic meaning having changed from bondage to bonding. During the twentieth century, the innovation called "a double-ring ceremony" popularized a ring also for the man. Some churches urge a plain gold band, to symbolize everlasting love. Others allow for a ring of any design or expense. In many Christian weddings, the rite includes a solemn blessing of the rings. Some contemporary married couples choose not to wear wedding rings, which they view as denying each person's individuality, and the conservative Amish wear no wedding rings because they take literally the advice in 1 Timothy that Christian women wear no "gold, pearls, or expensive clothes." Many other wedding symbols and rituals are, like rings, not essential to a Christian rite, but have their own history of usage and meaning.

Many world religions also conduct rites of passage at birth, welcoming the infant into the community, and at puberty, acknowledging to the whole community that a person has become sexually mature and thus will now function as an adult. Some Christians have developed forms of these classic rites. Some churches that practice believer's baptism conduct a service of thanksgiving at the birth of a child, with a prayer that God will keep the child safe until its baptism many years in the future. Perhaps because Christians have historically baptized infants, something of a classic rite of passage at birth has become incorporated into local baptism rituals. A cultural puberty ritual popular among some family with Spanish roots is the *quinceañera*, which celebrates the fifteenth birthday of a young woman. In a religious family, the elaborate party may include a worship service led by an ordained minister. Historically, Roman Catholics and Protestants situated a ceremony at puberty at which one was confirmed in the vows made at baptism. However, currently many churches find that in our culture, the age of twelve seems too young for a child to be recognized as an adult, and so churches are inquiring whether and when any such rituals should be conducted.

> The priest invites the quinceañera to make an act of thanksgiving and of a personal commitment to lead a Christian life, in these or similar words:
>
> Heavenly Father, I thank you for the gift of life
> for creating me in your image and likeness
> and for calling me to be your daughter through baptism....
> With your grace I commit myself to serve my brothers and
>   sisters all my life.
> Mary, Mother of Jesus and our Mother, I dedicate myself to
>   you....
>
> —*Roman Catholic blessing of a young woman on her fifteenth birthday*[8]

A third occasion, similar to a classic rite of passage, that accounts for services of worship throughout the week concerns healing. Rites of healing are commonplace in the religions of the world. The title Savior, a beloved way that Christians refer to Jesus, derives from the Greek idea that God saves, that is, brings healing and wholeness, and according to the Gospels in the New Testament, Jesus was renowned as a faith healer. Already in the ancient church, groups of Christians gathered at the bedside of those who were sick to pray for their healing, to lay hands on them, and to anoint their body with oil as a symbol of life. A renewed sense of the healing power of a community of prayer has helped to revive rituals of healing for those with serious or chronic illness. Pentecostal churches are among those for whom prayers and rituals of healing are central to worship. In some denominations, recent worship resources provided for the clergy include a prayer service intended for use at the hospital bed when the family gathers to turn off life-support machines. In other denominations, however, any such a cessation of life support is viewed as tantamount to murder and thus could not be accompanied with prayer.

Far more important to the film industry than to contemporary Christian churches in the United States are exorcisms. Some churches provide a rite in which the clergy and concerned Christians gather to pray that a person be

A typical daily crowd prays for healing at Lourdes, France.

released from the power of the devil. In the United States, however, full rituals of exorcism are now rare. Contemporary medicine suggests that much of what was historically viewed as demon possession is mental instability, and attending clergy consult health care professionals for advice. Yet some Christians assert that even a person diagnosed as mentally ill can be helped toward wholeness by some ritual of prayer.

Worshiping at occasional times and for specific needs

A list of all the possible occasions at which Christians gather for worship is beyond the scope of this chapter, but here are descriptions of those most common in the United States.

Some such occasions are led by clergy and sponsored by the congregation, while others are lay-led events. Some rely on printed ecclesiastically approved texts, while others are impromptu and regarded as authoritative precisely because they come from the heart and not from published church resources. Some are scheduled in church buildings or other sacred places, and others occur anywhere that Christians may be gathered.

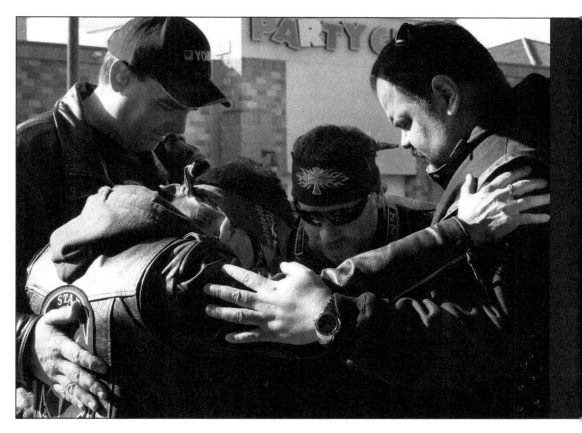

Bikers join in a prayer circle.

Some Christians assemble to bless not only persons, but also things. European fishing villages have long practiced the blessing of the fleet, and some American coastal cities continue this practice. Some Christians ritualize their move into a new home by hosting a house blessing. Roman Catholics have long gone to church on February 3, the day of St. Blase, famous for having saved a boy from choking to death on a fish bone, to have their throats blessed.

Increasingly ecumenically popular is an event held at churches on or near October 4, the death day of Francis of Assisi, to which people bring their pets for an annual blessing. At the Episcopal Cathedral of St. John the Divine in New York City, this blessing of the animals has included an elephant and a python borrowed from the Bronx

Components of a Christian healing service:

1. Praise to God who gives life and cares for the sick
2. A reading from the Bible pertaining to trust and health
3. A statement of faith that Christ's death and resurrection saves
4. Petitions for the health and wholeness of the sick

Zoo, and the immense church is filled with cages of cats, dogs, birds, and an astonishing array of animals that New Yorkers keep as pets.

Some Christians assemble to bless persons that other Christians refuse to bless. Around the world there are Christians who hold commitment ceremonies for homosexual couples. Sometimes but not always called weddings, these services embody the idea that God creates some persons to be homosexual. Rather than the church requiring their celibacy, the blessing of homosexual couples invites Christians to pray together that gays and lesbians can be enriched by covenant commitments, just as heterosexuals are. What God thinks of homosexual activity and how the church is to deal with same-sex couples are highly contentious issues. Churches that welcome commitment ceremonies are proud of what they view as God's word for these believers, and other churches, even in the same denomination, condemn homosexuality activity as a sin that could not be blessed by God.

The children of Christian homes may attend parochial schools in which worship is scheduled daily or weekly. If they attend public schools, the churches to which they belong may urge them to attend a weekly after-school program of religious instruction that includes worship. A week or two at a church-sponsored summer camp is a popular American option, and sometimes the worship at camp can be formative for a child's sense of the bonding power of religion.

Many churches sponsor social activities for teenagers that include worship. Often the teens are asked to help design the worship. The Greek language includes two words for time: *chronos*, that is, clock time, and *kairos*, that is, a period of extraordinary time. Weekend events called Kairos retreats have proven to be compelling to many American teens. Some religiously affiliated high schools and colleges conduct prayer at the beginning of sports events. Usually the intent of the prayer is aimed toward the safety of the players.

A worship event that has been a beloved fixture in the United States since the Christian settling of the American frontier is the week-long revival. Even in urban centers where many churches are available, this practice has continued. Such revivals usually feature daily evening services, inspired preaching, and enthusiastic singing, and can play a significant role in encouraging Christians toward deeper spirituality.

Many people, especially Roman Catholics, make retreats at monasteries or centers for spirituality at which some historic pattern of intense prayer is provided. Perhaps most famous are the spiritual exercises of St. Ignatius, a four-week, or at least four-unit, set of reflections that help the believer to examine to what degree one is living the life of Christ.

During Lent it is common for churches to sponsor special services that focus on confession of sin and amendment of life. Roman Catholics, who are encouraged to confess serious sin before communing, have instituted services of reconciliation that offer a communal option to the practice of private confession. Some Christians go to their clergy for private counseling, and such sessions with the minister include prayer. An ecumenical cycle of prayer called the Week of Prayer for Christian Unity is scheduled each year from January 18, kept by some churches as the feast of the Confession of St. Peter, through January 25, the day that commemorates the Conversion of St. Paul. Because traditionally Peter has been associated with the pope and the Roman Catholic church and Paul with preaching and the Protestant churches, these festivals bracket a week that brings together the two branches of the Western church. In some communities, Christians from various denominations meet during this week to pray for the unity of the church.

> The first method of making a wise and good choice contains six points:…The second point: I must have as my aim the end for which I am created, which is the praise of God our Lord and the salvation of my soul.…The third point: I must ask God our Lord to deign to move my will and to reveal to my spirit what I should do to best promote His praise and glory in the matter of choice…
>
> —*The Spiritual Exercises of St. Ignatius*[9]

For some Christians, pilgrimage provides an emotionally intense occasion for worship. Although not a requirement of the faith, pilgrimages arose in the early centuries of the church as believers walked to places that were deemed sacred by their connection with Christ or a saint. Currently, Protestant pilgrimages are likely to be to the Holy Land in Israel, Eastern Orthodox pilgrimages to a regional monastery, and Roman Catholic pilgrimages either to Rome or to a site where Mary is said to have appeared. Such pilgrimages become a metaphor for the journey of life, and many people who have gone on pilgrimage describe it as a life-changing experience. One might distinguish tourist travel from pilgrimage precisely by the amount of worship that the trip entails.

An increasingly popular substitute for pilgrimage is the labyrinth. Prehistoric labyrinth images have been found incised on the walls of caves around the world. Ancient labyrinths were constructed in preliterate societies, and so scholars can only speculate about their original meanings. Several medieval European cathedrals, most notably the thirteenth-century cathedral in Chartes, France, included a labyrinth in the design of their stone flooring. Walking these labyrinths functioned as a penitential option for persons who could not walk across the continent to a sacred site. Dozens of labyrinths have been constructed in recent decades, mostly to serve as places for meditation. The discipline of walking the labyrinth means to assist the individual in self-reflection. Christians have built labyrinths, or set one out on canvas for a period of time, and some of these labyrinths have been adapted with explicitly Christian meaning added to the interior exercise toward self-awareness.

The Chalice Labyrinth is an example of the labyrinth adapted for Christian devotion.

Whether one plans to hold a wedding or walk a labyrinth, there is no particular need for even devout Christians to use an explicitly Christian way to conduct any such ritual exercises. Especially conservative churches discourage members from participating in activities that have religious overtones but are not essentially Christian. In some American communities, evangelical Christians have objected to the celebration of Halloween in public schools. The most ancient version of this ritual, Samhain, was a northern European pagan festival that meant to ward off death over the coming winter and to placate the spirits of the dead. The Western church later altered the focus to be a memorial of the saints. Similar to community disputes about the Christmas tree, questions about the religious content of Halloween persist, especially in light of a revival of neo-pagan religious practice.

There are yet other occasions for communal prayer that only some Christians promote. Ecumenical prayer services on the Fourth of July or Thanksgiving Day are encouraged by some churches as promoting concern for the nation, and discouraged by others who fear an implicit message that God approves of the government or prefers the United States over other countries. Interfaith prayer services memorializing the destruction of the World Trade Center, for example, are welcomed by some churches as a move toward religious tolerance, and they are boycotted by other Christians who teach that prayer must be in the name of Jesus, and thus any prayer with non-Christians is problematic. Some liberal Christians hold prayer services for occasions such as before and after an abortion or at the winter and summer solstices. These Christians believe that worship occasions need to keep pace with the contemporary society in order for the religious faith to remain pertinent to people's lives. What is a religious ritual and what is not? What is Christian and what is not? When is one's belief central to a celebration and when is it not? Christians do not agree on the answers to these questions.

Suggestions

1. Review the chapter's vocabulary: Advent wreath, bless, canonical hours, churchyard, columbarium, communion of saints, daily office, devotion, folk religion, grace, Jesus prayer, liturgy of the hours, mantra, mysteries, novena, pall, retreat, unity candle, and wake.
2. Research one of these devotional options: a novena; the rosary; the Jesus prayer; exorcisms; blessing of the animals; a Kairos weekend; an Ignatian retreat; a pilgrimage.
3. Write a Christian devotion to accompany walking the labyrinth.
4. Present arguments for and against the blessing of same-sex couples.
5. Write a personal essay analyzing a funeral or wedding you have attended about which you have critical concerns.
6. Biblical passages have been cited by churches as a mandate for a life of prayer. Describe Christian prayer in light of 1 Thessalonians 5.
7. Discuss the prayers described in Sandra Cisneros's short story "Little Miracles, Kept Promises."[10]
8. Discuss the 1993 film *Shadowlands,* which chronicles several years in the life of theologian C. S. Lewis, the author of the Narnia stories, and includes examples of seven different occasions of worship discussed in this chapter, including a wedding and a funeral. An alternate is the 2007 documentary *Into Great Silence,* which depicts life at a contemporary strict Carthusian monastery.
9. Attend and write a report of a midweek evening prayer service held at a church or a college chapel.

For further study

Anderson, Herbert, and Edward Foley. *Mighty Stories, Dangerous Rituals: Weaving Together the Human and the Divine.* San Francisco: Jossey-Bass, 1998.

Bell, James S., Jr., and Tracy Macon Sumner. *The Complete Idiot's Guide to Christian Prayers and Devotions.* New York: Alpha, Penguin, 2007.

Chase, Steven. *The Tree of Life: Models of Christian Prayer.* Grand Rapids: Baker Academic, 2005.

Clifton, F. Guthrie, ed. *For All the Saints: A Calendar of Commemorations for United Methodists.* Akron, Ohio: OSL, 1995.

Dicharry, Warren F., C.M. *Praying the Rosary: The Joyful, Fruitful, Sorrowful, and Glorious Mysteries.* Collegeville, Minn.: Liturgical, 1998.

Geoffrion, Jill Kimberly Hartwell. *Christian Prayer and Labyrinths: Pathways to Faith, Hope, and Love.* Cleveland: Pilgrim, 2004.

Matus, Thomas. *Yoga and the Jesus Prayer Tradition: An Exercise in Faith.* New York: Paulist, 1984.

Pfatteicher, Philip. *Praying with the Church: An Introduction to Prayer in Daily Life.* Burlington, Vt.: Ashgate, 2003.

Sheppy, Paul P. J. *Death Liturgy and Ritual. Volume II: A Commentary on Liturgy Texts.* Burlington, Vt.: Ashgate, 2004.

Stevenson, Kenneth. *Nuptial Blessing: A Study of Christian Marriage Rites.* London: Alcuin Club, 1982.

How is Christian worship like or unlike the practices of other religions in America?

Lumpers and splitters

Some people who examine the world's many religious symbols and rituals are lumpers. That is, they are inclined to see similarities, to lump together things that, although at first glance seem to be different, are in some way parallel. A lumper notes that the symbols and rituals of most world religions serve the same intention: to situate the individual within a community of belief; to honor that which is prized as ultimate; and to monitor behavior so that the community prospers. The lumper points out that, for example, Christians, Jews, Muslims, Hindus, Buddhists, Daoists, and Sikhs all have sacred scriptures that serve as the basis for many of their symbols and rituals. Because those sacred texts were penned centuries ago in androcentric societies, a lumper is not surprised that many holy writings show a preference for males over females. Most world religions use the archetypal symbol of the tree of life, and most religions include rituals of washing and of eating. Because symbolic meaning and ritual intention are ambiguous and complex, the lumper is aware of a history of change and contemporary disagreements in the classic world religions.

Other thinkers are splitters. That is, they identify even small shades of difference, and they split each religion into several forms, interested in variations of belief and practice. The consummate splitter recognizes the role that education, social class, gender, nationality, wealth, and other such nonreligious phenomena play in the practice of any religious community, and so a splitter does not assume that any local worshiping group is an accurate representation of that world religion. Many textbooks of world religions are written by splitters. The hundreds of details that fill each chapter attest to the many unique aspects of each religious tradition. Granting the religious diversity available in the United States today, every practitioner of any religion is to some degree a splitter, having chosen one tradition over others, and even one local congregation over another.

Never before in the history of humankind have so many different, even mutually contradictory, religious practices thrived within the same residential area. The usual historic situation was that everyone in a single locale practiced, with more or less precision and fervor, the same religion, which provided much of the glue that held the society together. However, today in the United States people are practicing religions that arose in all corners of the earth. American society tends to urge citizens toward a policy of tolerance, that is, putting up with something with which one does not agree. Many households are marked by diverse religious practices, and American converts from one world religion to another eagerly explain how their new religious home is more personally or socially beneficial than was their previous one. Some social analysts compare the current religious situation to a mall: some individuals choose one symbol here, one ritual there, in order to invent a unique pattern of religious practice.

In such a society, it is useful for the student of religion to be both lumper and splitter, both recognizing diverse practices as reaching for similar goals and also distinguishing among the many options now available on Main Street. The academic study of religion may move a student from lumper to splitter or vice versa. This chapter does not intend to describe the world's countless religious symbols and rituals. Rather, it discusses some of the symbols and rituals practiced by American Jews, Muslims, Hindus, Buddhists, Native Americans, Wiccans, and several **syncretistic** groups, with the hope that such comparison clarifies what Christian worship is.

syncretism
the merging of ostensibly contradictory ideas or practices

Symbols and rituals in Judaism

Because both modern Judaism and Christianity evolved from biblical Judaism, it is not surprising that Jewish symbols and rituals are similar to those of Christianity. Both Jews and Christians claim that the worship of the one God is primarily a communal act of praise and petition for God's continuing gift of life. Both religious traditions affirm that this God has been revealed through the words of the Bible. The Jewish Bible, called the Tanakh, is called the Old Testament or the Hebrew Scriptures by Christians, and it constitutes two-thirds of the Christian Bible. Participants in both religions study this Bible and regularly pray the poems found in the Jewish book of Psalms. Because God is understood as bound to the people in a covenant, both religions hold weekly meetings at which the sacred scripture is read and the power of the word of God is shared. In both religious traditions, the Scriptures are accorded high reverence. Among Jews, this respect is indicated by the precious biblical scrolls, written out by hand, that are used in synagogue worship. Like a church, the synagogue has a podium for the reading of the Bible, and one task of the rabbi, like that of the Christian preacher, is to interpret the biblical reading for the congregation. Both Jews and Christians claim roots in the biblical story, and so for both, biblical characters such as Abraham, Sarah, King David, and Queen Esther play symbolic roles in forming contemporary identity.

Yet Jews and Christians interpret the Hebrew Scriptures in different ways. When encountering biblical passages about Jerusalem, Jews think of the literal contemporary city as symbolic of historic identity and future hopes, while Christians use "Jerusalem" as a metaphor of the church or heaven. When the Hebrew Scriptures speak of a coming messiah, Christians think of Jesus, while most contemporary practicing Jews understand "messiah" as a metaphor that designates the people's task to bring justice and peace to the world. Many Jews either require or prefer the use of Hebrew in prayer, while most Christians normalize translations into their vernacular.

Nearly all Jewish synagogues refuse to depict God in paintings and sculptures. Judaism teaches that representing God in art disobeys the command in Exodus 20:4 and inevitably reduces God to human imagination. Eastern Orthodox Christians and strict followers of John Calvin agree with the Jews about this, while other Christians have hoped that depicting God in a recognizable form will assist believers in approaching the divine. For those Christians who accept art that portrays the divine, Christian belief in the incarnation provides the legitimization: since God became human in Jesus, then the things of creation can to some degree carry the divine to the gathered assembly.

In both religions, people unite over food. At the opening of a formal Jewish meal, God is praised for the sustenance of bread, and at the close of the meal, for the joy of wine. The Creator has provided the grain and grapes, which the human community has manufactured into staple food and festive drink. The Jewish pattern of praising God over bread and wine was also the practice of Jesus and so came to constitute the communion meal of Christians. For both religions, God's gifts of bread and wine stand for everything through which God gives life to the people. Both Jews and Christians are encouraged to give thanks to God at the beginning of every meal. Both religions believe that since God has provided food, the community must share its food with the hungry. Both synagogues and churches regularly collect money for hunger relief and urge members to work to help those in need.

Judaism and Christianity celebrate similar annual rituals. Easter is the Christianizing of the high holy day of the Jewish Passover. At these festivals God is praised for having saved the people, and the community prays for all who are in need. Although the meaning of God's liberation differs, the theologians of both Judaism and Christianity teach that this springtime festival of life from God is their primary annual ritual. Another Jewish holy day is Shavuot, also called Pentecost, at which God is praised for descending from heaven in fire on top of a mountain and speaking to the chosen people in words that are called the Torah. Christians use Pentecost to celebrate the gift of the Holy Spirit. An increasingly important annual festival in the United States is Hanukkah. Set near the time of the Northern Hemisphere's winter solstice, Hanukkah has become the Jewish alternative to Christmas, which, like the story of the birth of Jesus, praises God for the miraculous gift of light in a dark world. The Jewish festival of Simchat Torah celebrates the Torah, and its celebrations of song and dance can be likened to the joyous rituals of Christians at Christmas, a time to thank God for the gift of the word made flesh. The most solemn religious holy day for Jews is Yom Kippur, the Day of Atonement, during which everyone prays for forgiveness of sin. Parallel in some ways to Ash Wednesday, the day is marked by rituals of confession such as fasting, and by honesty about death.

Reminiscent of the different Christian branches and denominations, synagogues in the United States may be Reform, Reconstructionist, Conservative, Orthodox, or Ultra-Orthodox, and Jews can choose with which synagogue to affiliate. These branches differ in their level of observance—that is, the degree to which biblical patterns of behavior and ritual are maintained, adapted, or discarded. For example, synagogues differ as to the ritual roles of women in communal prayer, so that Ultra-Orthodox Jewish women can be seen as resembling Amish women in some ways and their liberal Jewish sisters in others.

We abuse, we betray, we are cruel. We destroy, we embitter, we falsify.
We gossip, we hate, we insult. We jeer, we kill, we lie.
We mock, we neglect, we oppress. We pervert, we quarrel, we rebel.
We steal, we transgress, we are unkind. We are violent, we are wicked, we are xenophobic.
We yield to evil, we are zealots for bad causes.

—*The confession on Yom Kippur*[1]

An essential difference between Judaism and Christianity lies in the religious role of family. Normally, a person is born into Judaism, and the word *Jewish* can refer to an ethnic identity as well as to a religious persuasion, in a way that the noun *Christian* cannot. The central ritual at Passover is a family meal, because the home is the locus of Jewish religious life. Jews understand Sabbath as primarily a day of family rest. Strictly observant Jews dedicate Saturday to a family meal, home prayer, and quiet relaxation with other family members, and for many Jews the family meal on Sabbath is a more important religious ritual than attendance at a synagogue service.

In contrast, although many Christians pray at home, Christian worship is centered not in the family, but in a volunteer communal group. One is not born Christian but must instead join the church or be baptized to become Christian, and except in emergencies, baptism is not a home ritual, but is conducted in an assembly of nonfamily members of the church. The New Testament quotes Jesus as saying that his followers must leave father and mother to become part of what is metaphorically called the family of the church. For Christians, Sunday is the day for members to assemble, usually in a house of the church, to worship God, either with or without other natural family members.

Because Jews see religion as centered in the family, rites of passage are more religiously important than they are for most Christians. An infant boy is circumcised in a bris, and in some Jewish communities an infant girl is named at a brit, a home ritual that welcomes the newborn into the Jewish family. A popular Jewish ritual is the Bar or Bat Mitzvah, a puberty ritual in which the young teenager is made a son or a daughter of the commandment. The ritual requires the teenager to read, publicly and in Hebrew, the biblical text in the synagogue service, but in recent times many Bar and Bat Mitzvahs have become lavish family festivals. These rituals recognize the family and the age of its members as fundamental features of religious practice. A mikveh is a communal bathing place, a kind of Jewish spa, that Ultra-Orthodox Jewish

The most important annual event for Jews is the Passover seder meal in one's home.

men visit before Friday evening services, as if to wash away all that is outside the religion before weekly prayers. For the most conservative Jewish women, a visit to the mikveh occurs after a wife's menstrual period is over, and it intends to purify her body to return to active sexual intercourse with her husband. The desire of American Jews to visit Jerusalem follows from the ancestral connection between the contemporary Jew and the historic family home.

The ritual practice for which Jews are most known is their attention to kosher eating. By the word *kosher*, Jews mean religiously acceptable. It makes sense that a religion centered in the home has developed rules about what to eat and how to prepare it. There is considerable range among Jews as to how completely the biblical and traditional rules about food govern one's life. By maintaining the strictest eating patterns, Ultra-Orthodox Jews keep their religious community separated from all outside groups. The practice of some Jews called eco-kosher adapts traditional concerns into contemporary ecological ones. Thus, how much money the pickers were paid and how much land was required for the production of the foodstuffs become issues of religious concern. However, the Jewish understanding of kosher is explicitly rejected in the New Testament. In Acts 11, Peter has a dream in which God tells him to eat foods that are *treif*, not kosher, and Paul wrote that Christians can eat whatever foods they choose to, as long as they share food equally at their communal meals and meet the needs of the poor.

Symbols and rituals in Islam

Jews and Christians say that their traditions descended from the ancient patriarch Abraham through Sarah and their son Isaac, and Muslims understand themselves as children of Abraham through Hagar and their son Ishmael. Accepting this tradition literally makes Muslims half-brothers and half-sisters of Jews and Christians. Like Christians, Muslims believe that there is one God who alone is to be worshiped and that God has spoken to the people through the words of a holy book. The Muslims believe that their book, the Qur'an, was dictated to Mohammad by an angel, and it functions as the central divine symbol in the Muslim faith. The Qur'an includes versions of some of the stories of the Hebrew Bible, and it names Jesus as a central prophet of monotheism. Muslims are invited to gather weekly on Friday at a mosque to pray in community and to hear their leader of prayer, their imam, preach a sermon on the text from the Qur'an. Muslims teach that the unified worship of the one God creates one worldwide community of faith in which all believers are equal under God. The understanding of the symbolic power of the book can lump Islam with some forms of Christianity.

One characteristic of Islam that distinguishes it from general Christian practice is its linguistic conservatism. Muslims say that the Qur'an cannot be translated; any version in a language other than its original is only a paraphrase. Muslims of all languages pray five times daily in Arabic using traditional formulas, and many American Muslims prefer the Arabic word *Allah* rather than the English word *God*. Thus, Islam is not concerned with updating the language of prayer, and bookstores do not market diverse materials with contemporary renditions of Islamic prayer. By contrast, American Christians do not pray in Aramaic, the language Jesus spoke, and very few pray in New Testament Greek. Christian usage is marked by a preference for translation into the vernacular, and most denominations encourage both personal prayer and contemporary devotional guides as supplements to authorized worship texts.

Muslims strictly reject any pictorial representations of the divine. Instead, passages from the Qur'an are written on walls in elaborate scripts of various artistic schools. Thus, Muslims surround themselves with the very inscription of the words of the holy book. Many mosques also rely on geometric designs or stylized plant designs to adorn their walls. The tradition opposing pictorial symbols extends also to Muslim prayer rugs. To kneel on the rug in daily prayer is symbolically to kneel in paradise. Some prayer rugs are adorned with an arabesque pattern reminiscent of the tree in paradise, but the rug ought not depict angels, humans, animals, or God. In this Muslims are more like Jews than Christians.

axis mundi
the symbolic center
of the world

In the city of Mecca in Saudi Arabia is a sacred building called the Kaaba, which is reverenced as having been associated with Abraham and Ishmael and functions as an **axis mundi**. When Muslims kneel for their daily prayers, they are to face their body toward the Kaaba. In every mosque, a niche in one of the walls marks the direction to Mecca. All Muslims who are financially and physically able are to make a pilgrimage, at least once in life, to Mecca for a five-day communal ritual that honors the importance of that city as the birthplace of Mohammad, the site of the Kaaba, and the location of sacred places associated with Ishmael. These several ways that Mecca is symbolically honored help maintain the geography of the Near East as a world center of the religion that is unlike anything in Christianity. Some Christians have maintained an ancient pattern of aligning their churches toward the east, as if to face Christ when he comes from the sunrise at the end of time, and some Christians choose to visit the Holy Land, but no Christian denomination teaches that the homeland of Jesus is the geographic center of the Christian faith.

The daily prayer that is expected of all Muslims, called salat, is a fully prescribed ritual. The memorized Arabic prayers are to be precisely repeated five times each day and are accompanied with designated body postures and hand gestures. The idea is that the prostration of one's body brings the whole individual into submission to God: indeed, the word *Islam* means "submission." After repeating the prayers, the believer may add personal prayers in the vernacular. A precise ritual washing of face, hands, neck, arms, and feet precedes this prayer. Thus, like Christians, Muslims employ washing as a preparation for entering into the presence of God, but unlike Christians, the washing is repeated daily, rather than administered once in one's life.

Similar to some Protestants, Islam recognizes the individual as directly connected with God, and one's personal piety is seen and rewarded by God. Yet the emphasis on the individual is balanced by the symbol of Mecca and the mosque, both of which unite the individuals into a people under God. During Friday prayers at the mosque, individuals kneel in rows to conduct their prayer simultaneously. Everyone prays equally, together, yet individually, and no ordained clergy is required to lead the ritual. Through a lifetime of such prostrations before the majesty of the Almighty, Muslims experience peace with God, and by attention to the Qur'an they receive direction for

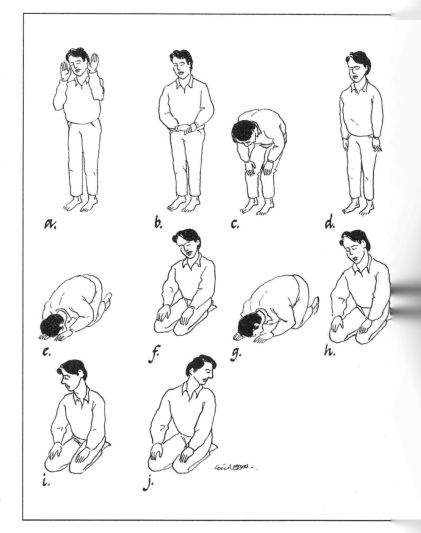

The words and gestures in Muslim daily prayer are precisely prescribed

faithful living. The weekly assembly of both Muslims and Christians includes the verbal greeting of peace. Muslim devotions can include meditation on the ninety-nine attributes of God, and some Muslims use a rosary to assist them in this prayer. At some mosques there is a growing use of Arab clothing at Friday prayers, to symbolize the importance of Muslim origins.

Muslims keep a lunar calendar, the most important month being Ramadan, a time of intense communal devotion, revered as the time during which the Qur'an was revealed to Mohammed. Its ritual of fasting is in some ways similar to the fasting practiced by some Christians during the weeks of Lent. Other annual festivals also commemorate events in the life of Mohammad.

I do not need to attend a mosque to talk to God. I have my time with God whenever I want. When I do pray, I pray directly to God. In Islam, God has no partners or intermediaries. He alone is the final judge of us all.

—Asma Gull Hasan[2]

Because all Muslims are united to one another in faith, Muslims have made charitable giving explicit by requiring a 2.5 percent contribution from one's net income as one of the five essential pillars of Muslim religious practice. These five pillars constitute the essential Muslim modes of religious practice: the confession of faith, daily prayers, charity to the poor, fasting during Ramadan, and pilgrimage to Mecca. More like Jews than Christians, many Muslims maintain classic rites of passage as ways to observe their faith.

Many Americans have heard of the traveling performances of whirling dervishes, Muslim mystics who employ ritualized dance as a technique to reach a state of ecstatic prayer. Such ecstasy can been seen as functioning like the speaking in tongues of Pentecostal Christians. Some Muslims are skeptical of the ritual of dervishes, however, since it purports to unite the believer with God in a mystical way that is beyond and beside the power of the Qur'an. Similar to the variations among churches, the role of women varies considerably in different groups of Muslims, with especially the symbol of veiling women a disputed issue. Again similar to Christianity, proponents of the various practices use scripture and tradition to substantiate their preferred methods of symbol and ritual.

Symbols and rituals in other religions

What Western scholars call Hinduism is an amalgamation of beliefs, symbols, and rituals practiced in India for thousands of years. Rooted in local varieties of nature religions in which the divine is seen as permeating all things, Hinduism has developed into a world religion in which worship of the divine is a high priority. Most Hindus use the word *Brahman* to denote what might be called the Ultimate Energy or the Absolute Reality. Some American Hindus call this divine energy God. The word *karma* refers to the Hindu belief that all actions have cosmic ramifications, and the veneration of the divine assists the worshiper in rejecting what is false and in living the ethical life, thus creating karma that is good rather than evil. Hindus agree with the Christian tradition that focusing on what is ultimate is not natural or easy without the assistance of religious symbols and rituals.

While Christians are monotheists, Hindus, who see the divine in all things, speak the language of polytheism; some Hindus say that there are three hundred million gods and goddesses. Hindus believe that humans need release from error and illusion, and multiple incarnations of the divine have entered human history to free those who are somehow enslaved and to teach the true meaning of life. All the manifestations of the divine are faces of the one Brahman, facets of the single Absolute; some Hindus say that Christ is yet another incarnation of the divine. Most Hindus focus on one aspect of the divine for their worship. Perhaps the deity worshiped is the one most honored in their ancestral home; some students honor especially Sarasvati, the goddess of learning. This can be compared with a Christian preference to pray to the one God as Father, Son, or Holy Spirit, and Roman Catholics may see the devotion to the many aspects of Brahman as similar to their invocation of the saints.

Hindus believe that since Brahman imbues all that is, the divine is found in each person's inner self, called the Atman. This belief allows the Hindu to speak of God as including the self in a way that classical Christianity has consistently denied. Christians say that the Spirit of God has entered the self through baptism and is nurtured in one's heart through the life of worship, but not that the self is in any way the same as God.

The Hindu sacred scriptures are filled with ancient tales of the adventures of the deities, divine incarnations, demons, animals, and human beings. These imaginative, even fantastic stories are beloved as metaphors for the continuing conflict between life and death, rich and poor, light and darkness, male and female, that prevail in society and inside each person. Similar to the use of the Bible in Christian worship, these traditional sacred texts are rehearsed in chant, story, mime, and art during Hindu festivals. Christians have understood at least some narratives in the Bible as historically accurate, and some churches use biblical historicity to legitimize the importance of the Bible. Such a concern about historicity is shared by some Orthodox Hindus, who are not likely to be encountered in the United States. Most Hindus value the sacred mythology found in the Hindu ancient scriptures for the truths contained therein. The worshipers learn the lessons of the story and so reject what is false and choose what is right. Liberal Christians may find this approach to sacred scriptures familiar.

Because the divine is in everything, Hindu deities are symbolized in a great variety of ways, as humans, animals, fantasy creatures, monsters, plants, and natural phenomena such as a river or fire. Statues and pictures of the gods and goddesses are placed on home altars and line the walls of the many Hindu temples now found in the United States. A Hindu

The spirit of the Hindu gods is as eternal as the desire to seek truth. The gods are gifts from what Hindus call nirvana—the state of absolute freedom, God, liberation, or truth. Kept alive in the hearts of Hindus through centuries of storytelling, these gods breathe humanity and humor into an everyday religiousness. They breathe understanding into existential questions and wisdom into all aspects of life.

—*Priya Hemenway*[3]

temple is literally a home of the gods rather than, like a Christian church, an assembly hall for communal worship. Because the Hindu statue or painting is understood as embodying the divine, the images of the gods and goddesses are adorned, washed, fed, and put to bed at night. Splitters may find these rituals quite alien to Christianity, while lumpers may see this attention to symbol as similar to how some Christians revere the bread and wine of Eucharist.

To restore one's necessary connection to the Ultimate, Hindus are urged to offer daily devotion to the divine. Called puja, this ritual can take place at one's home altar or at a local temple. During puja, Hindus offer praises to the divine, present petitions to the deities, chant a Sanskrit mantra, walk around the image a number of times, or present gifts of incense, flowers, or symbolic foods. Worship is about the need to be devoted to what is ultimate, to create more good than harm in the world, and to make symbolic offerings as part of daily life. Even when done at a temple, puja is a personal rite. The devotee faces the image of the deity, both seeing through to the divine and being seen by the divine. A Hindu pouring milk on an image is somewhat similar to the Eastern Orthodox Christian kissing an icon: the symbol carries the worshiper into the divine reality beyond. The idea is that devotion to the divine is essential for profound human life. To achieve this, Christians partake of the sacraments, and Hindus do puja before an image of the divine. At calendar festivals, the community also joins in several days of music, dance, drama, costume, parade, and feasting. The primary annual festivals celebrate the stories of the most important deities, and a priest leads these elaborate rituals. An important annual festival lasts nine days in the fall: the focus on three Hindu goddesses calls worshipers to cleanse themselves of all that is false, rededicate themselves to a selfless life, and reach for wisdom.

One method of religious symbolism among Hindus is called bhakti, which means the devotion of love. In bhakti, the believer comes to love the divine more deeply: the ritual is saying, "I love you completely." Since the divine is found in both male and female, some Hindu iconography uses sexual imagery: one's humble surrender to Brahman is something like the adoration between lovers. At many shrines, the divine is sexually imaged by an upright post set within a circular base. In medieval Christianity, some monastics employed sexual imagery in their mystical reveries, and some Western **rubrics** suggested that, reminiscent of sexual intercourse, the

A good example of faith-based action would be the fact that all Hindus worship Ganesha at the start of any activity. He is a corpulent elephant-headed deity with a protruding belly, and he rides a rat. To the believer, Ganesha is the perfect symbol of unstoppable power (elephant), prosperity (rotund body and potbelly), and protection (the rat, which is a pest, has been domesticated and turned into his vehicle). He opens the doorway to material success and spiritual growth.

—*Devdutt Pattanaik*[4]

base of the candle at the Easter Vigil be raised and lowered into the baptismal font, with some wax spilled into the water. Some contemporary praise songs refer in oblique ways to the intense love between the worshiper and God, but Christians have avoided explicit use of erotic imagery.

Newly popular in America is Buddhism, a religion that arose in northeast India and shares much of the worldview of Hinduism. The story of the Buddha tells of a prince who, discovering that the world is filled with sickness, suffering, and death, rejected the belief that there were deities who assist humankind in finding truth and overcoming suffering. Since religious symbols are usually containers of the divine, and since Buddhists dismiss any belief in supernatural reality or faith in a God who gives life to this world, there are few symbols in Buddhism. Some Buddhists participate in the elaborate ceremony of tea. Meticulous attention to the design of the tea utensils, the flowers in the vase, and the sweets on the tray aids the individual in seeing life as it really is. During the tea ceremony, what functions as a religious symbol is, for example, the sound made by hot or cold water being poured from a dipper. A statue of the Buddha is a religious symbol by being a reminder of the goal of transformation.

According to Buddhist belief, humans habitually see only what they want to see rather than what truly is. They are caught in a web of illusion, a false worldview, which is epitomized by the Western idea of a personal immortal soul. Buddhist ritual trains practitioners to get beyond focus on the self so as to live with compassion for others. Christians share this commitment to compassion, and they agree with Buddhists that the process of personal transformation from selfishness to compassion is immensely difficult. For some Buddhists, the Buddha provides a model for life's journey of life, and the Tibetan Buddhist Dalai Lama has become an internationally famous symbol of the meaningful life. Although for most Buddhists there is no god to save you, the form of Buddhism that more closely resembles Christianity is Pure Land Buddhism, in which Amida Buddha can assist those who will eventually join him in an existence beyond suffering.

In Buddhist homelands, the search for truth is centered in the phenomenon of monasticism, and a monk begging for food at one's front door is an invitation to selflessness. Although there are some Buddhist monastic centers in the United States, it is mostly the ritual of meditation that is a popular religious practice in America. Buddhists who hope to glimpse and finally

rubric
a rule or suggestion for ritual practice, called from the Latin word for "red" because originally written in liturgical texts in red ink

On their home altars, many American Hindus set up an image of Ganesha, who signifies the overcoming of obstacles.

to grasp the truth of selflessness attend regular meditation sessions at Buddhist meditation centers, some of which teach precise body posture and meticulous attention to breathing as part of the religious discipline. Although meditation is an individual exercise, meeting in groups assists each person in attaining the goal of transformed consciousness. In classical Buddhism the rigorous discipline leads to the acceptance of the suffering inherent in all things, while most American Buddhist meditation centers propose that the goal of meditation is peacefulness of the interior life.

Buddhists speak of personal transformation as enlightenment, a term that was used by early Christians to denote baptism. One Buddhist saying states the goal this way: "May all beings be free from suffering. May all beings abide in boundless equanimity, liberated from greed, hatred, and illusion." In hoping to escape captivity to selfishness, the strictest forms of Christian monasticism also require considerable practice in meditation as part of one's religious

---

Buddhist meditation develops mind control—control of one's own mind. Why is control of one's mind so important? Where the mind goes, the body tends to follow. A controlled mind can be directed skillfully, while an uncontrolled mind chatters like a "drunken monkey" and its misperceptions lead to unskillful behavior and unnecessary suffering.

—*Venerable Adrienne Howley*[5]

These Americans are practicing Eastern meditation. Note their precise body posture.

ritual. For the Christian, however, meditation begins with a reading from the Bible: the believer travels through the words, into the silence beyond the words, to arrive finally at God. Although some Christian mystics have spoken about the experience of absolute nothingness as being God, usually the destination of Christian meditation is an encounter with God. Different from Buddhists, Christians speak in a positive way about the self. Through the grace of baptism God enters the self. Indeed, God loves that self and can transform that self.

American interest in Buddhist meditation is influencing some Christian worship patterns. Some Christians spend private time in contemplation, perhaps sitting before a religious icon. Some churches schedule events in which persons meditate in silence or listen to Eastern chants. On Sunday morning, some churches are instituting times of silence, perhaps by sounding a Buddhist temple gong to mark a period of quiet contemplation. The ritual of walking the labyrinth, perhaps one that is Christianized, gives the American something to do with the body while meditating.

In the millennia before the historic world religions such as Buddhism developed, most **indigenous religion** focused on nature as the essential divine power to counter suffering and death. The particular geological landscape of an area, its weather patterns, and its native plants and animals constituted the people's home and food, and whether these natural phenomena were personified into divinities or not, a primary intent of the religion was to honor the earth for the maintenance of health and wholeness. Because nature religions were originally oral traditions, there is massive diversity within and among them. But lumpers have shown that generally such religions share a vision of nature as dynamic and all living things as interdependent. Humans are not in some way divine, but are a part of nature and must live in balance with all other natural elements so that individuals can be at peace and the community can thrive. It is usual that the dead are considered a continuing natural force. In the twenty-first century, many Native Americans are reviving their ancestral tribal practices. Some Native Americans are practicing Christians and are adding nature symbols and rituals into their Christian worship patterns. Others reject Christianity as a hierarchical, otherworldly religion that has oppressed the American natives and despoiled the earth, and these Native Americans practice only their restored nature religion.

indigenous religion
historically original religion of a geographical area

Originally, the symbols in nature religions reflected the local natural realities. If the tribe relied on cornmeal for sustenance, cornmeal was used in rituals of purification. If the spruce tree grew in well-watered terrain, the desert tribe used it to symbolize fecundity. The number four has high significance, because nature is said to have four directions, four

The Pueblo guide on the Taos, New Mexico, Indian reservation said to the visitors, "We are Catholics, since Mary is the Corn Mother."

divisions of time, four elements, and four human races. Costuming in feathers and animal hides symbolizes the human interdependence with local animals and honors their desirable powers. Rituals in nature religions tend to be scheduled either according to the cosmos—thus at the full moon, the solstices, and the equinoxes—or to mark changes in an individual's life, such as a ritual for healing. The rituals mean to harness the power of the earth for wholeness in the community and health for the individual. Some rituals mean to restore the world to a primal perfection, and so a story of creation is retold to call life back to an intended unity.

Some symbols and rituals now practiced are specific to a tribe. The Lakota assemble for the annual Sun Dance, once outlawed by the United States government but now restored. The Sun Dance is famous for its ritual during which men are pierced and hang from a tree pole for hours of dancing in the summer sun: their suffering is understood as healing for the entire community. When a Navaho shaman creates a sand painting, the suffering individual is seated inside the center of a mythic design that symbolizes wholeness. Some Apache young women hold a several-day dance of endurance at the celebration of their first menstruation. The Hopi hold rain dances during the drought of summer at which the drumming and dancing mean to function as sympathetic magic, calling the clouds to come from the west and water their land.

Even some Indian people must be reminded of our four cardinal principles: respect for Wakan Tanka, respect for Mother Earth, respect for our fellow man and woman, and respect for individual freedom.

—Ed McGaa, Eagle Man[6]

Intertribal sharing of traditional and contemporary symbol and ritual is developing into what is called Native American spirituality. Many groups now use the term *Wakan Tanka* to refer to the Great Spirit or the Great Mystery. Commercially available books suggest prayers to Mother Earth and describe rituals of address to the four corners of the earth. Prayer circles mean to replicate in the group the circle of wholeness that is the earth itself. Retreats welcome participants to experience the sweat lodge. Powwows that are open to visitors host dancers elaborately adorned in symbolic identification with the other animals of earth.

Another contemporary nature religion is Wicca, also called the Craft. Wicca attracts educated women and men and sometimes is marked by an adamant rejection of things Christian, especially the reference to God as Father, any male dominance, and a preference for the supernatural over the natural world. Wiccans characteristically meet in groups of no more than thirteen, called covens, thus ensuring intimacy within the group. When Wiccans personify nature, Goddess is usually the dominant deity. Goddess is within each person, and all things female symbolize the life of nature. An example of a

Wiccan ritual is croning, at which the post-menopausal woman is honored as having arrived at her time of wisdom. This ritual is seen as directly countering contemporary and Christian devaluing of older women.

Some contemporary Christians are heeding the message of nature religions by urging an end to all Western cultural patterns that ignore the health of the cosmos, as if only heaven or the self mattered. Recent publications by churches include prayers for animals and plants. Some church leaders include reference to the winter solstice at Christmastime and to the spring equinox at the Easter Vigil. Fundamentalist Christians continue to teach the six-day supernatural creation described in Genesis; other Christians accept a continuing evolution of God's creation as a process in which humans participate. Within both types of Christian belief, some churches are addressing current ecological concerns in serious ways, honoring the earth as a gift from God and recognizing all animals as beloved by God. The rituals of nature religions tend to be highly participatory. Since these rituals are not authorized by any hierarchy, some Christians see them as models of worship that is alive to the current assembly and easily adapted. This flexibility is attractive to many Christians who fear that much of what has been repeated for 100,000 Sundays may be inaccessible to the contemporary worshiper. Yet contemporary nature religions usually claim roots in the ancient world, thus valuing the symbols and rituals of prehistoric cultures more than those of recent times.

There remains a fundamental distinction between the practices of nature religions and those of Christianity. The Christian belief in God inevitably opens its members to the mystery of an existence other than this earth. Nature is finally not enough. Because the human problem is so absolute, the community of faith uses symbols and rituals that reach beyond the sun and moon and that go

Native American dancers celebrate the connection between humans and other animals.

The Goddess continually offers us challenges, but knowing that she is within us as well as around us, we find the strength to meet them, to transform fear into power-from-within, to create communities in which we can grow, struggle and change, to mourn our losses and celebrate our advances, to generate the acts of love and pleasure that are her rituals.

—*Starhawk*[7]

deeper than the roots of a tree. Christians honor the earth not because it can provide salvation, but because it is created by an ultimate God whose practice of forgiveness is not natural and who promises a life that is in some way other than the natural processes of birth, growth, aging, and death.

Examples of syncretistic religions that blend nature religion with some elements of Christianity are the Native American Church, Vodou, and Santería. The Native American Church reads from the Bible and teaches that Jesus is the primary intercessor for human needs. What is distinctive about the Native American Church is its ritual use of peyote: at an all-night ritual the peyote bud is ingested to induce an altered state of consciousness. When Africans were kidnapped from the Yoruba area and forced into slavery in the Americas, many of them layered Christian symbol and ritual onto essential aspects of their African tribal religions. Vodou developed in Haiti, and Santería in Cuba, and both are now practiced in the United States and marked by traditional African practices such as drumming, dancing, spirit and demon possession, and divination. Each accepts a distant God along with a pantheon of divinities that, usually bearing the names of biblical angels or Roman Catholic saints, are aspects of the nature religion of their African homeland. The symbols connect the people with the continuing power of the ancestors, and their rituals of healing resemble nature religions more closely than they resemble historic Christianity. A controversial religious practice in Santería is animal sacrifice, seen as an offering to the spirit world. Splitters point out that for Christians, the death and resurrection of Christ, celebrated weekly in word and sacrament, has replaced such religious rituals. However, lumpers recall that Christians also speak of making offerings to God, even calling the Eucharist, charity contributions, or devotional practices "sacrifice," and suggest that money as a substitute for an animal indicates the type of economy present, rather than the religious intent behind the ritual.

> In the act of giving birth, blood was spilled to facilitate your birth. The sacrificial animal blood is symbolic of the blood that is spilled at birth. It is the blood that gives life. The community of initiates also eats, ensuring that members of the family will never go hungry. In the Santeria religion the life force of animals used in rituals is revered because it brings spiritual rebirth as well as nourishment to the community.
>
> —*Marta Moreno Vega*[8]

This chapter has introduced some of the many complex questions that arise when comparing and contrasting Christian worship—itself a diverse phenomenon—with the many religious symbols and rituals currently available in the United States. A value in the American polyglot culture is to keep one's mind knowledgeable about one's neighbors. Yet an open mind ought not refuse to see differences or make judgments between sets of religious symbols and rituals. Such an ability is one of the goals of the study of the 100,000 Sundays of Christian worship.

Suggestions

1. This chapter contains many terms that are central to other world religions. Review especially these few terms: *axis mundi*, indigenous religion, rubric, syncretism.
2. Become acquainted with the practice of Judaism or Islam in your locale.
3. Present arguments for and against conducting Christian prayer during which everyone faces north, then east, then south, then west.
4. Learn about Scientology, argue whether or not it is a religion, and compare and contrast its practices with those of Christianity.
5. Write a personal essay explaining whether and why you are either a lumper or a splitter in the area of religious symbol and ritual.
6. In the Bible, the narratives in Acts 17:1—18:4 describe early Christian encounters with Judaism and with Greco-Roman polytheism. Discuss whether these narratives have any wisdom to offer Christians in the twenty-first century.
7. Discuss Leslie Marmon Silko's short story "The Man to Send Rain Clouds,"[9] a description of a syncretistic burial on an Indian reservation.
8. Discuss the 1994 film *Little Buddha*, which narrates the encounter between an American family and several Tibetan Buddhist monks who are searching for a new lama.
9. Attend a Hindu temple or a Buddhist dharma meditation center, and report on the symbols and rituals that you observe. If you can, interview one of the participants as part of your research.

For further study

Gallagher, Eugene V., and W. Michael Ashcraft, ed. *Introduction to New and Alternative Religions in America*. 5 vol. Westport, Conn.: Greenwood, 2006.

Griffith, R. Marie. *American Religions: A Documentary History*. New York: Oxford University Press, 2008.

Neusner, Jacob, ed. *World Religions in America*. 3d ed. Louisville: Westminster John Knox, 2003.

Porterfield, Amanda. *The Power of Religion: A Comparative Introduction*. New York: Oxford University Press, 1998.

A liturgical spirituality

This textbook has focused on the event of Sunday worship, on the continuing development of its symbols and rituals, and on the various ways that different Christians understand the meaning of their worship. Some Christians stress the activity of God during worship; others focus on the actions of the participants; and some do both. However, all Christians make claims about what influence Sunday worship has on Monday through Saturday, on the values held, decisions made, and the actions undertaken by participants as a result of worship. For 100,000 Sundays, Christians have said that worship flows out of the time allotted. When they meet for worship, they receive God, who creates life anew, saves the community from sin and death, and inspires their days with hope and love. The effect of this worship is to transform the consciousness of the participants, and through their daily living, to change the world that is outside the church. Worshiping is similar to eating a meal, which not only satisfies one's momentary hunger but also strengthens the body for the hours ahead; also, the quality and amount of food eaten over the years affects

See Plate 11 in the gallery. Compare this church art with others in the gallery.

not only one's health and well-being, but also the livelihood of farm workers and the ecology of the planet. Activity in the present influences the future.

First, a disclaimer: it is often true that worship does not achieve all that its proponents desire. Worship may be conducted so poorly that its symbols are opaque and its rituals seem hollow. Repetition may so bore the participants that they have interiorized nothing. Some worshipers may have no interest in religious devotion or personal transformation, and the minimal or begrudging participation of such persons may diminish the power of the communal experience. Even those persons we might call the worship professionals—the clergy, the musicians—have weeks, perhaps months, when they doubt that what they are being paid to do has much influence on anything once the event is concluded.

> What, then, is the point of "church-going"? Ask a theologian and you'll get one kind of answer. Ask overworked parents of young children and you'll get another. For me, it's an opportunity to acknowledge by being in the presence of others that I'm not alone in believing in the divine, in expressing gratitude for the Spirit's presence in my life, and in seeking ways to respond more fully to that spirit.... Churches can be energizing places for dialog and discovery. Most worship traditions also provide a framework for marking and celebrating the cycles of the year.... I was also looking for a spirit of joy. I'm not talking about the good time that a bar-hopper might look for.
>
> —*Gail Reitenbach*[1]

Yet the practice of Christian worship continues, indeed, thrives, in the United States. Many adherents value its symbols, welcome its rituals, and consciously or unconsciously enact something of the experience during the week. The type of religious piety that is rooted in communal worship is called **liturgical spirituality**. For those with a liturgical spirituality, the enlightenment of baptism, the practice of praising and praying to God, regular attention to the Scriptures, and participation in the meal of communion create an energy that empowers the assembly, and through that inspiration, improve the self and the world. In one way or another, worship will affect the individual, the community, the social order, and perhaps even the cosmos.

liturgical spirituality
a way of living religiously that is centered in and flows out of weekly or daily worship

Faithful Christian worshipers who claim a liturgical spirituality tell quite different stories about how worship affects their lives. The same Gospel reading may inspire quite diverse behavior in the days following. Yet those who adopt a liturgical spirituality somehow connect their worship experience with their thoughts and actions throughout life. Some Christians assert that after years of routine worship, God worked through a single Sunday's service to transform their worldview and alter their actions. Other Christians claim that the positive results received from worship depend upon the knowledge and skills gained from a discipline of regular worship.

This final chapter outlines twelve ways that worship may affect what happens outside of worship. The list summarizes various claims that Christians advance, and each claim is supported by a seminal scriptural passage that Christians use in teaching what worship is about. The proposals are organized around a simple outline of Sunday worship, what some Christians call the four-part **ordo**: the assembly gathers, hears the word, at least sometimes participates in the meal, and is sent to live out the meaning of the event.

When I opened up my heart to receive the eloquence with which he spoke, there likewise entered, although only by degrees, the truth that he spoke.

—*Augustine, in c. 400 describing the preaching of Ambrose*[2]

ordo
a term taken from Latin that outlines Christian worship as gathering, word, meal, and sending

Gathering

The study of symbol leads to proposal #1: *Honoring significant symbols makes the life of Christians more profound.* The task of identifying what has genuine significance is part of a well-directed life. Since a symbol is a shared designation of meaning, the individual needs the community for symbol to function. Especially in a culture as cluttered with options as is twenty-first-century America, shifting through the options to select what has ultimate importance is not an easy task and is helped by communal participation.

In Acts 2:1-42, the author identified as Luke describes an event that occurred to the early Christian community on the Jewish festival called Pentecost, fifty days after Passover. Pentecost celebrated God's giving of the law to the ancient Jews from Mount Sinai. As told in Exodus 19, God descended onto the top of the mountain in fire. Luke records that on Pentecost, now described as fifty days after Christ's resurrection, believers were transformed by an experience of the overwhelming presence of the Spirit of God. Luke writes that "divided tongues, as of fire, appeared among them, and a tongue rested on each of them." Like the sacred scriptures of many world religions, Acts uses fire to symbolize divine presence. Luke assumes that not only have his readers experienced the transformative might of fire—its light, its heat,

From *The Boy Who Could Sing Pictures*: "It will be the last time I will ever sing for them," Ben thought. "I must make it good." And it was. He sang colors they had never seen, in a land they had never seen. He even sang a giraffe and that not even he had ever seen. He sang sugar cane from another country, melons and cherries and all summer fruit in the winter snow, still fresh and good. . . . He sang babies born in times to come. And oxen and warm fire and the sea gulls along the shore. And on and on he sang the Promised Land. The weary, he sang rested. The hungry, he sang full. The cold, he sang warm. And the great sadness, he sang all away. And then he sang no more.

—*Seymour Leichman*[3]

its ferocity, its power to comfort the community—but also they know the story of Sinai. God was in the fire on the mountain, and God is in the fire on the forehead of each believer. The symbol ignites both ancient Jewish stories and this narrative of the early Christian assembly, and when contemporary Christians gather on Pentecost Sunday to celebrate the presence of the Spirit of God, the symbol of fire beckons their consciousness toward the mystery called God. Such attention on each Sunday to central symbols means to deepen personal awareness around what is important in communal life.

The study of ritual leads to proposal #2: *By ritualizing their faith, Christians come to embody their values.* To ritualize something is to practice its intent. When a community gathers for ritual, whether Sunday worship or Monday football, the assembly is held together in actions that propose a worldview worthwhile for the individual and the group. When a group joins together to sing, whether a Christian hymn or "The Star Spangled Banner," the song unites the individuals into a single body of faith and practice. A secular society offers little to assist the individual to live a religious life. However, worshiping with the community strengthens one's resolve to believe, because in the ritual, the Christian worldview is enacted.

In ritual and symbol we "act as if" this were a world already governed by God's shalom. And we hope that this eucharistic feasting in the liturgy of the church might lead us to a like feasting in the liturgy of the world. We hope that it will help us rediscover the transformative power of even our daily meals in the sharing of food with our families and friends, but, perhaps more importantly, with our enemies and strangers as well.

—*Richard R. Gaillardetz*[4]

One way that Christians examine ritual is by studying the biblical story of the institution of Passover in Exodus 12. According to Jewish memory, God was readying to punish the Egyptians for enslaving the Israelites by killing all the firstborn, both humans and animals. To save the Jews from the angel of death, God set out the details of an elaborate ritual: they were to slaughter a perfect lamb or goat, cook it according to precise directions, wear certain clothing for the feast, and mark their doorposts with the blood of the animal. The blood that signified the death of the lamb substituted for the death of the firstborn, and so God's chosen people were saved. Of the ritual, God says, "Throughout your generations you shall observe it as a perpetual ordinance." The people lived because the angel had passed over their homes, and to recall this salvation, they are to repeat the Passover ritual each year. And they do, and Jesus did. By repeating the ritual, the story is told, its lessons repeated, its inspiration revived, its worldview practiced. Christians center their year on the Passover of Christ, and each Sunday, in celebration of the resurrection, they enact the values arising from their salvation.

Proposal #3: *Participation in a weekly gathering reminds us that the individual does not, cannot, ought not, exist alone.* I did not birth myself, feed myself, shelter myself. Regular worship enacts the truths that we need one another for life and that attending to our own needs and the needs of others consumes some or a great deal of our time. The idea is that the group will miss the individual who is absent and that each person's presence enriches the experience of everyone. The awareness that the human is a communal animal may lead worshipers to adopt countercultural ways of thought and life in a culture as individualistic as twenty-first-century America.

It takes a long time to learn a church, and I have not learned All Angels' yet. There are still many people's names I don't know, although I now nod and bustle and chat when I walk into services. A vestryman died this year, a pillar of the church, and everyone was sad, shaken. That is how I knew I was still new: I knew the man's name, but couldn't have picked him out of a crowd.

—*Lauren Winner*[5]

An important biblical passage about the communal nature of religious life is 1 Corinthians 12:1—13:13, in which Paul uses the metaphor of the human body to describe the Christian community. All are part of one. "The eye cannot say to the hand, 'I have no need of you.'" Christians do not live as isolated individuals; rather, they receive the word from others, share it with others, are baptized by another, are handed the bread and wine by another. Paul continues his exhortation on the body with the famous chapter describing Christian love, which concludes with the claim that love is more fundamental to the Christian life than either faith or hope. For love to be preeminent, there must be a community, for it is other people whom we love. According to Christian faith, it is the Spirit of the risen Christ who forms the assembly into a body destined for love.

Word

Proposal #4 reflects the fact that at Sunday worship Christians read and contemplate the Bible:

CH CH
What's missing?
UR
Join us for Sunday Liturgy

Attending to Scripture trains the assembly to value the records of the past. William Faulkner is quoted as saying that the past is not dead; it isn't even over. American values sometimes suggest that newness is of sole significance for human life. Yet human cultures have always searched their past for help in finding a meaningful existence, and a community assembled to listen carefully to texts written two to three thousand years ago opens the contemporary listeners to truths that may have been forgotten. For some worshipers, interest in this word will suggest not only weekly, but daily, reading and meditation of the Bible.

In Matthew 12:38-40 Jesus is asked for a sign to authenticate his teaching. He tells the people to recall Jonah. In the short book of Jonah, God calls a prophet to preach to a city that was an enemy of Israel. Jonah instead takes ship heading in the opposite direction. In an attempt to calm a ferocious tempest that is interpreted as expressing divine rage, the mariners throw Jonah overboard, and God sends a great fish that swallows him and, after three days, coughs him up on dry land, after which he does, finally, travel to the enemy city to proclaim the word of God. Jesus is using the famous story as a metaphor for his being thrown into death and, after three days, being raised by God to new life and mission. Following the Gospel of Matthew, the church has referred to the story of Jonah as testimony to God's power of resurrection, and many medieval churches and manuscripts depicted side by side Jonah coming out the mouth of the fish and Jesus arising from the tomb. The ancient story offers us a truth we ought not miss.

Proposal #5: *Christians acknowledge that, individually and communally, we need help making moral decisions.* Morality functions within communities of shared discourse, and in our society, religious groups offer a rare occasion for such discourse. Any appeal to conscience is, after all, an appeal to what one has heard before, perhaps learned in childhood, and as one's conscience matures, more data must always be considered, other people heard, and their positions discussed. Sermons are one vehicle for sharing wisdom about complex ethical matters, and the deliberation of the wider church is an essential part of the decisions made by Christian individuals.

What is perhaps the most famous parable of Jesus illustrates this proposal. In Luke 10:25- 37, Jesus is asked a moral question: To love my neighbor, I must know who my neighbor is. Who then is my neighbor? The context of the parable indicates that even people who heard the teachings of Jesus needed to inquire about the ethical life. In the parable of the Good Samaritan, the priest and the Levite, religious professionals who serve in the Temple rituals, walk past the man lying in the ditch, but a man who is an ethnic and religious outsider assists the stranger in need. The answer that Jesus gives is not only surprising, but in some ways upsetting, for it is counter to usual definitions of "neighbor." Repeatedly over 100,000 Sundays, this story has been proclaimed to call the Christian assembly into the difficulty of the ethical life, and countless preachers have used this story to help the community think through current moral issues.

There's a lovely Hasidic story of a rabbi who always told his people that if they studied the Torah, it would put Scripture on their hearts. One of them asked, "Why **on** our hearts, and and not **in** them?" The rabbi answered, "Only God can put Scripture inside. But reading sacred text can put it on your hearts, and then when your hearts break, the holy words will fall inside."[7]

Proposal #6: *Hearing the word reminds the assembly that in every time and place, humans have suffered.* Individual sinfulness, personal sickness, family sorrow, social disruption, natural catastrophe: such suffering has always marked human life, and persons ignore this reality to their peril. Only a religion that looks death in the eye is worth one's time and energy. Upon hearing the word, one response of the assembled community is to lament before God; another is to intercede for all the needy. But many worshipers then do something over the coming week to alleviate the suffering of others, misery that, apart from attending church, they may be able to block out of their privileged or happy life.

The book of 1 Kings tells of the building of the Temple in Jerusalem during the reign of King Solomon. Following the practices of other ancient Near Eastern societies, the king functioned as head of both government and religion, and in chapter 8 Solomon himself offers the prayer at the dedication of the Temple. The prayer begins with thanksgiving for centuries of God's care for the people. But then comes a lengthy prayer of intercession. The people will need continual forgiveness, and the future will bring drought, famine, plague, sickness, warfare, captivity, interaction with foreigners, defeat. Not even on the glorious occasion of the dedication of the Temple can the people forget that human

When you have partaken of this sacrament, or desire to partake of it, you must in turn share the misfortunes of the fellowship. As love and support are given you, you in turn must render love and support to Christ in his needy ones. You must feel with sorrow all the dishonor done to Christ in his holy Word, all the misery of Christendom, all the unjust suffering of the innocent, with which the world is everywhere filled to overflowing. You must fight, work, pray, and—if you cannot do more—have heartfelt sympathy.

—*Martin Luther, 1519*[8]

In 1951 Fritz Eichenberg printed this depiction of the Lord's Supper in the newsletter The Catholic Worker.

life contains much suffering. This comprehensive prayer has inspired many Christian worshipers always to be aware of the tragedies of their neighbors.

Meal

Since at Sunday worship Christians eat and drink, here is proposal #7: *One is what one eats* (to translate a German phrase, *man ist was man iss*). Fast-food restaurants now indicate what is in the food that is served. The Jewish practice of kosher prohibits the eating of animals that are scavengers, such as pigs, vultures, or lobsters, since if we eat an animal that ate garbage, we also eat that garbage. Weekly eating and drinking of a symbolically significant meal reminds worshipers that food, whether the meal of the church or American junk snacks, contributes to both the body and the spirit. Simple bread and clear wine are transparent foods that link the community to the goodness of the earth, filling the body of the self and of the community with the natural food God gives, and modeling a universe in which everyone can be sustained by eating good food.

It is not surprising that the fresco of Jesus eating his last supper with his disciples painted by Leonardo da Vinci is a beloved Christian image. For many Christians, the primary biblical reference for the meal of bread and wine is the narrative of the Last Supper as told in Matthew 26:17-29, Mark 14:12-25, and Luke 22:7-19. The three accounts are not identical, and scholars assume that since Jesus spoke Aramaic, none of these narratives written in Greek can be a verbatim transcript of the words of Jesus. But despite the interesting complications raised by the comparative texts, Christians for most of 100,000 Sundays have said that the bread and cup partake of the mystery of the Last Supper. The bread is "my body," the wine is "my blood of the covenant," or as Paul writes in 1 Corinthians 11:25, "the new covenant in my blood."

Throughout Christian history theologians have proposed ways to understand these words. Using their own scholarly or vernacular languages and their current philosophical and scientific categories, they taught their followers to understand these odd words in their one approved way, and history tells of Christians martyring other Christians who explained the mystery with different words. Yet all Christians agree that God visits the meal, whether the food itself, the process of the meal, or the participants, so that in, with, and under the bread and wine comes the extraordinary presence of the Spirit of Christ. Yes, the bread is the body of Christ: but no, Christians are not cannibals. Churches say yes to one explanation, no to another one. Paul leads the church to say that into the body of each participant comes the body of Christ, making of the assembly the body of Christ. By sharing in the body of Christ, the community becomes that very body. We are what we eat.

Proposal #8: *Communion reminds the assembly that food is best consumed when it is equally shared.* Food shared makes the community united in its eating, which is why so many peoples have developed regulations about whom one can

> At first Edmund tried to remember that it is rude to speak with one's mouth full, but soon he forgot about this and thought only of trying to shovel down as much Turkish Delight as he could, and the more he ate, the more he wanted to eat. . . . The Queen knew, though Edmund did not, that this was enchanted Turkish Delight and that anyone who had once tasted it would want more and more of it, and would even, if they were allowed, go on eating it till they killed themselves.
>
> —C. S. Lewis, The Lion, the Witch, and the Wardrobe[9]

> The Biblical writers chose wine as the classic symbol of joy. Wine is to make our hearts glad, and it works very well. Drunkenness is always condemned in the Biblical community but wine is to be shared as a communal symbol of joy.
>
> —Jeff Smith, the Frugal Gourmet[10]

The Chinese artist He Qi depicts Jesus sharing food with the woman and the man of Emmaus.

eat with. Families that include a recovering alcoholic know the discomfort of enjoying wine when not all at the table can drink. At the weekly sharing of a bite of bread and a swallow of the fruit of the vine, each has a little, and all have the same. Communion enlivens the assembly toward the hope that the increasing gap between the menus of the rich and the fare of the poor is not what God intends. Regular worship might help the American consumer to consume less, contribute more for hunger relief, and advocate for policies that attend to the growing problem of starvation around the world.

Some Christians look to all the meals of Jesus as precursors of the Sunday meal of the church. The four Gospels tell of Jesus feeding several thousand people with five loaves of bread and two fish, and beloved narratives of the ministry of Jesus include the stories of Jesus eating with Zacchaeus and with Mary and Martha. Indeed, in Matthew 11:19 and Luke 7:34, he is accused of being "a drunkard and a glutton." Some contemporary liturgical theologians focus on Jesus' meals after the resurrection as models of each Eucharist, especially the dinner with the disciples at Emmaus told in Luke 24:13-35. Jesus, unrecognized by the travelers, has walked with them on the road. He has opened the Hebrew Scriptures to them, teaching them about the Messiah, but it was at table, when Jesus "took bread, blessed and broke it, and gave it to them," that they experienced the risen Christ in their midst. At each Sunday's sharing of bread and wine, the assembly experiences the body of Christ in their midst, around the table, on the table, in their bodies.

Most Christians have taught that the reason that Jesus suffered and died was to forgive sin and that the Eucharist is a visible sign of God's forgiveness of our sin. Thus

Following one of her episodes of sobbing after participating in communion, the lady's priest came to her, saying, "Woman, Jesus is long since dead." When her crying had ceased, she said to the priest, "Sir, his death is as fresh to me as if he had died this same, day, and so, I think, it ought to be to you and to all Christian people. We ought always to remember his kindness, and always think of the doleful death that he died for us."

—The Book of Margery Kempe, *ca. 1400*[11]

proposal #9: *Worship reminds us that all people are sinners and need forgiveness.* There is much in contemporary culture that tries either to explain misbehavior or inculcate guilt, but less that assists people to acknowledge sin and work for restitution. Weekly participation in communion seeks a more honest appraisal of both sin—we are all sinners—and guilt—some guilt is appropriate and some not, and communion comforts participants with the assurance of God's mercy. If God can forgive us and others, so can we.

For some Christians, the primary biblical story standing behind each Eucharist is the crucifixion, told in Matthew 27:27-61, Mark 15:16-41, Luke 23:26-49, and John 18:16-30. As with the narratives of the Last Supper, these four accounts are in interesting ways distinct, each portraying Jesus in its own way. For example, in Mark the single quote from Jesus on the cross shows him abandoned by God, while in Luke, Jesus continues his ministry of reconciliation and mercy from the cross. For churches that think of communion as expressing the crucifixion, the very reason God became incarnate in Jesus of Nazareth was to provide forgiveness of sin, and communion, like the crucifixion, enacts the forgiveness of sin. Divine justice demands that God cannot merely wipe the slate clean: there must be suffering and death, and so Jesus offered his life in obedience to God. His offering is recalled, perhaps repeated, each time the Eucharist is celebrated, and many Christians ritualize this need for forgiveness by kneeling to receive communion.

Sending

Proposal #10: *Praising God at the beginning of each week cultivates in worshipers an attitude of gratitude.* In a culture that popularizes satire and utilizes complaints as the road to improvements, it is not easy to live in gratefulness. When Americans refuse to say "thank you" for gifts because they did not like the present, individual opinion has become more important than habits of thankfulness. Yet in the second century, Justin wrote, "We always thank God," and he described Sunday worship as the preeminent occasion for expressing such perpetual gratefulness. The historic title for the meal of bread and wine is Eucharist, the Greek word for thanksgiving. Some theologians have taught

> To his secret delight, the final hymn was the Old Hundredth, one of the first poems ever to have moved him, when he was little boy of twelve or so. It seemed to have the local vote as well; when the congregation launched into "All people that on earth do dwell," the building seemed actually to vibrate as it absorbed the noise...."Praise, laud and bless his name always, for it is seemly so to do." Emerging at the far end of the doxology, he felt as shaky and exhilarated as if he had been on a long run.
>
> —Jane Stevenson[12]

that the primary purpose of Sunday worship is giving thanks to God, after which worshipers are sent home to live out that gratitude.

Psalm 100 sounds throughout Christian time and space as exuberant praise to God. This one short psalm calls the assembly to joy, gladness, singing, thanksgiving, praise, and blessing, because God cares for the people like a shepherd with steadfast love and faithfulness. For the churches that use a lectionary, Psalm 100 is appointed especially on festival occasions, and many Protestant churches use Psalm 100 as the opening call to worship. It has become beloved especially in its sixteenth-century versification by William Kethe as the hymn "All People That on Earth Do Dwell," and its tune is named Old Hundredth. Some churches appoint this hymn for their fall Thanksgiving Day celebration, since this is a hymn that the Pilgrims did sing. Like many other psalms, Psalm 100 calls believers to give thanks to God simply because God is. There need not be specific personal reasons to incite gratitude: standing before the presence of the divine is reason enough for praise.

Proposal #11: *Praying for others can be powerful.* Christians trust that God will hear their prayers and will move heaven and earth to answer them. But Christians also see the influence of prayer on those who pray. That churches pray for world peace and for justice in every nation leads some worshipers to dedicate their lives to the political process, run for office, urge legislators to moral choices, and find alternatives to violence and warfare. Petitions for the care of the earth, newly regularized in some churches, lead some worshipers to creative approaches to ecological issues. That God cares for the soil and the rivers, the plants and the animals, and not only humans, inspires Christians to reverse centuries of disregard for the earth. That worshipers pray for all the needy leads others to visit the sick, provide housing for the homeless, organize food distribution centers, since in their prayers they stood before God with those who would otherwise have stood alone.

Some churches have understood that each week the church replicates the preaching of the prophets. Like Isaiah, Jeremiah, Hosea, Joel, Amos, Micah, and John the Baptist, the preacher calls the people to newness of life, and the hearers embody that life in the week following. In Micah 6:6-8, a poem probably from

---

One early, cloudy morning when I was forty-six, I walked into a church, ate a piece of bread, took a sip of wine. A routine Sunday activity for tens of millions of Americans—except that up until that moment I'd led a thoroughly secular life, at least indifferent to religion, more often appalled by its fundamentalist crusades. This was my first communion. It changed everything. . . . I took communion, I passed the bread to others, and then I kept going, compelled to find new ways to share what I'd experienced. I started a food pantry and gave away literally tons of fruit and vegetables and cereal around the same altar where I'd first received the body of Christ.

—*Sara Miles*[13]

---

the eighth century before Christ, the speaker questions the meaning of worship: What is the intention of the burnt offerings that God has commanded? Should believers, like their Canaanite neighbors, practice even child sacrifice to please God? The prophet responds that worshipers are "to do justice, to love kindness, to walk humbly with your God." The trajectory of worship is the doing of justice, the loving of kindness. Worship with no future has little use in the present. Inspired by passages such as Micah 6, Christians have taken onto themselves the concerns for which the assembly prays, as if from Monday through Saturday each worshiper embodies one petition from Sunday's communal prayer.

Proposal #12: *Part of the Christian life is preparation for death.* Some social critics claim that American optimism leads to a national difficulty in accepting the reality of death. However, the weekly remembrance of the death of Christ, petitions for those who grieve, and thanksgiving for the beloved dead are ways to practice for one's own death and to see death as not only inevitable, but even a natural part of the life that God created. To live without fear of death gives each day a freedom in God, and to be able to deal with the death of those we love without a fruitless search for closure extends the peace of God into the sadness that comes with times of grieving.

The last book of the Bible, the Revelation to John, is in large part a complex apocalyptic vision of the horrors accompanying the end of the earth and the joys experienced after death in the presence of God. Throughout the descriptions of the final battles are glimpses of life in heaven, where the dead join the angels to praise God. The poems throughout Revelation have been sung by Christians who think of worship as joining the living with the dead in praise. In Revelation 4:6-11, the four mysterious creatures sing a hymn like one that many Christians sing every Sunday, beginning "Holy, holy, holy." The poem in 7:9-17, proclaimed at many Christian funerals, speaks of the hope that after death God will "guide them to springs of the water of life" and "wipe away every tear from their eyes." Finally, in chapters 21 and 22 is a description of the heavenly city, with the tree of life offering its twelve fruits for all to eat. Such biblical readings help worshipers to confront death honestly by offering them images of divine life that is far greater than their own fragile human existence.

In the lectionary for the Sunday liturgy it would be hard to find a single set of readings that does not have at least one mention of or allusion to death. The hymns of the church, on the whole, also possess a remarkable range of serious language for death. "Time, like an ever-rolling stream, soon bears us all away . . . ," we sing, in Isaac Watts' widely used "O God Our Help in Ages Past." Taught by the language of the Scriptures and the creeds, the preacher will also speak of death, avoiding the euphemisms so common in current speech. It would be painfully ludicrous to say that Jesus Christ "passed away." It is similarly inaccurate and unhelpful to so speak of the death of any of us.

—*Gordon Lathrop*[14]

After the beloved rabbi's death, his disciples came together and talked about the things he had done. When it was Rabbi Schneur Zalman's turn, he asked them: "Do you know why our master went to the pond every day at dawn and stayed there for a little while before coming home again?" They did not know why. Rabbi Zalman continued: "He was learning the song with which the frogs praise God. It takes a very long time to learn that song."[15]

In conclusion

A high school English teacher said to the class, "For your exam, write about the wide truths of life in *Moby Dick*," and she left the room. Christians with a liturgical spirituality testify that weekly worship opens them up not only to the Spirit of God and the power of Christ's resurrection, but also to the "wide truths of life," and they claim that these truths affect their thoughts and actions throughout the week. In summary form, here are twelve of the truths of life that worshiping on Sunday may instill in church-goers for the remainder of their week:

1. Honoring significant symbols enriches human life.
2. Through ritual, the community practices its worldview.
3. Individuals need community.
4. The words of the past speak in the present for the future.
5. The community searches together for the ethical life.
6. Together humans face the reality of sorrow and suffering.
7. The food one eats shapes the person one becomes.
8. Eating is best when shared with others.
9. Everyone needs forgiveness.
10. Living in gratitude transforms experience.
11. Society needs persons who help those in need.
12. It is wholesome to prepare for death.

Like training for a marathon, or nurturing a relationship toward marriage, or ending the abuse of women, or becoming a physician, many activities that are worth the effort are not easily or quickly achieved. For earth's last 100,000 Sundays, groups of Christians have agreed that a weekly meeting over word and meal illumines their lives and focuses their energies. The symbols and rituals experienced on Sunday mean to birth and sustain meaningful personal lives and beneficial communal engagement. For students completing this textbook, it is hoped that a semester of attention to this continuing phenomenon has been at least educationally useful and perhaps even spiritually significant.

Suggestions

1. Review the chapter's vocabulary: liturgical spirituality and ordo.
2. Analyze the Web site or printed materials of a local church to determine what activities it sponsors and which attitudes outside of Sunday worship it means to cultivate.
3. Interview an active lay Christian to determine the role that worship plays in that person's lifestyle and daily choices; or interview someone who has left the church to determine where outside of worship that person finds the values that this chapter discusses.
4. Write an essay commenting on this quote from Annie Dillard: "I often think of the set pieces of liturgy as certain words which people have successfully addressed to God without their getting killed. In the high churches they saunter through the liturgy like Mohawks along a strand of scaffolding who have long since forgotten their danger. If God were to blast such a service to bits, the congregation would be, I believe, genuinely shocked."[16]
5. Write a personal experience essay in which you support or dispute one of the chapter's twelve proposals.
6. The biblical chapter Romans 16 is seldom read on Sunday morning. Discuss the relationship between this conclusion to Paul's epistle and the contents of this chapter.
7. Read "Collection,"[17] a transcription of one of Garrison Keillor's radio monologues about a Sunday service in his fictional Lake Wobegon, Minnesota.
8. Discuss the 1989 film *Saint Maybe*, in which attendance at a church service changes the life of the protagonist and those he cares for.
9. Attend a Sunday service of your choice, and write a report identifying anything in the service that would lead to specific action during the week.

For further study

Anderson, E. Byron. *Worship and Christian Identity: Practicing Ourselves.* Collegeville, Minn.: Liturgical, 2003.

Bass, Diana Butler. *Christianity for the Rest of Us: How the Neighborhood Church Is Transforming the Faith.* New York: HarperOne, 2006.

Byars, Ronald P. *What Language Shall I Borrow? The Bible and Christian Worship.* Grand Rapids: Eerdmans, 2008.

Gallagher, Nora. *Things Seen and Unseen: A Year Lived in Faith.* New York: Vintage, 1998.

Lamott, Anne. *Traveling Mercies: Some Thoughts on Faith.* New York: Anchor, 1999.

Madigan, Shawn. *Spirituality Rooted in Liturgy.* Rev. ed. Portland, Ore.: Pastoral, 1988.

McNamee, John. *Diary of a City Priest.* Kansas City, Mo.: Sheed & Ward, 1995.

Miles, Sara. *Take This Bread: A Radical Conversion.* New York: Ballentine, 2007.

Neumark, Heidi. *Breathing Space: A Spiritual Journey in the South Bronx.* Boston: Beacon, 2004.

Norris, Kathleen. *The Cloister Walk.* New York: Riverhead, 1996.

Saliers, Don E. *Worship Come to Its Senses.* Nashville: Abingdon, 1996.

Torvend, Samuel. *Luther and the Hungry Poor: Gathered Fragments.* Minneapolis: Fortress Press, 2008.

Van Dyk, Leanne, ed. *A More Profound Alleluia: Theology and Worship in Harmony.* Grand Rapids: Eerdmans, 2005.

Wilson, Jonathan P. *Why Church Matters: Worship, Ministry, and Mission in Practice.* Grand Rapids: Brazos, 2006.

Yancey, Philip. *Church: Why Bother? My Personal Pilgrimage.* Grand Rapids: Zondervan, 1998.

Chronology toward
American Christian worship

787	Seventh Ecumenical Council approves use of icons
843	Byzantine Empress Theodora restores icons to Orthodox churches
1000	Cathedral building begins in Europe
1054	Great Schism between Eastern Orthodox and Western Catholic churches
1100	Anselm proposes a theory of atonement based on divine justice
c. 1100	Western Catholic fathers and brothers begin European preaching tours
1100–1400s	Western Catholic mystics access God apart from the sacraments
1123	Western Catholic council mandates clerical celibacy
1137	Building of Gothic cathedrals in Europe begins
1215	Western Catholic Council promulgates doctrine of transubstantiation
1400s	Stations of the Cross devotions spread through Europe
1450	Invention of printing press
1454	Gutenberg Bible printed
1523	First Reformation liturgies celebrated; some Protestants destroy church art
1525	Reformed church in Strasbourg provides text of liturgy in people's book
1525	Ex-monk Martin Luther marries ex-nun Katerina von Bora
1526	Martin Luther publishes a German vernacular order for Sunday worship
1536	Tyndale's English Bible printed
1542	John Calvin publishes a service order for Geneva, Switzerland
1549	Thomas Cranmer oversees publication of the *Book of Common Prayer*
1555	German citizens required to adopt the religious practice of their prince
1570	Roman Catholic Council of Trent mandates Tridentine mass
1580–1610	Jesuit Mateo Ricci introduces inculturation in Japanese mission
1609	John Smyth's congregation institutes believer's baptism
1611	Publication of the English Bible authorized by King James
1630	Pilgrims establish theocratic colony in Plymouth, Massachusetts
1670	Beginning of Pietism

1686	William Penn's Pennsylvania colony establishes religious tolerance
1723–50	J. S. Bach serves as music director in Leipzig, Germany
1734	America's Great Awakening begins
1738	John Wesley's religious experience
1773	First Baptist church for slaves founded on Georgia plantation
1779	Thomas Jefferson's bill for establishing religious freedom
1780	Selection of John Wesley's 7,000 hymns published
1787	Richard Allen's walk-out leads to African Methodist Episcopal Church
1801	Revival camp meetings at Cane Ridge
1835	Alexander Campbell's restorationist movement founds Disciples of Christ
1853	Antoinette Brown Blackwell ordained in the Congregational Church
1869	Thomas Welch discovers method of producing grape juice
1895	C. H. Mason founds Church of God in Christ, black Pentecostal church
1900	Invention of the microphone
1906	Azusa Street revival in Los Angeles, birth of Pentecostalism
1923	Aimee Semple McPherson founds charismatic Foursquare Gospel Church
1940s	Ecumenical monastery established in Taizé, France
1950s	Billy Graham crusades exemplify postwar revivalism
1962–65	Second Vatican Council modernizes Roman Catholic liturgy
1970s	Renewals in Protestant churches inspired by reformed Roman mass
	Copy machines become commonplace
1973	United Church of Christ ordains openly gay William Johnson
1975	Willow Creek Community Church popularizes seeker services
1988	Episcopal Church consecrates Barbara Harris its first female bishop
21st cen.	Christians keep worshiping on Sundays in old and new ways

Notes

1. Why study Christian worship?

1. Ralph Waldo Emerson, "The Divinity School Address," vol. 1 of *The Collected Works of Ralph Waldo Emerson*, ed. Robert E. Spiller (Cambridge, Mass.: Belknap, 1971), 86, 89.
2. Emily Dickinson, "Some keep the Sabbath," #324, in *The Complete Poems of Emily Dickinson*, ed. Thomas H. Johnson (Boston: Little, Brown, 1960), 153–54.
3. Philip Larkin, "Church Going," in *Collected Poems*, ed. Anthony Thwaite (New York: Farrar, Straus & Giroux, 2003), 58.
4. Nica Lalli, *Nothing: Something to Believe In* (Amherst, N.Y.: Prometheus, 2007), 132.
5. Margaret Forster, *Keeping the World Away* (New York: Ballantine, 2006), 216.
6. Annie Dillard, *Holy the Firm* (New York: Bantam, 1977), 65.
7. C. G. Jung, *Psychology and Religion* (New Haven: Yale University Press, 1938), 113.
8. Anne Lamott, "Why I Make Sam Go to Church," *Traveling Mercies: Some Thoughts on Faith* (New York: Anchor, 2000), 99–105.

2. What is a symbol?

1. See for example the thesis of Brian Hayden, *Shamans, Sorcerers and Saints: A Prehistory of Religion* (Washington, D.C.: Smithsonian, 2003), 3.
2. Russell Hoban, *Riddley Walker* (New York: Washington Square, 1980), 124, 126.
3. Aidan Kavanagh, *Elements of Rite: A Handbook of Liturgical Style* (New York: Pueblo, 1966), 5.
4. Anonymous, "The Pasch History," in *The Paschal Mystery: Ancient Liturgies and Patristic Texts*, ed. A. Hamman (Staten Island, N.Y.: Alba House, 1969), 64–65.
5. See, for example, Nathaniel Altman, *Sacred Trees: Spirituality, Wisdom & Well-Being* (New York: Sterling, 2000); Roger Cook, *The*

Tree of Life: Image for the Cosmos (New York: Thames and Hudson, 1974); and E. O. James, *The Tree of Life: An Archaeological Study* (Leiden, Netherlands: E. J. Brill, 1966).

6. Thomas Aquinas, *Summa Theologiae*, 1 A, Question 13, 3, and 10.

7. Sigmund Freud, *New Introductory Lectures on Psychoanalysis*, trans. James Strachey (New York: Norton, 1965).

8. C. G. Jung, *Psychology and Religion* (New Haven: Yale University Press, 1938).

9. Mircea Eliade, *Images and Symbols: Studies in Religious Symbolism*, trans. Philip Mairet (Princeton: Princeton University Press, 1991).

10. See Mari Womack, *Symbols and Meaning: A Concise Introduction* (Walnut Creek, Calif.: Alta Mira, 2005).

11. Susanne K. Langer, *Philosophy in a New Key: A Study in the Symbolism of Reason, Rite, and Art* (New York: Mentor, 1942), 61.

12. *Egeria: Diary of a Pilgrimage*, trans. and ed. George E. Gingras, vol. 38 of *Ancient Christian Writers* (New York: Paulist, 1970), 111.

13. Margaret Elphinstone, *The Sea Road* (Edinburgh: Canongate, 2000), 181.

14. Christopher Irvine, ed., *The Use of Symbols in Worship*, Alcuin Liturgy Guides 4 (London: SPCK, 2007), 16.

15. Charles Schultz, "Peanuts," *The Philadelphia Inquirer*, May 30, 1996.

16. Paul Ricoeur, *The Rule of Metaphor: Multi-disciplinary Studies of the Creation of Meaning in Language* (Toronto: University of Toronto Press, 1977), 22.

17. Mark Searle, "Liturgy as Metaphor," *Worship* 55 (1981): 104–05.

18. Robert Jones, "Metaphor and Sacrament," *The Christian Century*, 100: 18 (June 1, 1983), 548.

19. John Donne, *Devotions upon Emergent Occasions*, XIX Expostulation (Ann Arbor: University of Michigan Press, 1959), 124.

3. What is a ritual?

1. See Robert Putman, *Bowling Alone: The Collapse and Revival of American Community* (New York: Simon & Schuster, 2000).

2. Judith Manners, *Miss Manners' Guide for the Turn-of-the-Millennium* (New York: Simon & Schuster, 1990), 442–43.

3. *Hsun Tzu: Basic Writings*, trans. Burton Watson (New York: Columbia University Press, 1969), 94–95.

4. Pema Chödrön, *The Wisdom of No Escape* (Boston: Shambhala, 2001), 77–78.

5. Ed McGaa, Eagle Man, *Mother Earth Spirituality: Native American Paths to Healing Ourselves and Our World* (San Francisco: Harper, 1990) 91, 93, 94.

6. Victor Turner, *The Ritual Process: Structure and Anti-Structure* (Chicago: Aldine, 1969), 131–65.

7. Robert G. Hamerton-Kelly, ed., *Violent Origins: Walter Burkert, René Girard, and Jonathan Z. Smith on Ritual Killing and Cultural Formation* (Stanford: Stanford University Press, 1987).

8. Catherine Bell, *Ritual: Perspectives and Dimensions* (New York: Oxford University Press, 1997), 80–83.

9. Roy A. Rappaport, *Ritual and Religion in the Making of Humanity* (Cambridge: Cambridge University Press, 1999), 70–74.

10. Nora Gallagher, *Things Seen and Unseen: A Year Lived in Faith* (New York: Vintage, 1998), 129.

11. John Wesley, "Directions for Singing," in *The United Methodist Hymnal* (Nashville: The United Methodist Publishing House, 1989), vii.

12. Ruth Boling, et al., *A Children's Guide to Worship* (Louisville: Geneva, 1997); Joyce Carol Thomas, *Shouting!*, illus. Annie Lee (New York: Hyperion Books for Children, 2007); Gail Ramshaw, *Sunday Morning* (Chicago: Liturgy Training Publications, 1993).

13. Shirley Jackon, "The Lottery," *The Lottery and Other Stories*, 2nd ed. (New York: Farrar, Straus & Giroux, 2005).

4. Which symbols and rituals have Christians used for 100,000 Sundays?

1. Chaim Potok, *My Name is Asher Lev* (New York: Ballantine, 1972), 163.

2. Pliny the Younger, www.earlychristianwritings.com/text/pliny.

3. See "Trinity Affinity" in Carmen Renee Berry, *The Unauthorized Guide to Choosing a Church* (Grand Rapids: Brazos, 2003), 56–60.

4. Kurt Niederwimmer, *The Didache*, Hermeneia, trans. Linda M. Maloney (Minneapolis: Fortress Press, 1998), 144, 155.

5. Augustine, Sermon 272, *The Works of Saint Augustine, Sermons*, III/7, trans. Edmund Hill, O.P. (New Rochelle, N.Y.: New City, 1993), 300.

6. Justin, trans. Gordon Lathrop, *Central Things: Worship in Word and Sacrament* (Minneapolis: Augsburg Fortress, 2005), 78–79.

7. Ursula LeGuin, "The Barrow," *Orsinian Tales* (New York: Harper & Row, 1976), 5–14.

5. What comes down to us from 75,000 Sundays ago?

1. Cited in Edward Foley, *From Age to Age: How Christians Have Celebrated the Eucharist* (Chicago: Liturgy Training Publications, 1991), 47.
2. Irenaeus, "Against Heresies," *Early Christian Fathers*, ed. Cyril C. Richardson (New York: Macmillan, 1970), 382, 383.
3. See *The Apostolic Tradition*, commentary by Paul F. Bradshaw, Maxwell E. Johnson, and L. Edward Philips (Minneapolis: Fortress Press, 2002), 38.
4. "Sermon on the Sacrament of the Altar," *The Mass: Ancient Liturgies and Patristic Tests*, ed. Adalbert Hamman, O.F.M. (Staten Island, N.Y.: Alba House, 1967), 211–212.
5. Cyril of Jerusalem, in Edward Yarnold, S.J., *The Awe-Inspiring Rites of Initiation* (Collegeville, Minn.: Liturgical, 1994), 90.
6. Theodore of Mopsuestia, in *The Awe-Inspiring Rites of Initiation* (Collegeville, Minn.: Liturgical, 1994), 222.
7. Cited in Foley, *From Age to Age* (Chicago: Liturgy Training, 1991), 57.
8. Richard Rodriguez, "Credo," *Hunger of Memory: The Education of Richard Rodriguez* (Boston: David Godine, 1982).

6. What comes down to us from 50,000 Sundays ago?

1. Cited in Geoffrey Wainwright and Karen B. Westerfield Tucker, ed., *The Oxford History of Christian Worship* (New York: Oxford University Press, 2006), 266.
2. Alexander Schmemann, *For the Life of the World* (Scarsdale, N.Y.: St. Vladimir's Seminary Press, 1973), 26–27.
3. Elizabeth Zelensky and Lela Gilbert, *Windows to Heaven: Introducing Icons to Protestants and Catholics* (Grand Rapids: Brazos, 2005), 124–25.
4. The anaphora, *The Divine Liturgy according to St. John Chrysostom* (New York: Russian Orthodox Greek Catholic Church of America, 1967), 56–57.
5. Romanos, "On the Resurrection IV," *Kontakia of Romanos, Byzantine Melodist*, trans. Marjorie Carpenter (Columbia: University of Missouri Press, 1970), 1:285.
6. Symeon of Thessalonika, cited in Robert Taft, S.J., *Through Their Own Eyes: Liturgy as the Byzantines Saw It* (Berkeley: InterOrthodox, 2006), 154.

7. Thomas Aquinas, "God with Hidden Majesty," *Worship: A Hymnal and Service Book for Roman Catholics* (Chicago: GIA, 1986), #489.

8. Romano Guardini, *Sacred Signs* (Wilmington: Michael Glazier, 1979), 80–81.

9. Preface for Eucharistic prayer II, www.catholic-resources.org.

10. Robert Coles, *Dorothy Day: A Radical Devotion* (Reading, Mass.: Addison-Wesley, 1989), 76–77.

11. Andre Dubus, "A Father's Story," in *A Celestial Omnibus: Short Fiction on Faith*, ed. J. P. Maney and Tom Hazuka (Boston: Beacon, 1997), 15–33.

7. What comes down to us from 25,000 Sundays ago?

1. O. E. Rolvaag, *Giants in the Earth* (New York: Harper & Bros., 1927), 242.

2. See, for example, dozens of the entries in Suzanne Strempek Shea, *Sundays in America: A Yearlong Road Trip in Search of Christian Faith* (Boston: Beacon, 2008).

3. Ulrich Zwingli, "Action or Use of the Lord's Supper," in *Liturgies of the Western Church*, ed. Bard Thompson (Minneapolis: Fortress Press, 1980), 150.

4. *Martyrs Mirror*, compiled by Thieleman J. van Braght, trans. Joseph F. Sohm (Scottsdale, Penn.: Herald, 1972), 482.

5. Martin Luther, "Concerning the Communion of the People," in *Liturgies of the Western World*, 119.

6. *The Book of Common Prayer* (New York: Seabury, 1977), 335.

7. Ibid., 371.

8. *Enriching Our Worship* (New York: Church, 1998), 60.

9. Graydon F. Snyder and Doreen M. McFarlane, *The People Are Holy: The History and Theology of Free Church Worship* (Macon, Ga.: Mercer University Press, 2005), 121.

10. Joe Wittmer, *The Gentle People: An Inside View of Amish Life*, 3d ed. (Washington, Ind.: Black Buggy, 2007), 43.

11. Gottlieb Mittelberger, "Journey to Pennsylvania," in *Pennsylvania Dutch Folk Spirituality*, ed. Richard E. Wentz (New York: Paulist, 1993), 72.

12. "Preaching" and "The Bible," in Kathleen Norris, *Amazing Grace: A Vocabulary of Faith* (New York: Riverhead, 1998), 180–96.

8. What comes down to us from the last 10,000 Sundays?

1. John D. Witvliet, *Worship Seeking Understanding: Windows into Christian Practice* (Grand Rapids: Baker Academic, 2003), 166.
2. Marlea Gilbert, Christopher Grundy, Eric T. Myers, and Stephanie Perdew, *The Work of the People: What We Do in Worship and Why* (Herndon, Va.: Alban Institute, 2007), 75.
3. James White, *A Brief History of Christian Worship* (Nashville: Abingdon, 1993), 155.
4. "The Love Feast," *The United Methodist Book of Worship* (Nashville: The United Methodist Publishing House, 1992), 582.
5. "Religious Experience and Journal of Mrs. Jarena Lee," *Spiritual Narratives*, ed. Sue E. Houchins (New York: Oxford University Press, 1988), part 2, 28.
6. Joseph Jones, *Why We Do What We Do: Christian Worship in the African-American Tradition* (Nashville: R. H. Boyd, 2006), 48–49.
7. Michael Horton, *A Better Way: Rediscovering the Drama of Christ-Centered Worship* (Grand Rapids: Baker, 2002), 177.
8. Irene V. Jackson-Brown, "Gospel Music and Afro-American Worship," *The Landscape of Praise: Readings in Liturgical Renewal*, ed. Blair Gilmer Meeks (Valley Forge, Pa.: Trinity International, 1996), 249.
9. Ruth C. Duck and Patricia Wilson-Kastner, *Praising God: The Trinity in Christian Worship* (Louisville: Westminster John Knox, 1999), 146.

9. What is baptism?

1. Glaucia Vasconcelos-Wilkie, "The *Ordo* of Liturgical Space," *Ordo: Bath, Word, Prayer, Table*, ed. Dirk G. Lange and Dwight W. Vogel (Akron, Ohio: OSL, 2005), 135.
2. Ingrid Hill, *Ursula, Under* (New York: Vintage, 2005), 146.
3. Fredric Klees, "Brethren, Schwenkfelders and Other Plain People," www.horseshoe.cc.
4. "Holy Baptism," in *Evangelical Lutheran Worship* (Minneapolis: Augsburg Fortress, 2006), 229.
5. Zeno, "Seven Invitations to the Baptismal Font," *Baptism: Ancient Liturgies and Patristic Texts*, ed. Andre Hamman, O.F.M. (Staten Island, N.Y.: Alba House, 1967), 66.
6. Bryan D. Spinks, *Reformation and Modern Rituals and Theologies of Baptism* (Burlington, Vt.: Ashgate, 2006), 158–60.
7. Flannery O'Connor, "The River," in *The Complete Stories of Flannery O'Connor* (New York: Farrar, Straus and Giroux, 1971), 157–74.

10. What Christian worship takes place between Sundays?

1. Kurt Niederwimmer, *The Didache*, 8:2-3, trans. Linda Maloney, Hermeneia (Minneapolis: Fortress Press, 1998), 134.
2. *Hippolytus: A Text for Students*, trans. Geoffrey J. Cuming (Bramcote, Notts.: Grove, 1976), 30.
3. Rick Warren, *The Purpose-Driven Life: What on Earth Am I Here For?* (Grand Rapids: Zondervan, 2002), 84.
4. Anne Lamott, *Traveling Mercies: Some Thoughts on Faith* (New York: Anchor, 1999), 82.
5. Justin, *1 Apology* 67, trans. Gordon Lathrop, in *Holy Things* (Minneapolis: Fortress Press, 1993), 45.
6. Martin Luther, "Preface to the Burial Hymns," trans. Paul Zeller Strodach and Ulrich W. Leupold, in *Luther's Works* 53 (Minneapolis: Fortress Press, 1965), 326.
7. Cited in James F. White, *Documents of Christian Worship: Descriptive and Interpretive Sources* (Louisville: Westminster, 1992), 227.
8. "Order for the Blessing on the Fifteenth Birthday," www.usccb.org/liturgy/Quinceañera.pdf.
9. The *Spiritual Exercises of St. Ignatius*, trans. Anthony Mottola (New York: Image, 1964), 85.
10. Sandra Cisneros, "Little Miracles, Kept Promises," in *A Celestial Omnibus: Short Fiction on Faith*, ed. J. P. Maney and Tom Hazuka (Boston: Beacon, 1997), 3–14.

11. How is Christian worship like or unlike the practices of other religions in America?

1. Confession, in *Mahzor for Rosh Hashanah and Yom Kippur*, ed. Rabbi Jules Harlow (New York: Rabbinical Assembly, 1972), 403.
2. Asma Gull Hasan, *Why I Am a Muslim: An American Odyssey* (London: Element, HarperCollins, 2004), 22.
3. Priya Hemenway, *Hindu Gods: The Spirit of the Divine* (San Francisco: Chronicle, 2003), 9.
4. Devdutt Pattanaik, *Indian Mythology: Tales, Symbols, and Rituals from the Heart of the Subcontinent* (Rochester, Vt.: Inner Traditions, 2003), 10.
5. Venerable Adrienne Howley, *The Naked Buddha: A Practical Guide to the Buddha's Life and Teachings* (New York: Marlowe & Company, 2003), 93.
6. Ed McGaa, Eagle Man, *Mother Earth Spirituality: Native American Paths to Healing Ourselves and Our World* (San Francisco: HarperSanFrancisco, 1989), 51.

7. Starhawk, *Spiral Dance: A Rebirth of the Ancient Religion of the Great Goddess*, rev. ed. (San Francisco: HarperSanFrancisco, 1989), 11.

8. Marta Moreno Vega, *The Altar of My Soul: The Living Traditions of Santeria* (New York: One World, 2000), 129–30.

9. Leslie Marmon Silko, "The Man to Send Rain Clouds," in *A Celestial Omnibus: Short Fiction on Faith*, ed. J. P. Maney and Tom Hazuka (Boston: Beacon, 1997), 49–53.

12. How might Sunday worship affect daily life?

1. Gail Reitenbach, *How My Neighbor Worships: A Grand Tour of Faith Communities* (Santa Fe: Right Hand Communications, 2006), 174–75.

2. Augustine, *The Confessions of St. Augustine*, trans. John K. Ryan (New York: Image, 1960), 131.

3. Seymour Leichman, *The Boy Who Could Sing Pictures* (Garden City, N.Y.: Doubleday, 1968), 57.

4. Richard R. Gaillardetz, *Transforming Our Days: Spirituality, Community and Liturgy in a Technological Culture* (New York: Crossroad, 2000), 124.

5. Lauren F. Winner, *Girl Meets God: A Memoir* (New York: Random House, 2002), 36–37.

6. *The Collects of Thomas Cranmer*, ed. C. Frederick Barbee and Paul F. M. Zahl (Grand Rapids: Eerdmans, 1999), 4.

7. Cited in Anne Lamott, *Plan B: Further Thoughts on Faith* (New York: Riverhead, 2006), 72.

8. Martin Luther, "The Blessed Sacrament of the Holy and True Body of Christ, and the Brotherhoods," in *Luther's Works*, vol. 53. ed. E. Theodore Bachmann, (Philadelphia: Fortress Press, 1960), 54.

9. C. S. Lewis, *The Lion, the Witch and the Wardrobe* (New York: Macmillan, 1950), 29.

10. Jeff Smith, *The Frugal Gourmet Keeps the Feast: Past, Present, and Future* (New York: William Morrow, 1995), 12.

11. *The Book of Margery Kempe*, trans. B. A. Windeatt (New York: Penguin, 1985), 187.

12. Jane Stevenson, *The Empress of the Last Days* (Boston: Houghton Mifflin, 2004), 178.

13. Sara Miles, *Take This Bread: A Radical Conversion* (New York: Ballantine, 2007), xiii.

14. Gordon Lathrop, *The Pastor: A Spirituality* (Minneapolis: Fortress Press, 2006), 127.

15. Martin Buber, *Tales of the Hasidim: The Early Masters* (New York: Schocken, 1947), 111.

16. Annie Dillard, *Holy the Firm* (New York: Bantam, 1979), 60.

17. Garrison Keillor, "Collection," *Leaving Home: A Collection of Lake Wobegon Stories* (New York: Viking, 1987), 79–83.

Acknowledgments

I offer my thanks to many people: to Daniel Brockopp, who in 1965 encouraged my study of liturgy; to Nader Ata, OFM Conv., who in March 2006 urged me to write such a textbook; to the administration of La Salle University, for granting me leave in fall 2007 to write the first draft; to the students in Religion 226 in 2008, whose use of the draft led to many improvements; to Vivienne Angeles, Vyshnavi Suntharalingam, William Grosnick, Mark Mummert, and Frank Senn, for their helpful expertise; to the Liturgical Language seminar and the Philadelphia caucus of the North American Academy of Liturgy, for their suggestions and enthusiasm; to Miriam Schmidt, Glaucia Vasconcelos-Wilkie, and Martin Seltz, for their attentive reading of the text, their questions and recommendations; to Fortress editor-in-chief Michael West, for his unfailing encouragement of this project; to Andrew DeYoung, for months of skillful and cordial multitasking as project manager; to Lynette Johnson, for securing permission for the images; and to David Lott, for his careful editing. And thanks to Gordon Lathrop, for gracious assistance in a multitude of ways.

June 1, 2008, Justin's Day

Image Credits:

p. 9: Photo © Osservatore Romano / Associated Press.
18: Photo copyright © 2007 Brian C. Lee. Used by permission.
25: Photos courtesy Artistic Manufacturing, Holbrooks Stoneware, and Alviti Creations.
34: Calvin and Hobbes © 1993 Watterson. Dist. by Universal Press Syndicate.
  Reprinted with permission. All rights reserved.
38: Photo © Musdeq Sadeq / Associated Press.
40: Photo © Chris Gardner / Associated Press.
42: Photo © Shakil Adil / Associated Press.
46: Reprinted by permission from *Liturgical Year: Supplemental Liturgical Resource 7,*
  © 1992 Westminster/John Knox Press.
57: Photo © Erich Lessing / Art Resource, NY.
59: Photo © Scala / Art Resource, NY.
61: Photo © Gerri Hernandez / iStockphoto.
64: Photo © Gail Ramshaw.
72: Text © 2000 Augsburg Fortress.
74: Text and music © 1978, 2006 Augsburg Fortress.
77: Photo courtesy Diocese of St. Asaph, UK.
78: © www.CartoonStock.com.

80: Photo © Franky De Meyer / iStockphoto.

91: Photo © Scala / Art Resource, NY.

95: Photo © Martí Sáiz / iStockphoto.

101: Copyright © 2006 by Roz Chast, reprinted with permission of the Wylie Agency LLC.

106: Photo courtesy of Saint Michael's Evangelical Lutheran Church, Sellersville, PA.

110: Photo courtesy Library of Congress.

111: Photo © iStockphoto.

116: Excellent Sermon: © The New Yorker Collection 2005 Tom Cheney from cartoonbank.com. All Rights Reserved.

119: Text © 1978 *Lutheran Book of Worship,* admin. Augsburg Fortress.

128: Photo © Susan Walsh / Associated Press.

134: Photo by Lonnie Timons III © Religious News Service.

135: Photo © Kenneth Griesemer.

144: Photo courtesy of Matt Huprich and Son.

145: Photo © Scott Leigh / iStockphoto.

151: Photo © Joel Johndro / iStockphoto.

157: Photo courtesy of Saint Malachy Parish, UK.

162: Photo by Joe Epstein / The Star-Ledger of Newark, N.J. / © Religion News Service

168: Photo courtesy of Clearwater Stone and Columbaria. Used by permission

172: Photo © Jocelyn Mathewes.

174: Photo © Chris Gardner / Associated Press.

175: Photo by Paritosh Bansal © Religion News Service.

178: Photo © Jill Geoffrion. Used by permission.

182: Worship 10 am: © The New Yorker Collection 2004 Edward Koren from cartoonbank.com. All Rights Reserved.

186: Photo © age fotostock / SuperStock.

189: Illustration by Sureyya Aydin, Norway. Reprinted under the terms of the GNU Free Documentation license.

193: Photo © Exotic India.

194: Photo © Peter Kretzmann.

197: Photo © SuperStock, Inc. / SuperStock.

205: © LaSalle University Campus Ministry. Used by permission.

208: Fritz Eichenberg Collection. Graphic Arts Division. Department of Rare Books and Special Collections. Princeton University Library.

210: *Supper at Emmaus,* by He Qi (China). For more information and art by He Qi, please visit www.heqigallery.com.

Plate 1: Photo © Scala / Art Resource, NY.

Plate 2: Photo © David J. Hetland. Used by permission.

Plate 3: Photo © Scala Art Resource, NY.

Plate 4: Photo © Scala / Art Resource, NY.

Plate 5: © SuperStock, Inc. / SuperStock.

Plate 6: Photo © Scala / Art Resource, NY.

Plate 7: Copyright by Monastery Icons—www.monasteryicons.com.

Plate 8: © Blake Debassige.

Plate 9: Photo © Scala / Art Resource, NY.

Plate 10: Yale University Art Gallery. Dura-Europos Collection.

Plate 11: Photo © David Sanger Photography. Used by permission.

Index

About the Cover Artist

Los Angeles artist John August Swanson is noted for his finely detailed, brilliantly colored paintings and original prints. His works are found in the Smithsonian Institution's National museum of American History, London's Tate Gallery, the Vatican Museum's Collection of Modern Religious Art, and the Bibliothèque Nationale, Paris.

Full-color posters and cards of Mr. Swanson's work are available from the National Association for Hispanic Elderly. Proceeds benefit its programs of employment and housing for low-income seniors. For information, contact: National Association of Hispanic Elderly, 234 East Colorado Blvd., Suite 300, Pasadena, CA 91101, (626) 564-1988.